Jethro Tull's *Thick as a Brick* and *A Passion Play*

PROFILES IN POPULAR MUSIC

Jeffrey Magee and Felicia Miyakawa, editors

Unlocking the Groove: Rhythm, Meter, and Musical Design in Electronic Dance Music
Mark J. Butler

Neil Young and the Poetics of Energy
William Echard

Johnny Cash and the Paradox of American Identity
Leigh H. Edwards

Jazzwomen: Conversations with Twenty-One Musicians
Wayne Enstice and Janis Stockhouse

Choro: A Social History of a Brazilian Popular Music
Tamara Elena Livingston-Isenhour and Thomas George Caracas Garcia

Rush, Rock Music, and the Middle Class
Chris McDonald

Five Percenter Rap: God Hop's Music, Message, and Black Muslim Mission
Felicia M. Miyakawa

The Songs of Jimmie Rodgers: A Legacy in Country Music
Jocelyn R. Neal

The Megamusical
Jessica Sternfeld

Radiohead and the Resistant Concept Album
Marianne Tatom Letts

THICK AS A BRICK
and
A PASSION PLAY

INSIDE TWO LONG SONGS

TIM SMOLKO
FOREWORD BY ADRIAN STONE-MASON

INDIANA UNIVERSITY PRESS   *Bloomington & Indianapolis*

This book is a publication of

INDIANA UNIVERSITY PRESS
Office of Scholarly Publishing
Herman B Wells Library 350
1320 East 10th Street
Bloomington, Indiana 47405 USA

iupress.indiana.edu

Telephone orders 800-842-6796
Fax orders 812-855-7931

© 2013 by Timothy J. Smolko

All rights reserved

No part of this book may be reproduced or utilized in any form or by any means, electronic or mechanical, including photocopying and recording, or by any information storage and retrieval system, without permission in writing from the publisher. The Association of American University Presses' Resolution on Permissions constitutes the only exception to this prohibition.

∞ The paper used in this publication meets the minimum requirements of the American National Standard for Information Sciences–Permanence of Paper for Printed Library Materials, ANSI Z39.48–1992.

*Manufactured in the
United States of America*

*Library of Congress
Cataloging-in-Publication Data*

Smolko, Tim, author.
  Jethro Tull's Thick as a brick and A passion play : inside two long songs / Tim Smolko.
   pages cm. – (Profiles in popular music)
  Includes bibliographical references and index.
  ISBN 978-0-253-01026-1 (cloth : alkaline paper) – ISBN 978-0-253-01031-5 (paperback : alkaline paper) – ISBN 978-0-253-01038-4 (ebook) 1. Jethro Tull (Musical group) 2. Rock music – England – 1971-1980 – History and criticism. 3. Progressive rock music. I. Title. II. Series: Profiles in popular music.
  ML421.J5S66 2013
  782.42166092'2 – dc23

2013010486

1 2 3 4 5   18 17 16 15 14 13

Contents

- List of Illustrations *vii*
- Foreword by Adrian Stone-Mason *xi*
- Preface *xiii*
- Acknowledgments *xvii*

1 Life Is a Long Song: Providing a Context for *Thick as a Brick* and *A Passion Play* 1

2 Galliards and Lute Songs: The Influence of Early Music in Jethro Tull 19

3 Geared toward the Exceptional Rather than the Average: The Album Cover and Lyrics of *Thick as a Brick* 33

4 The Music of *Thick as a Brick:* Form and Thematic Development 57

5 The Music of *Thick as a Brick:* Other Features 91

6 The Château d'Isaster Tapes and the Album Cover and Lyrics of *A Passion Play* 111

- 7 The Music of *A Passion Play*   130
- 8 *Monty Python*, Reception, and Live Versions   158
- · Conclusions   176
- · Epilogue: Whatever Happened to Gerald Bostock?   179

- · Appendix 1. The Complete Lyrics to *Thick as a Brick*   185
- · Appendix 2. The Complete Lyrics to *A Passion Play*   195
- · Appendix 3. Analysis of the Instrumental Passages   205
- · Notes   211
- · Bibliography   223
- · Discography   229
- · Videography   231
- · Index   233

Illustrations

FIGURES

3.1. Cover of *Thick as a Brick* 38

3.2. Comic on p. 7 of the *St. Cleve Chronicle* 45

3.3. Article on p. 8 of the *St. Cleve Chronicle* 47

3.4. Lyrics to *Thick as a Brick* from the *St. Cleve Chronicle* 50

6.1. Front cover of *A Passion Play* 119

6.2. Back cover of *A Passion Play* 120

6.3. Inside gatefold of *A Passion Play* 121

6.4. Inside gatefold of *A Passion Play* with mock theater program 121

MUSICAL EXAMPLES

Example 4.1 *Thick as a Brick*, melody in first A section of Vocal 1, 0:11 side 1 76

Example 4.2 *Thick as a Brick*, melody in second A section of Vocal 1, 1:00 side 1 76

Example 4.3 *Thick as a Brick*, Motive 1 78

Example 4.4 *Thick as a Brick*, Motive 2 80

Example 4.5	*Thick as a Brick,* Motive 2 in $^6_8$ meter, 0:48 side 2	*80*
Example 4.6	*Thick as a Brick,* Motive 2 *fortspinnung* passage, 18:42 side 2	*81*
Example 4.7	*Thick as a Brick,* Motive 3	*82*
Example 4.8	*Thick as a Brick,* Motive 3 on organ, 17:31 side 1	*82*
Example 4.9	*Thick as a Brick,* Motive 4, 11:23 side 1	*83*
Example 4.10	*Thick as a Brick,* Motive 2 interrupted by Motive 4, 19:46 side 2	*84*
Example 4.11	*Thick as a Brick,* Motive 5, 16:35 side 1	*85*
Example 4.12	*Thick as a Brick,* Motive 6	*85*
Example 4.13	*Thick as a Brick,* Motive 6 layered onto Motive 2, 20:04 side 2	*86*
Example 4.14	*Thick as a Brick,* Motive 7	*87*
Example 7.1	*A Passion Play,* Overture Theme 1	*131*
Example 7.2	*A Passion Play,* Overture Theme 2	*132*
Example 7.3	Johann Sebastian Bach, *French Suite in E♭ major BWV 815,* "Gigue"	*134*
Example 7.4	Hector Berlioz, *Symphonie Fantastique,* "Dream of a Witches' Sabbath," mm 21–25	*135*
Example 7.5	"Neapolitan Tarantella," *Traditional*	*136*
Example 7.6	*A Passion Play,* Motive 1: Heartbeat	*142*
Example 7.7	*A Passion Play,* Motive 2	*144*
Example 7.8	*A Passion Play,* Motive 3	*145*
Example 7.9	*A Passion Play,* Motive 4	*146*
Example 7.10	*A Passion Play,* Motives 4 and 3 combined, 17:41–17:58, side 1	*146*
Example 7.11	*A Passion Play,* Motive 5	*147*
Example 7.12	*A Passion Play,* Story Theme 1	*153*
Example 7.13	*A Passion Play,* Story Theme 2	*153*

ILLUSTRATIONS

TABLES

Table 4.1 Song forms in *Thick as a Brick*   65

Table 4.2 Large-scale form of *Thick as a Brick*   66

Table 4.3 Multiple climaxes in *Thick as a Brick*   69

Table 4.4 Vocal sections of *Thick as a Brick* with local repetition   75

Table 4.5 Appearances of *Thick as a Brick* Motive 1   78

Table 4.6 Metrical progression from 16:18–17:41, side 1   79

Table 4.7 Appearances of *Thick as a Brick* Motive 2   80

Table 4.8 Appearances of *Thick as a Brick* Motive 3   82

Table 4.9 Appearances of *Thick as a Brick* Motive 6   85

Table 4.10 Appearances of all *Thick as a Brick* Motives throughout side 1   87

Table 4.11 Appearances of all *Thick as a Brick* Motives throughout side 2   87

Table 5.1 Instrumentation of *Thick as a Brick*   100

Table 5.2 Instrumentation legend of *Thick as a Brick*   101

Table 5.3 Flute paired with other instruments in *Thick as a Brick*   103

Table 5.4 Chord progressions in the first eleven minutes of *Thick as a Brick*   109

Table 6.1 Lyrics about the parallels between human and animal behavior   113

Table 6.2 Lyrics about the theater as a conceit for human life   114

Table 6.3 Settings of the four acts of *A Passion Play*   122

Table 6.4 Subtitles on the MFSL Gold CD release of *A Passion Play*   129

Table 7.1 Musical events in the Overture to *A Passion Play*   133

Table 7.2	Song forms in *A Passion Play*	137
Table 7.3	Large-scale form of *A Passion Play*	139
Table 7.4	Multiple climaxes in *A Passion Play*	141
Table 7.5	Appearances of *A Passion Play* Motive 1	143
Table 7.6	Appearances of *A Passion Play* Motive 2	144
Table 7.7	Appearances of *A Passion Play* Motive 3	145
Table 7.8	Appearances of *A Passion Play* Motive 4	146
Table 7.9	Appearances of *A Passion Play* Motive 5	147
Table 7.10	Appearances of the phrase "Passion Play"	148
Table 7.11	Appearances of all *A Passion Play* motives throughout side 1	149
Table 7.12	Appearances of all *A Passion Play* motives throughout side 2	149
Table 7.13	Instrumentation of *A Passion Play*	152
Table 7.14	Instrumentation legend of *A Passion Play*	153
Table 7.15	Appearances of the two themes in "The Story of the Hare Who Lost His Spectacles"	154
Table 8.1	Form of *Flying Circus* episode: "How to Recognize Different Types of Trees from Quite a Long Way Away"	164
Table 8.2	Form of *Thick as a Brick*, Live at Madison Square Garden 1978 version	170
Table 8.3	Form of *Thick as a Brick*, live "Out in the Green" Festival version (1986)	171
Table 8.4	Form of *Thick as a Brick*, 25th Anniversary Box Set studio version (1992)	172

Foreword by Adrian Stone-Mason, BA (Hons), FRICS, RIBA

(with a little helpful encouragement from Mr. Ian Anderson)

TIM SMOLKO'S BOOK ON THE SUBJECTS OF *THICK AS A BRICK, A Passion Play,* and *The Chateau D'Isaster Tapes* makes for a scholarly but vigorous insight into the sometimes wacky but always considered and adventurous world of Ian Anderson's rather extreme musical meanderings of the early '70s.

Exploring the background to the advent of progressive rock and the often uneasy parallels with many of Anderson's musical contemporaries, Smolko keeps this rounded, grounded, well-founded, and contextual picture of Jethro Tull's record album excesses continually entertaining for the reader.

Doubtless Anderson himself would take issue with some of the analysis and historical detail, but the level of research and cross-referencing in the preparation of this book makes for convincing factual evidence to support the musicology.

But what is the point, we might ask, of such painstaking and, perhaps, even obsessive attention to the minutiae of detailed reference? The point must be, surely, that when an even half-keen listener next sits down to listen to these "big" rock albums, there is now an educated companion potentially at his or her side. A step-by-step guide to the flora and fauna of Anderson's jungle creation. A road map for the exquisite journey on the back roads. A recipe book to explain the banquet feast of musical delights.

So don't be put off by the seriousness of this book or reject its good intentions. It is a vivid insight into the Anderson creative force and the efforts of his often-changing band of merrie men.

From codpiece to coda, from flutter-tongue to fugue, from B-flat to, er, D-sharp... Tim Smolko covers the ground, dots the i's, and crosses the bridges when he comes to them.

Prepare for the journey. Take reading glasses, smelling salts, and a wee dram of something smoky from the peat bogs of the Western Isles. Take a friend. If you have one left, that is, after playing *A Passion Play* too loudly through the open window after Matins last Sunday.

Adrian Stone-Mason
St. Cleve
Somerset
December 2012

Preface

MOST RECORD COLLECTORS REMEMBER IN VIVID DETAIL THE first time they discover a favorite album. Many years ago when I first saw Jethro Tull's *Thick as a Brick* in the stacks at Jerry's Records in Pittsburgh, I was intrigued. Why did they make the album cover into a newspaper? What was all the text about? Who was this strange little bloke, Gerald Bostock, staring back at me from the cover? When I saw that the album folded out into a full-size, twelve-page newspaper and realized how hilarious and absurd it was, I was fascinated. Then when I looked at the record itself and saw only "Thick as a Brick" on the label instead of a numbered list of songs, and noticed the continuous groove on both sides ("Is it really just one long song?"), I was hooked. It took me less than a minute to decide to buy it.

Before I bought the album, I had heard the "Thick as a Brick" three-minute single many times on the radio and on the first Jethro Tull greatest hits compilation, *M.U. The Best of Jethro Tull*, which I owned. When I discovered the *Thick as a Brick* album that day in Jerry's Records, it came as a complete shock to me that the "single" was simply the first three minutes of a continuous forty-three-minute song.[1] When I began listening to the music and lyrics, they seemed to be serious and studied, in contrast to the cover, which was silly and surreal. The music struck me as being raw and refined at the same time. Thus began my fascination with this unusually long rock song.

This book began as an exploration of just *Thick as a Brick*, but it's hard to do a study of that album without also considering the band's next one, *A Passion Play*, an even more outrageous sonic adventure. They are close cousins in that both consist of an album-length song, both contain some of Jethro Tull's most difficult music and lyrics, and, ironically, both are the band's only albums to hit number one on the U.S. *Billboard* 200 Album Chart. So I expanded the book to explore *A Passion Play* and thought I was finished. I wasn't. On the day I signed the publishing contract for this book, Ian Anderson announced on Jethro Tull's website that he was releasing a full-fledged sequel to *Thick as a Brick* titled *Thick as a Brick 2: Whatever Happened to Gerald Bostock?* complete with an online version of the spoof newspaper. The sequel was also released as an LP. The years 2012–2013 brought an eighteen-month world tour with the complete performances of both the original work and its sequel, a sonically improved edition of the original *Thick as a Brick,* and a new solo album by Anderson. Thus, this book comes at a fortuitous time, when Anderson and his band – forty-five years after their first album – are as creative and active as they have ever been.

PURPOSE AND STRUCTURE OF THE BOOK

While rock journalists have been writing reviews, articles, biographies, and discographies of progressive rock bands since the 1970s, it was only in the 1990s that progressive rock – and rock music in general, for that matter – began to receive any significant attention from musicologists. In 1997 Edward Macan published his definitive study *Rocking the Classics: English Progressive Rock and the Counterculture.*[2] Other scholars such as Nors Josephson, Allan Moore, Walter Everett, and John Covach laid the groundwork for musical analyses of the longer pieces by bands such as the Beatles, Pink Floyd, Frank Zappa and the Mothers of Invention, Yes, Genesis, and King Crimson. These scholars showed that the analytic methodologies used to explore classical music were also useful in analyzing the large-scale structures found in progressive rock. Since the early 2000s, a growing number of musicologists, including Mark Spicer, John Sheinbaum, and Kevin Holm-Hudson, have been doing thorough analyses of many progressive rock pieces.

The purpose of this book is primarily to explore the musical content of *Thick as a Brick* and *A Passion Play,* two of the most complex and compelling pieces of rock music ever recorded. Jethro Tull have sold over sixty million records and have played more than three thousand concerts worldwide in over fifty countries in their forty-five-year career. They are one of the few rock bands originating in the 1960s that are still recording and performing. They appeal to a broad range of music lovers because they have fostered an eclectic, yet accessible, style embracing rock, folk, jazz, blues, world, and classical music. Yet, out of all the major British progressive rock bands, they have received the least attention in terms of musical analysis. The majority of writings on the band have consisted of histories, biographies, and discographies, the best being Greg Russo's *Flying Colours: The Jethro Tull Reference Manual*.[3] Allan Moore does some analysis of the style characteristics of Jethro Tull's music in his book *Rock: The Primary Text,* but no album or song receives a thorough analysis.[4] Moore's book *Aqualung* is a detailed study of that album and is the only such scholarly work on a specific Jethro Tull album.[5] John Covach wrote a short article on *Thick as a Brick* in the progressive rock periodical *Progression Magazine,* but it is only an introduction to the piece.[6] Several fans, including Jan Voorbij, Andrew Jackson, and Neil Thomason, have created elaborate websites with thorough analyses of the lyrics of both albums but not the music. This book, with its lengthy analysis of the music of *Thick as a Brick* and *A Passion Play,* is designed to fill that gap. While the emergence of progressive rock as a distinct style of rock music and Jethro Tull's place within this style have been well documented, much more needs to be said about how significant a milestone these two albums were in the early 1970s, a period that saw great expansion in the boundaries and possibilities of rock music.

The opening chapter of the book discusses the two albums in the context of late 1960s and early 1970s rock music, their chart success, their length, and the origins and development of Jethro Tull. Chapter 2 shows how the band integrated elements of medieval and Renaissance culture, literature, and music into their lyrics, music, album covers, and live shows. Chapters 3, 4, and 5 examine the album cover, lyrics, and music of *Thick as a Brick*. Chapter 6 considers *The Château d'Isaster Tapes,* the recordings from an aborted first attempt at what would become *A Passion Play*. The chapter also examines the album cover and lyrics of *A Passion Play,* while chapter 7 analyzes the music. Lastly, chapter 8 shows how the structure and flow of the two albums is similar to the structure and flow of the British television show *Monty Python's Flying Circus* and describes how the albums were received by fans, critics, and the musicians themselves. It also considers the live versions of the two pieces, which Jethro Tull performed in their entirety during their 1972 and 1973 tours. The epilogue discusses the sequel album *Thick as a Brick 2: Whatever Happened to Gerald Bostock?* and the accompanying live show.

Acknowledgments

FIRST OFF, I'D LIKE TO THANK MY WONDERFUL WIFE, JOANNA, for encouraging me, editing me, and acclimating her ears to the din of loud electric guitars and drums. I owe so much to you and I love you!

I'd also like to thank:

My editors at Indiana University Press, Raina Polivka and Darja Malcolm-Clarke, along with series editors Felicia Miyakawa, and Jeffrey Magee. Thanks also to Jill R. Hughes for an excellent copyedit.

Ian Anderson, who granted me a phone interview, wrote the foreword, and gave me permission to include the lyrics of the two songs and scans of the album covers in the book. Thanks to all the members of Jethro Tull, past and present, for forty-five years of superb and inspiring music. Thanks also to Anne Leighton and Jenny Hughes at Jethro Tull management, and Julie McDowell at Hal Leonard, for their assistance with various details of the book.

The music professors at the University of Georgia, especially Dr. David Haas, Dr. David Schiller, and Dr. Leonard Ball. Special thanks to Dr. Robert Greenberg for his Teaching Company lectures and to Dr. Stephen Valdez, rock scholar extraordinaire and all-around cool guy.

UGA Library colleagues Neil Hughes, Kelly Holt, and Gil Head for their input, encouragement, and support.

My small-town parents, who encouraged me to pursue big-city dreams. My parents-in-law, Rich and Deb Hastings, for providing a piano upon which I picked out many a Tull melody.

Friends who have greatly inspired me, both in music and life in general: Dan Cush, Brent and Molly Stater, Sal Manzella, and my church families at Grace Orthodox Presbyterian Church in Pittsburgh and University Church in Athens, whom I stand beside in praise of our Savior.

Friends and colleagues who have given me good advice: Deane Root, Kathy Miller Haines, Jim Cassaro, Jessica Sternfeld, Alan Shockley, Kevin Holm-Hudson, and Ed Macan.

Jerry Weber, owner of Jerry's Records in Pittsburgh, on whose shelves one can always find a pristine copy of *Thick as a Brick*, complete with newspaper.

Karen Paddison, who first introduced me to *Monty Python's Flying Circus* and various other British eccentricities.

Andrew Jackson (Jethro Tull Press), Jan Voorbij (Cup of Wonder), and Neil Thomason (Ministry of Information) for their well-designed, accurate, and exhaustive websites on Jethro Tull. Greg Russo, David Rees, and Scott Allen Nollen for their excellent biographies of the band. Special thanks to Blackpool rock historian Pete Shelton.

Lastly, thanks to our five-year-old twins, Ian and Elanor, who, when they are teenagers, will probably introduce me to their friends in this manner: "This is my dad. He likes to listen to forty-five-minute rock songs (groan)."

Except where indicated, all the musical examples in the book are my own transcriptions of the music from the remixed CD of *Thick as a Brick* (Chrysalis Records 5099970461923, 2012) and the remastered CD of *A Passion Play* (Chrysalis Records 7243 5 81569 0 4, 2003).

Thanks to Ian Anderson, BMG/Chrysalis, and Hal Leonard for permission to include the complete lyrics in the book.

"Thick as a Brick"
Words and Music by Ian Anderson.
Copyright ©1976 Chrysalis Music Ltd.
Copyright Renewed.
All Rights for the U.S. and Canada Administered by Chrysalis Music.
All Rights Reserved. Used by Permission.
Reprinted by Permission of Hal Leonard Corporation.

"Passion Play"
Words and Music by Ian Anderson.
Copyright ©1973 Chrysalis Music Ltd.
Copyright Renewed.
All Rights for the U.S. and Canada Administered by Chrysalis Music.
All Rights Reserved. Used by Permission.
Reprinted by Permission of Hal Leonard Corporation.

Jethro Tull's *Thick as a Brick* and *A Passion Play*

ONE

Life Is a Long Song: Providing a Context for *Thick as a Brick* and *A Passion Play*

IN THE LATE 1960S AND EARLY 1970S, BRITISH PROGRESSIVE rock bands such as King Crimson; Emerson, Lake & Palmer; Yes; Genesis; and Jethro Tull were imbuing their music with a broadened harmonic palette, large-scale forms, polyphonic textures, avant-garde sensibilities, virtuoso technique, and the use of the latest advances in instrument and studio technology. All of these ingredients are in evidence on Jethro Tull's *Thick as a Brick* (1972) and *A Passion Play* (1973). Each of these albums is one continuous song – composed of numerous vocal sections interspersed with instrumental passages – lasting over forty minutes. Their complex yet accessible music, perplexing lyrics, and unique LP packaging place them among the most creative albums in the history of rock music. Although they are quite innovative, one would not expect such oddities to achieve success with the mainstream popular music audience. Amazingly, they did. "Jethro Tull's back-to-back Number One albums, 1972's *Thick as a Brick* and 1973's *A Passion Play*, are arguably the most uncommercial and uncompromising albums ever to top the *Billboard* album chart."[1] So writes Craig Rosen, author of *The Billboard Book of Number One Albums*. *Thick as a Brick* reached number one on the U.S. *Billboard* 200 Album Chart in June 1972, where it remained for two weeks, and reached number five on the UK Albums Chart.[2] *A Passion Play* hit number one for one week on *Billboard* in August 1973. How can these "uncommercial and uncompromising" albums have been so popular?

In the mid to late 1960s the Beatles and other bands fostered an atmosphere of artistic freedom within the music industry and created a new style of popular music in which active and concentrated listening was valued. A simple comparison between an early Beatles album (*Meet the Beatles!* from 1964) and a later Beatles album (*Sgt. Pepper's Lonely Hearts Club Band* from 1967) illustrates how quickly this spirit of inventiveness arose. The first album is a collection of singles primarily for dancing, while the second is an eclectic and experimental album made primarily for listening. The fact that both Beatles albums reached number one on the U.S. *Billboard* 200 Album Chart shows the drastic shift in artistic expression in popular and rock music from the mid to late 1960s. In this period the rock album was becoming quite an experimental art form, with bands and musicians like Pink Floyd, the Doors, the Velvet Underground, Miles Davis, and Frank Zappa taking it into uncharted territory. It was in this period, and because of this artistic freedom, that progressive rock arose as a distinctive style of rock music.

Yet even in this time of creativity and innovation, it is still remarkable that a band like Jethro Tull could release albums like *Thick as a Brick* and *A Passion Play* and see them become number one hits. The ability to compose extended pieces of music that are both challenging to the listener and accessible to the general popular music audience is something that few bands have accomplished. Of all the progressive and experimental rock bands in the 1960s and 1970s – besides the Beatles – only the Jimi Hendrix Experience (*Electric Ladyland*, 1968), Jethro Tull (*Thick as a Brick, A Passion Play*), and Pink Floyd (*Dark Side of the Moon*, 1973; *Wish You Were Here*, 1975; *The Wall*, 1980) had number one albums on the U.S. *Billboard* chart.[3] Chart success was a little easier in England for these types of bands and musicians, with Jethro Tull (*Stand Up*, 1969), Emerson, Lake & Palmer (*Tarkus*. 1971), Pink Floyd (*Atom Heart Mother*, 1970; *Wish You Were Here*, 1975), Yes (*Tales from Topographic Oceans*, 1974; *Going for the One*, 1977), Rick Wakeman (*Journey to the Centre of the Earth*,1974), and Mike Oldfield (*Hergest Ridge*, 1974; *Tubular Bells*, 1974) having albums that reached number one on the UK Albums Chart.[4] While such charts are not a critical assessment of music, they are a good indication of what is in vogue at a particular time. In the early 1970s it seems that the popular music audience was interested in listening to a forty-minute-plus rock song – perhaps if only for the novelty of it.

THE RISE OF PROGRESSIVE ROCK IN THE LATE 1960S

While the early days of progressive rock have been well documented by Edward Macan, Paul Stump, and Bill Martin, a brief overview would not go amiss. Progressive rock grew out of the psychedelic rock of the British counterculture of the mid to late 1960s. The Beatles, Pink Floyd, the Yardbirds, Cream, and the Jimi Hendrix Experience (who were based in London even though Hendrix was American) established psychedelic rock in the years 1965–1967. The psychedelic bands from the American West Coast, such as the Byrds, the Grateful Dead, and Jefferson Airplane, were also an influence. While there was a commonality between the British and American aspirations of the counterculture, much of the music that came out of the American counterculture addressed divisive issues such as politics, racial tensions, and, especially, the war in Vietnam. The numerous antiwar protest songs from the period, like "I-Feel-Like-I'm-Fixin'-to-Die Rag" by Country Joe and the Fish (1967), bear this out. Although these issues were important to the British hippies, they didn't have the immediacy they did to their American counterparts. As a result the British psychedelic bands developed a form of expression more rooted in escapism, a music in which "art for art's sake" was celebrated. Thus, the first few albums by progressive groups like the Moody Blues, Pink Floyd, Yes, Jethro Tull, and King Crimson had some, and often many, psychedelic elements, such as surreal lyrics and album covers; extended song structures and instrumental soloing; and the use of phasing, tape reversal, and other studio effects.

Progressive rock's other essential elements, listed below, grew out of the experimentation of the psychedelic era, even if they were not directly influenced by psychedelic music. The music stretched beyond American rock 'n' roll, blues, and R & B and incorporated aspects of folk, jazz, classical, and Eastern music. The instrumentation expanded beyond the usual guitar, bass, and drums to encompass classical instruments (even a full orchestra), a vast array of keyboards, and ethnic instruments from other cultures. The music blended both acoustic and electric instruments, and often pitted them against one other. The lyrics tended toward the symbolic and surreal, rather than the literal and real, with utopianism, fantasy, science fiction, mysticism, and mythology becoming common themes. Album cover designs reflected this escapist aesthetic by depicting fantastical landscapes, such as Roger Dean's album covers for Yes. The surrealism and escapism in the lyrics and albums covers were also brought to the concert stage. Extravagant lighting systems, lasers, and fog machines were used to create other-worldly settings for the music. Yet for all this escapism, as Edward Macan points out, there is a palpable strain of confrontational social critique in the lyrics that has often been overlooked.[5] This social critique is evident in the lyrics of Jethro Tull's *Thick as a Brick*, as will be discussed in chapter 3.

One element that was common in the music of the counterculture on both sides of the Atlantic was the influence of drugs, especially marijuana. Macan describes the close connections between the psychedelic drug experience and the elements of progressive rock music:

> The consistent use of lengthy forms ... underscores the hippies' new, drug-induced conception of time. The intricate metrical and wayward harmonic schemes of the music ... reflect the elements of surprise, contradiction, and uncertainty that the counterculture prized so highly. The juxtaposition within a piece or an album of predominantly acoustic with predominantly electric sections, one of the hallmarks of the progressive rock style, seems to encapsulate ... the contrast of the pastoral and organic with the technological and artificial, the conflict between matriarchal and patriarchal values, between ancient and modern ways of life ... that were of great significance to the counterculture.[6]

Rather, drug use is one area in which Jethro Tull stood apart from their peers. Most of the members of the band, especially Ian Anderson, had a negative view of the drug culture and never took drugs. Yet, because of the band's scraggly appearance, long mangy hair, and general freakiness, they were immediately pegged as potheads. Anderson's manic stage presence – as can be seen on the DVD *Nothing Is Easy: Live at the Isle of Wight 1970* (2004) – prompted the music press to assume he consumed huge quantities of drugs, something he continually felt compelled to deny. Anderson said in 1977, "I've never smoked marijuana or taken any of those drugs. The main reason I don't do it is because everybody else does – it strikes me as boring."[7] Noting the obvious influence of LSD on the Beatles' *Sgt. Pepper's Lonely Hearts Club Band,* Anderson quips "most of mine have been Löwenbräu albums."[8] Psychedelic influences can be found in early Jethro Tull, but they are not overbearing. The most overt instances are the swirling effect on Martin Barre's guitar in "A New Day Yesterday" from *Stand Up* (in which Anderson swung a microphone in a circle in front of Barre's guitar amplifier) and the tape reversal in "With You There to Help Me" and "Play in Time" from *Benefit* (1970). The elements that Macan describes (lengthy forms, intricate metrical and wayward harmonic schemes, acoustic vs. electric passages) are vital aspects of Jethro Tull's music, but they did not arise because of drug use.

A second area where the band stood apart from their countercultural peers was their view of free love, and they became notorious among rock groupies not for their sexual escapades, but for their lack thereof. Robert Plant and Jimmy Page from Led Zeppelin referred to the band as "Jethro Dull." Anderson said in 1969, "Sex . . . is something which I can probably only share with one person, [whom] I would want to marry. That's probably rather an unusual viewpoint for somebody in this day and age, particularly in my profession . . . where drug-taking and sex and the whole bit . . . is almost expected of you."[9] In 1991 he said, "We would go back to a hotel after a show, no groupies, no hangers-on, and . . . pick up something from the deli, and we would read aloud to each other . . . from Agatha Christie novels."[10] Yet, ironically, one can find dozens of sexual innuendos (some downright vulgar) in Anderson's lyrics, and among his favorite stage antics during concerts is to use his flute as a phallic symbol.

Jethro Tull achieved their first mainstream success in the summer and fall of 1969, and a closer look at this period reveals just how popular they became. The band was invited to play at the Woodstock festival in August of that year but declined because of conflicts with previously scheduled concerts. "Living in the Past" was a hit single and *Stand Up* reached number one on the UK Album Chart in August. In a reader poll in the September 20, 1969 issue of the leading British music magazine, *Melody Maker*, Jethro Tull was voted the second most popular group in the United Kingdom, an astounding accomplishment for them. The Beatles, who were just about to release *Abbey Road* on September 26, were unsurprisingly voted number one in the poll. The Rolling Stones were number three, having released *Beggar's Banquet* back in December 1968, but they had not yet released *Let It Bleed*, which would eventually hit number one with the help of "You Can't Always Get What You Want."

According to this poll, Jethro Tull was also more popular than the Who (who had released *Tommy* in May), Led Zeppelin (who released their first album in January but had not yet released *Led Zeppelin II*), Cream (who had already broken up but released two high-charting albums in 1969), and Pink Floyd (who were about to release their double album *Ummagumma*). Jethro Tull's early success with singles and albums, visceral live shows that continually sold out, positive reviews in the British musical papers, and subsequent success in American and Europe allowed the band the liberty, resources, and clout to create such innovative works as *Aqualung* (1971), *Thick as a Brick,* and *A Passion Play*.

Returning to the rise of progressive rock, most writers on the style see it coming into its own and branching off from psychedelia in 1969. In the early 1970s the overt influences of psychedelia gradually faded from progressive rock – and rock music in general – as the counterculture itself splintered and slowly disintegrated. Yet progressive rock became ever more popular with the ascendancy of the album over the single, the impact of FM radio stations that played longer songs, affordable concert tickets, and other factors. By the mid 1970s, Emerson, Lake & Palmer; Yes; Genesis; Jethro Tull; Pink Floyd; and North American groups like Rush, Kansas, and Styx were selling millions of records and playing in large arenas. Kevin Holm-Hudson succinctly describes the rise and fall of progressive rock, and its reception, this way:

> From 1969 to about 1977, progressive rock – a style of self-consciously complex rock often associated with prominent keyboards, complex metric shifts, fantastic (often mythological or metaphysical) lyrics, and an emphasis on flashy virtuosity – dominated FM radio and rock album charts. When punk became an ascendant force in popular culture in 1976–77, the excesses and high-cultural pretensions of progressive rock made it an easy target, hastening its demise.[11]

Although progressive rock has never died, it did fall headlong out of the mainstream in the late 1970s with the rise of punk, disco, and new wave music. Beginning in the late 1980s, there has been a resurgence of interest in the style with the mainstream success of adventurous bands such as Marillion, Dream Theater, and Radiohead. Three of the major progressive rock bands, Pink Floyd, Genesis, and Rush, have been inducted into the Rock and Roll Hall of Fame (in 1996, 2010, and 2013, respectively).

BAND MEMBERS AND THEIR BEGINNINGS

The British progressive rock bands of the late 1960s and early 1970s were prone to frequent lineup changes, with musical or personal differences being the common reason for a musician leaving a group. Jethro Tull is no different, with more than twenty-five musicians at one time or another being in the band. Guitarist Martin Barre, not one to sugarcoat a situation, bluntly remarks "the continuity is rubbish."[12] Yet each new musician brings a fresh perspective, an added dimension to the band's craft, and the group has always had an easily identifiable sound despite the personnel changes. The musicians who recorded *Thick as a Brick* and *A Passion Play* are Ian Anderson on vocals, flute, and acoustic guitar; Jeffrey Hammond on bass; John Evans on keyboards; Barrie Barlow on drums and percussion; and Martin Barre on electric guitar. In addition, David Palmer (who underwent a sex-change operation and became Dee Palmer in 2003) arranged and conducted all the orchestral parts for the band's early albums.[13] This group of musicians – which lasted from mid 1971 to late 1975 – is widely considered to be among the finest versions of Jethro Tull. They created some of the band's most popular and adventurous albums and reached a peak in popularity, especially in America. The recordings by this lineup are *Life is a Long Song* (a five-song British EP from 1971), *Thick as a Brick*, *Living in the Past* (a 1972 double album compilation that includes the five songs from the *Life is a Long Song* EP), *A Passion Play*, *War Child* (1974), and *Minstrel in the Gallery* (1975).[14] An important reason why this particular group of musicians achieved such musical heights is because four of the five began playing together when they were teenagers as the Blades (later called the John Evan Band and the John Evan Smash) years before Jethro Tull released their first album, *This Was*, in 1968. Martin Barre was the only member not in these early bands. He joined Jethro Tull for their second album, *Stand Up*.

The Blades, the earliest incarnation of what would become Jethro Tull, was a rhythm-and-blues band that was formed in Blackpool, England, in 1962 by Ian Anderson (vocals, harmonica, guitar), Jeffrey Hammond (bass), and John Evans (drums). Anderson was born in Dunfermline, Scotland, on August 10, 1947, grew up in Edinburgh, and moved with his family to Blackpool, England, in 1959 when he was twelve. He obtained his first guitar, a Spanish acoustic, around this time. In late 1962 Ian approached Jeffrey Hammond (later "Jeffrey Hammond-Hammond"), born on July 30, 1947, in Blackpool, about forming a band. Hammond, Anderson's schoolmate at Blackpool Grammar School, agreed and took up the bass guitar. John Evans (later "Evan"), another Blackpool native and school chum, joined the group on drums. Evans, born on March 28, 1948, began playing piano at the early age of four, since his mother was a piano teacher. The group played coffeehouses, youth clubs, and dance halls around Blackpool and were influenced by the Beatles, the Rolling Stones, and American R & B. In late 1963 and early 1964 Evans moved to keyboards, where he excelled under his mother's tutelage, and the band recruited Barrie (later "Barriemore") Barlow to play drums. Barlow was born in Birmingham on September 10, 1949, and at age fourteen moved to Blackpool, where he met the other members of the band. Thus, four of the five members of Jethro Tull who would eventually record *Thick as a Brick* and *A Passion Play* were playing together almost ten years earlier in 1964.

Blackpool, north of Liverpool and south of the Lake District on the west coast of England, has been a seaside resort since the middle of the eighteenth century. The advent of railways in the mid-nineteenth century gave factory workers the means to travel from the smoky industrial centers of Manchester and Birmingham to the waves at Blackpool's beaches.[15] Even today it remains England's most popular vacation destination after London. In the early 1960s a wave of a different sort hit its shores along with the rest of England: American music. Although it was not on par with Liverpool, which received into its ports the early rock 'n' roll records from America and was host to hundreds of bands and dozens of venues, Blackpool had its own thriving music scene. Bands such as Johnny Breeze and the Atlantics and the Rockin' Vickers were combining American rock 'n' roll, R & B, and soul with British skiffle to create an original style. Pete Shelton, a Blackpool music historian, sees this pursuit of originality as the key to the early success of these bands, one of which was the John Evan Band that eventually became Jethro Tull. Shelton writes: "The Beatles and the Stones had set the benchmark for progress ... and were beginning to develop their own musical style simply by creating their own image, and writing their own material. To succeed in music, a band need[ed] to constantly move forward. That was the feeling in Blackpool among the new bands being formed."[16]

Ironically, by 1968 when Jethro Tull recorded their first album, the only member from the original Blades remaining in the band was Ian Anderson. Hammond left in 1966 to go to the Blackpool College of Art and later studied painting for three years at the Central School of Art in London. He was replaced on bass guitar by Glenn Cornick, who played on the first three Jethro Tull albums. After Cornick was asked to leave the group in 1971, Anderson convinced Hammond to take a break from art, pick up his bass again, and join the band. Hammond's first album with Jethro Tull was *Aqualung*.

In late 1967 Evans and Barlow left the band together. They were both disenchanted with the blues direction that Anderson was taking with lead guitarist Mick Abrahams, and with the meager income they earned from playing gigs. Evans enrolled in the Chelsea College of Science (now King's College) and continued to study piano. He was asked by Anderson in December 1969 to play organ on Jethro Tull's single "Teacher" and piano and mellotron on "The Witch's Promise." In early 1970 he played organ and piano as a sideman on Jethro Tull's third album, *Benefit*. He left school and joined them full-time in April 1970, staying with the band for ten years until 1980. Barlow joined Jethro Tull in May 1971, replacing Clive Bunker, who left the band after the *Aqualung* album to get married and settle in England. Barlow played drums in various bands after leaving the Blades and also worked as a lathe turner. He first recorded with Jethro Tull on the five-song EP *Life is a Long Song* and then joined the band on the road to complete the *Aqualung* tour. His first full-length album was *Thick as a Brick,* and he played drums in the band until 1980.

The fifth member is the superb electric guitarist Martin Barre, who was born in Birmingham on November 17, 1946. By age seventeen he was playing saxophone, flute, and guitar, and studying architecture and surveying at Hall Green College in Birmingham. He first came into contact with Jethro Tull in 1968 when his band Gethsemane opened for Tull at a concert. Barre was asked to join the band in 1969 after Mick Abrahams left and has been the longest-standing member besides Anderson.

On a final biographical note, this book is just as much about the individual Ian Anderson as it is about the band Jethro Tull. While I am loath to give short shrift to the other band members, who are all brilliant in their own respects, Anderson deserves most of the credit for the accomplishments of Jethro Tull. In the band's forty-five-year career he has written practically all of the music and lyrics to their over three hundred songs, although various members have contributed ideas. He guided the designs for their almost fifty studio, live, and compilation albums; oversaw the stage designs for their more than three thousand concerts; and handled almost all of the band's promotion, including hundreds of interviews and personal appearances. Dee Palmer, in her succinct manner, puts it this way: "Jethro Tull *is* Ian Anderson."[17]

INFLUENCES ON JETHRO TULL

While the Beatles were a major influence on Barre, Barlow, Evans, and Hammond, they were not so on Ian Anderson. Anderson's early songwriting and performing were shaped mostly by American blues musicians such as T-Bone Walker, Muddy Waters, and John Lee Hooker; the jazz musician Rahsaan Roland Kirk; and the British folk musicians Bert Jansch and John Renbourn. Above all, though, was Roy Harper. Anderson says that Harper is his "primary influence as an acoustic guitarist and songwriter."[18] Jethro Tull biographer Greg Russo reports that in the early days Anderson owned only one LP, Roy Harper's first album, *Sophisticated Beggar* (1966), which he played on his mono record player plugged into a Vox guitar amplifier.[19] Anderson says that Harper's second album, *Come Out Fighting Genghis Smith* (1967), "spun endlessly on my Dansette turntable through the equally endless Summer of '68."[20]

Since Anderson was greatly inspired by Harper's songwriting craft and playing, it is easy to see certain similarities between the two musicians. First, their experiences living in the seaside city of Blackpool have been a subject in their songwriting. Harper's *Sophisticated Beggar*, contains his "Blackpool" while Anderson's "Up the 'Pool" is on Jethro Tull's *Life is a Long Song* and *Living in the Past*.[21] In fact, Harper recorded his version of "Up the 'Pool" for the Jethro Tull tribute album *To Cry You a Song: A Collection of Tull Tales* (1996), which convinced Anderson to begin playing his long-forgotten song in concert. Second, Harper's fingerpicking style on acoustic guitar, especially his mastery of picking out melodies within strumming patterns, is a vital component of Anderson's style. For example, Anderson's "Nursie" (on *Life is a Long Song* and *Living in the Past*) sounds much like Harper's "Girlie" from *Sophisticated Beggar*. A third similarity is both musicians' use of string ensembles to augment intimate acoustic songs. Some examples, of which there are dozens to choose from, are Harper's "All You Need Is" from *Come Out Fighting Genghis Smith* and Jethro Tull's "Reasons for Waiting" from *Stand Up*. Fourth, both artists wrote many songs that inveigh against authority figures and organized religion, such as Harper's "Circle" and "Come Out Fighting Genghis Smith" from *Come Out Fighting Genghis Smith* and Jethro Tull's "Wind Up" and "My God" from *Aqualung*. Lastly, both songwriters employ large-scale musical structures that stretch the boundaries of conventional folk and popular music song forms. Harper's longest song is the twenty-two-minute "The Lord's Prayer" from *Lifemask* (1973), while *Thick as a Brick* and *A Passion Play* clock in at forty-three and forty-five minutes respectively. The 2012 sequel album *Thick as a Brick 2: Whatever Happened to Gerald Bostock?* tops them both, being fifty-three minutes of continuous music. It is to this aspect of the band's craft that I will turn next.

THE ART OF THE LONG SONG

One of the defining characteristics of progressive rock is the use of large-scale forms to create works of extended length. In the late 1960s and early 1970s a number of bands integrated rock music with large-scale forms – typically found in classical music – using a variety of means. The most popular was the concept album, which, as Roy Shuker defines it, is "unified by a theme, which can be instrumental, compositional, narrative or lyrical."[22] The Beatles' *Sgt. Pepper's Lonely Hearts Club Band* is generally regarded by rock critics, scholars, and fans as being the first rock concept album, although John Lennon said, "It was not as 'put together' as it sounds."[23] The majority of concept albums from this period consist of separate songs that tell a story, such as the Who's *Tommy* from 1969. Some bands integrated classical music with rock by either recording with a symphony orchestra (the Moody Blues, Deep Purple, Procol Harum), interpreting classical works within a rock context (Emerson,

Lake & Palmer's version of Modest Mussorgsky's *Pictures at an Exhibition*), or quoting familiar themes by great composers in their songs.

While creativity and experimentation in rock music can take many forms, composing a piece of original music of formidable length without falling into the traps of predictable and mindless repetition, extended soloing, and vacuous studio wizardry is impressive. Writing a large-scale work that keeps the listener's interest requires a keen understanding of form, harmony, arranging, and instrumentation. Employing different styles of music, varying the mode of expression, and having a flair for dramatic storytelling are also important. John Covach points out two approaches to long rock songs that bands adopted in the late 1960s:

> The first is the "medley," in which a number of independent tunes are played one after the other with no break in the music and sometimes with a bit of transition to ease the way from one tune into the next. Perhaps the most famous rock medley of this type is the second side of [the Beatles'] *Abbey Road*, where tunes follow one after the other to fill up one whole side of the LP. A second way of creating pieces of extended length is to "stretch them from within," so to speak: in such a case a song of conventional length is extended by creating a long jam session in the middle, and something like [Iron Butterfly's] "In-A-Gadda-Da-Vida" is a pretty good example of this. Here the song and its reprise act as bookends surrounding the extended soloing in the middle.[24]

Thick as a Brick (TAAB) and *A Passion Play* (APP) have some similarities with the first approach, yet because they have numerous instrumental passages, they are much more than just medleys of tunes. TAAB has nineteen different instrumental passages that link the vocal sections, and APP has sixteen. Some of these passages are placed between sections of a particular tune. This is quite a bit more sophisticated than "a bit of transition," which characterizes the medley approach. In fact, the instrumental passages in TAAB take up approximately twenty-three minutes of music, while the vocal sections take up approximately twenty-one minutes, which makes the album more "transition" than "tune." Yet the relationship between the vocal and the instrumental sections is more complex than just thinking of the vocal sections as "tunes" and the instrumental passages as "transitions." (This will be discussed in more depth in chapters 4 and 7 with regard to the thematic development in both albums.)

The two Jethro Tull albums bear little resemblance to the second approach. In fact, they are marked more by concision than by extension, being tightly composed collages of many musical ideas rather than a stretching of a few musical ideas. Even the passages of improvised solos are short, and no section, neither vocal nor instrumental, lasts longer than five minutes. Concerning the stretching of musical material, Edward Macan writes: "When listening to the long instrumental jams of even the most gifted psychedelic bands – the Hendrix Experience, Cream, the Nice – one is initially wowed by the musicians' daunting virtuosity, but after two or three minutes a certain numbness sets in: one wishes for a greater variety of instrumentation and dynamics, a better balance between virtuoso solos and a more melodic approach, and ultimately a sense that the music was 'going somewhere.'"[25] Indeed, a long song that is composed and arranged well (i.e., that is "going somewhere") is often more satisfying than a long song that is made long simply by instrumental soloing. Although Anderson did indulge in dreadfully long flute solos in concerts, there is none of that on *Thick as a Brick* or *A Passion Play*. Yes, the songs are quite long, but they take the listener on a spacious musical journey that is satisfying from beginning to end. As a result, these two albums transcend Covach's categories because of their wealth of thematic development, their unique forms, and their stylistic diversity.

JETHRO TULL'S LONG SONGS

When one considers the progressive rock bands of the late 1960s and early 1970s, it seems unlikely that Jethro Tull would be the first to release an album that consisted of one continuous song. Not counting live recordings, the longest song the band wrote and recorded before *Thick as a Brick* was "My God" from *Aqualung*, which is just over seven minutes long. Several bands broke the "eighteen-minute sound barrier" (a continuous, unified song lasting the whole side of a record or more) before *Thick as a Brick*, and many composed concept albums before 1972. Yet practically all of these side-long pieces fit into Covach's two categories, being either songs strung together as a medley with linking material or conventional-length songs stretched by instrumental soloing.[26]

Thick as a Brick was a huge leap forward for Jethro Tull, but there are signs on *Aqualung* that the band was capable of a work of this magnitude. "Aqualung" and "My God" are dramatic pieces of music that employ different styles and modes of expression. Yet there are even clearer signs in "By Kind Permission Of," a piano solo recorded live at Carnegie Hall on November 4, 1970, and included on *Living in the Past*.[27] In this piece, pianist John Evans strings together bits of the first movement of Beethoven's Piano Sonata no. 8 in C minor ("Pathetique"), Debussy's "Golliwogg's Cakewalk" from *Children's Corner*, and Rachmaninoff's Prelude in C♯ minor Op. 3 No. 2, and combines them with his own tuneful vamping, improvising, and duetting with Anderson on flute. Because of its large-scale structure and merging of a number of different styles, this piece may be seen as a precursor to a work like *Thick as a Brick*.

In interviews Ian Anderson has expressed mixed feeling about progressive rock bands and their penchant for writing extended-length songs. On the one hand, he does not think of Jethro Tull as exclusively a progressive rock band. The band and Anderson as a solo artist have delved into several different styles of music throughout their career: blues rock, hard rock, electric folk, acoustic folk, electronic, world music, and classical music. Progressive rock is simply one of those styles. He maintains that *Thick as a Brick* was not envisioned from the start as a continuous forty-three-minute song (although *A Passion Play* was). On the other hand, he has expressed some regret that album-length compositions were no longer feasible for the band after *A Passion Play*. In an interview with Greg Russo, Anderson said, "I enjoyed the experience of working in that way. I'm very sad that it's been proved necessary to have to work in conventional song lengths again."[28]

The uniqueness of Jethro Tull's progressive phase is accentuated when one compares *Thick as a Brick* and *A Passion Play* to their next studio album, *War Child*. The songwriting on *War Child* is strikingly different from TAAB and APP and is a bit of a letdown. The foursquare melodies, the repetitive strophic and verse-chorus forms, and the lack of instrumental passages and counterpoint give the album a predictability, a conventionality, a blandness that pales in comparison to the audacity of the two prior studio albums. If the songwriting on TAAB and APP erred on the side of bombast and complexity, the songwriting on *War Child* erred on the side of reticence and simplicity. One gets the feeling while listening that the band is much better than the music on that album. Anderson says of "Bungle in the Jungle," the first single released from *War Child:*

> It's a rather odd song for Jethro Tull, I think. Every so often there are those songs that fall into the conventional pop-rock structure – songs like "Teacher," for instance – but that style isn't our *forte*. We're not very good at it because I'm not that kind of a singer, and it doesn't come easy to me to do that stuff. But "Bungle" is one of those songs that was nice to have done. It's got the Jethro Tull ingredients, but it's a little more straight-ahead. It's Jethro Tull in tight leather trousers.[29]

Yet this album of "straight-ahead" rock songs "in tight leather trousers" was a necessary step for Jethro Tull after negative critical reaction to *A Passion Play*. Another concept album consisting of one long song would have been too much cream in the coffee. But after *War Child* the band returned once again to longer, more involved song structures with *Minstrel in the Gallery*, the concept album/song cycle of aging rocker Roy Lomas on *Too Old to Rock 'n' Roll, Too Young to Die!* (1976), the compositionally dense folk trilogy of *Songs from the Wood* (1977), *Heavy Horses* (1978), and *Stormwatch* (1979), and the eclectic and underrated *A* (1980). Anderson continued to write long songs throughout the eighties and nineties, the best tracks being "Budapest" from *Crest of a Knave* (1987) and "At Last, Forever" from *Roots to Branches* (1995). In 2012 Anderson jumped headlong back into album-length concepts with *Thick as a Brick 2: Whatever Happened to Gerald Bostock?*

THICK AS A BRICK AND A PASSION PLAY COMPARED AND CONTRASTED

Now that the backdrop for progressive rock and Jethro Tull has been established, it is time to look a bit closer at the albums themselves. *TAAB* and *APP* have much in common. Both albums were composed and recorded within a year and a half of each other and, as a result, are cut from roughly the same musical cloth. They are a blend of rock, folk, and classical music with the five band members displaying expansive instrumentation and virtuoso technique. They both eschew the common forms of popular and rock music and consist of one continuous piece of music lasting over forty minutes with similar amounts of short vocal and instrumental sections. They are both unified by the periodic return of vocal melodies, lyrics, mode/key areas, and instrumental motives. They are intended to be concept albums and experienced as unified works, although portions have been extracted and released as three- or four-minute singles. Lastly, both works were accompanied by extravagant album packaging when they were first released, and both were played live in their entirety on the tours to promote them.

Yet there are many discernible differences that make them two distinct listening experiences. Regarding the overall musical impression of the two albums, *Thick as a Brick* sounds more organic and unified than *A Passion Play* because of its wealth of thematic development that binds it together from beginning to end. While APP contains thematic development, it doesn't have the unity and continuity of its sibling. TAAB maintains a nearly constant intensity throughout, even in the slower sections, while APP comes at the listener in fits and starts, with abrupt shifts in tempo that periodically stymie its forward progress. For instance, the most identifiable section of APP ("There was a rush...") appears several times, but its slow tempo and unvaried hymn-like setting continually deflate the momentum and energy of the music. The most identifiable section of TAAB (the opening acoustic guitar pattern) also returns a number of times throughout the piece, but it is continually varied in some fashion. This makes it sound fresh each time it is encountered and moves the music forward. "The Story of the Hare Who Lost His Spectacles" is another factor that compromises the unity of APP, since it is so stylistically different from the rest of the album, even though it provides a welcome respite from the dark, lyrical subject matter. "The Story," a spoken-word fable with orchestral accompaniment in the middle of APP, divides the piece into three sections – the first twenty-one minutes, the four-minute "Story," and the last twenty minutes – and has little, if anything, to do with the rest of the music and lyrics. TAAB also has sections that venture into divergent musical territory, but they are short and transitory. Although continuity, unity, thematic development, and forward progress are not necessarily markers of good music, they are musical ingredients in which Jethro Tull excelled. If Frank Zappa (on many of his albums) and the Beatles (on side 2 of *Abbey Road*) were masters of using abrupt transitions and divergent musical styles to create sound collages, Jethro Tull were masters of using gradual transitions and thematic development to create unified works.

Ironically, although the music of *Thick as a Brick* holds together better than that of *A Passion Play*, the *Thick as a Brick* lyrics can confound the listener with their bewildering and incoherent assortment of characters, settings, and narrative viewpoints. Because of their perplexing and obtuse nature, the average listener is likely to give up trying to make sense of the lyrics by the end. The lyrics to *A Passion Play*, on the other hand, are easier to follow, since they concern a central protagonist, Ronnie Pilgrim, who goes on a journey through his afterlife. Yet the narrative of APP also has its wayward moments and veers off course completely with "The Story of the Hare Who Lost His Spectacles."

Thick as a Brick is an album of paradoxes. The preposterous newspaper that comprises the album cover implies that it is a spoof of concept albums, yet it is a classic example of a concept album. Its music is complex and layered, yet it is tuneful and hummable. Its lyrics are fragmentary and puzzling, yet the music makes the barrage of disjointed images, characters, and ideas flow fluently. It is an experimental album not intended to please the general popular music audience, yet it hit number one on the *Billboard* chart. While *Thick as a Brick* was a milestone for the band, *A Passion Play* was something of a millstone. It is nearly as compelling a work as its predecessor in terms of music, lyrics, theme, and use of humor, but it suffered simply because the band had already recorded a monumental album-length composition, and a second attempt at this endeavor was bound to fall short. Anderson himself predicted this even before the band conceived *A Passion Play*. While on the *Thick as a Brick* tour in 1972, Anderson said, "I think every record and every year has to be different. If we ever turned out two successive records which were... in the same vein, the second wouldn't be good, I mean to me."[30] Although many fans – including myself – believe *A Passion Play* to be one of the band's greatest albums, it has always received negative reviews from the musical press, scarring its reputation. Ironically, Jethro Tull's two most difficult and perplexing albums were the only ones to hit number one on the U.S. *Billboard* 200 Album Chart.

Perhaps the greatest strength of the two albums, and the essential element that makes them worthwhile, is their wealth of melody and the sheer tunefulness in the music. Without this, listening to a continuous forty-five-minute piece of music of any type would tax the ears of even the most dedicated music lover. Eric Tamm effectively described the progressive rock of the 1970s as "a music in which the head of classical sophistication was grafted Frankenstein-like onto the erotic body of rock."[31] There are numerous musical monstrosities in the rock music of the 1970s, but, thankfully, Jethro Tull never abandoned simple and beautiful melodies in their desire to stretch the boundaries of the rock album.

TWO

Galliards and Lute Songs: The Influence of Early Music in Jethro Tull

THIS CHAPTER, WHICH BUILDS UPON CHAPTER 1 IN PROVIDING a context for *Thick as a Brick* and *A Passion Play*, first describes how an interest in medieval and Renaissance culture and music arose within the British folk and rock music of the late 1960s. It then considers how these influences began to show up early in Jethro Tull's career and on the two albums. By the early 1970s these influences became a defining characteristic of the band and were reflected not only in their music but also in their lyrics, live shows, and album covers. Although Ian Anderson has the uncanny ability to summon up vestiges of the past, he has never claimed to be a scholar of the music, literature, or culture of the British Middle Ages. He has never expressed any intention of authentically recreating the music of earlier periods, and thus his allusions and borrowings, especially on the earlier Jethro Tull albums, have a vagueness about them. He is a fusionist at heart, with a foot in both the past and the present. His performance of "The Witch's Promise" in 1970 on the British television show *Top of the Pops* demonstrates this.[1] He could pass for a hippie, a medieval strolling minstrel, or a Victorian-era tramp.[2]

Popular, rock, and folk musicians in the late 1960s expressed a desire to move society forward beyond the Vietnam War, beyond the conservative mind-set of their parents, beyond the din of industrial capitalism, and beyond the homogeny of the suburban sprawl. Many musicians found the answer in turning back to medieval and Renaissance music and culture, or at least an idealized version of it. Yet they found it difficult to completely abandon their electric guitars and amplifiers. Bill Martin expresses this Janus-like perspective when he writes that progressive rock bands were "performing works whose lyrics concern ecologism, pastoralism, and antitechnological romanticism ... even while employing the most up-to-date electronic musical gear; to say nothing of megavolts of electricity."[3] Jethro Tull was but one of several British bands to go "living in the past" in the late 1960s. This trend can be seen in progressive rock bands like King Crimson, Genesis, Gentle Giant, Renaissance, and the Strawbs; folk musicians and bands like John Renbourn, Bert Jansch, Pentangle, the Incredible String Band, Dolly and Shirley Collins; and electric folk bands like Fairport Convention and Steeleye Span.[4] Even more mainstream rock bands like Led Zeppelin showed this influence with their mythical "The Battle of Evermore" (from *Led Zeppelin IV*, 1971), on which singer Robert Plant is accompanied by Fairport Convention's Sandy Denny.

How did this interest in preindustrial culture arise within British folk and rock music of the late 1960s? The first strand of influence was broadly cultural while the second was more specifically musical. Two major factors in the first strand were the burgeoning ecology movement and popularity of fantasy/historical literature and film. Regarding the first, the late 1960s counterculture saw in the preindustrial period a people who lived closer to the earth. Although the first Earth Day was officially celebrated on April 22, 1970, the ecology movement can be traced to the early 1960s with the publication of Rachel Carson's *Silent Spring* (1962), which warned of the dangers of chemical pesticides. In an increasingly urbanized and industrialized 1960s, the predominantly rural population of the medieval/Renaissance period was seen as a type of utopia. Hippies from both sides of the Atlantic were "Going Up the Country" (as in the 1968 Canned Heat song) in order to get themselves "back to the garden" (as in Joni Mitchell's 1969 song "Woodstock").

The second factor in the cultural medievalism in the late 1960s was the popularity of fantasy/historical literature and film. J.R.R. Tolkien's *The Lord of the Rings* (1954–1955), with its borrowings from the medieval epic poem *Beowulf*, became a great source of lyrical inspiration. There was even a rock concert venue in London's Covent Garden in the late 1960s called Middle Earth, where psychedelic and progressive bands played (such as Pink Floyd, the Who, Fairport Convention, Jefferson Airplane, Captain Beefheart, Soft Machine, and Tomorrow).

T. H. White's book *The Once and Future King* (1958), a retelling of the King Arthur legends, was also popular in the 1960s and was the inspiration for the musical *Camelot* on Broadway (1960), in the West End (1964), and as a blockbuster film (1967). Paul Hardwick comments on the connection between progressive rock bands and the King Arthur legends: "the image of the mounted Arthurian knight has become ... an icon of the genre."[5] The film *A Man for All Seasons* (1966) portrayed Sir Thomas More in his stand against King Henry VIII's wish to annul the marriage to his first of six wives, Catherine of Aragon. *The Lion in Winter*, another play (1966) and blockbuster film (1968), dramatized the stormy relationship between King Henry II and his wife, Eleanor of Aquitaine, in twelfth-century England. Also in 1968, Franco Zeffirelli's adaptation of Shakespeare's *Romeo and Juliet* filled the ears and eyes of filmgoers with courtly life in the Renaissance era.

What influence did the ecology movement and the popularity of fantasy/historical literature and film have on Jethro Tull? Although Anderson was at odds with the free love and drug use of the hippies, as discussed in chapter 1, he did have their passion for ecology. The band shares its name with the British agriculturist who perfected the horse-drawn seed drill in 1701. Dozens of their songs either celebrate the beauty of nature ("Velvet Green," 1977; "A Winter Snowscape," 2004) or inveigh against the detrimental effects of industrialization ("Wond'ring Again," 1970; "Farm on the Freeway," 1987). Regarding medieval-influenced literature and film, Anderson's aesthetic sense was not enlivened so much by kings, queens, knights, or star-cross'd lovers, but by those at the other end of the social spectrum: the peasants, minstrels, and court jesters. It may be true to say that Anderson identified more with the medieval "counterculture," the minstrels and jesters, than with his late 1960s contemporaries, an idea that will be explored further below.

THE BRITISH FOLK REVIVAL:
"SPIN ME DOWN THE LONG AGES"

The second strand showing the influence of the Middle Ages in the late 1960s had a concerted focus on recreating the music of earlier periods. It would be helpful at this point to briefly trace the British folk revival, since it provided a foundation that bands like Jethro Tull built upon. The British folk revival came in two installments. The first gained its impetus from the work of Harvard professor and folklorist Francis James Child (1825–1896), who collected manuscripts of traditional English folk ballads and published them as *The English and Scottish Popular Ballads*. Most of these ballads are from the late fifteenth to the late seventeenth centuries, although some date to the thirteenth century. Child's collection, published in ten volumes between 1882 and 1898, contains 305 ballads and has long been a primary tool for scholarly research on English history and folklore as well as a rich resource for folk musicians. Cecil Sharp built on Child's work by transcribing and publishing collections of traditional British songs, instrumental music, and dances. He disseminated them within the British public school system, bringing the nation's folk heritage to its youth. In the early twentieth century he established what is known today as the English Folk Dance and Song Society (EFDSS), whose purpose is to preserve British folk manuscripts, music, instruments, and costumes. It was also during the early twentieth century that a new breed of English composers emerged (Ralph Vaughan Williams, Benjamin Britten, and Gustav Holst) with a keen interest in preserving, arranging, and borrowing traditional British folk music.

While the first British folk revival focused on written manuscripts and was a scholarly enterprise, the second revival's agenda was more of a populist movement and treated folk song primarily as an oral tradition. A pioneer in this second revival was Alan Lomax, who, with his cumbersome recording equipment, traveled all over the British Isles in the 1950s to record folk music in its natural habitat. The rise of folk clubs, mostly in London, and the establishment of a folk "scene" were crucial in creating a community where folk song could flourish. Record labels, radio shows, and television shows were also influential in propagating the music to this new audience. Lastly, the skiffle craze in the late 1950s played a huge role in putting inexpensive acoustic instruments, especially the guitar, into the hands of young musicians. Shirley Collins and John Renbourn both played in skiffle groups in the early 1960s before their encounters with medieval music. By the mid 1960s, folk music had reached a mainstream audience on both sides of the Atlantic with musicians like Bob Dylan, Joan Baez, and Simon and Garfunkel reaching the top of the record charts with their albums and singles.

Three albums released in 1969 provide examples of how fruitful the confluence between medieval music and contemporary folk music was in this period. The first of these albums is *Anthems in Eden,* which features the folksinger Shirley Collins on vocals, her sister Dolly Collins on portative organ, and several members of the Early Music Consort of London playing medieval instruments such as viols, crumhorns, and rebecs. One of these members, David Munrow, a musician and early music historian, was influential in developing and preserving period instruments and performing on them with British folk musicians. The centerpiece of *Anthems in Eden* is a twenty-eight-minute medley of eight traditional British folk songs called "A Song-Story." This medley has structural similarities to *Thick as a Brick, A Passion Play,* and the medieval *lai,* which is discussed at the end of the chapter.

The second landmark album from 1969 is Fairport Convention's *Liege and Lief,* which perfectly synthesizes medieval/Renaissance English ballads with folk and rock music. The band's original numbers, such as "Come All Ye" and "Crazy Man Michael," perfectly complement their renderings of Child ballads like "Tam Lin" and "Matty Groves." This album added an electric edge to the blending of 1960s folk and medievalism and is widely regarded as being the seminal "electric folk" album.

The third is Jethro Tull's second album, *Stand Up,* which reached number one on the UK Albums Chart. While the medieval and Renaissance influences on *Stand Up* are not nearly as overt as on the Collins and Fairport Convention albums, it was the first manifestation of this vital element in Jethro Tull's style and helped to bring an appreciation of early music to a mainstream audience. While the band explored many musical avenues besides medievalism, their early albums can be described, in Rob Young's words, as "music born out of the battle between progressive push and nostalgic pull."[6]

The remainder of this chapter will consider Jethro Tull's interest in the Middle Ages on the albums from *Stand Up* onward, as seen in their lyrics, live shows, album covers, and instrumentation.

LYRICS

From his earliest lyrical attempts on Jethro Tull's first few albums, Ian Anderson has been adept at writing in past literary styles and imbuing his lyrics with pastoral imagery found in preindustrial British literature and folklore. This type of lyric writing would come to full fruition on *Songs from the Wood* and *Heavy Horses,* but many early songs, such as "The Witch's Promise" (1970) and "Mother Goose" from *Aqualung,* use folkloric imagery that can be found in ballads, fables, nursery rhymes, and fairy tales. Many of Anderson's lyrics adhere to strict rhyme schemes and poetic meters and have an affinity with traditional British narrative forms. Several phrases in the lyrics of *Thick as a Brick* incorporate or allude to past literary genres; for instance, the folk and ballad tropes "Let me tell you" and "Come all ye" in Vocal 12.[7] In this regard, Jethro Tull was part of a larger group of electric folk bands – including Fairport Convention and Steeleye Span – who merged rock music with English folk music, folklore, and literature. Yet Jethro Tull differed from these groups in that they rarely performed versions of Child ballads or other traditional British folk songs. From *Stand Up* onward, Anderson clearly saw himself as an original songwriter and not an interpreter of others' material. The few pieces of early music that the band did create their own versions of are "Bourrée" (from J. S. Bach's Suite for Lute in E minor, BWV 996), "King Henry's Madrigal" (written by King Henry VIII and better known as "Pastime with Good Company"), the sixteenth-century English folk song "John Barleycorn," and some Christmas carols on *The Jethro Tull Christmas Album* (2003). In addition, Anderson was not deliberately trying to imitate any particular literary form or style. The form and content of the lyrics to *Thick as a Brick* and *A Passion Play* are unique and defy easy classification.

The late 1960s was a period in rock music when addressing contemporary issues like the Vietnam War was viewed as imperative. Anderson addressed contemporary social issues in his lyrics but did so obliquely, often adopting the tone of a medieval or Renaissance-era court jester. "Sossity; You're a Woman" from *Benefit,* much of the *Aqualung* album, and "Wond'ring Again" from *Living in the Past* all contain social critique delivered in this fashion. The lyrics to *Thick as a Brick* can also be viewed in this way, an oblique critique of society from the perspective of an eight-year-old boy genius (as discussed further in chapter 3 on the lyrics).

Specific references in Jethro Tull's lyrics to medieval/Renaissance life and culture begin to show up more often beginning with *A Passion Play*. The passion play itself was an early medieval invention. Maypole dancing – though not exclusively a medieval English tradition – is mentioned in the lyrics and was shown in the short film played during the tour for that album. "Back-Door Angels" and "Only Solitaire" from *War Child* contain references to fools and court jesters, and the lyrics to "Minstrel in the Gallery" (1975) are written from the perspective of a minstrel looking down on his audience. Most of the songs from *Songs from the Wood* and *Heavy Horses* are about rural life in preindustrial England and Scotland.

LIVE SHOWS

Early in the band's career, Anderson began to shape his iconic persona of the slightly mad minstrel flutist hopping up and down on one leg, as he was so often described. This can be seen on the DVD *The Rolling Stones Rock and Roll Circus*, recorded in December 1968 but not released until 2004. For Jethro Tull concerts in the early to mid 1970s, Anderson dressed in garb similar to that of a medieval or Renaissance-era strolling minstrel or jester, complete with tights and a codpiece. When speaking of his life as a touring musician, he often invokes minstrelsy: "It's something to do with being a gippo [gypsy], a troubadour, a traveling musician, that peculiar romanticism about traveling around and hawking your wares, which is what we do to a bunch of different people in different places."[8] In fact, Anderson conflated the itinerate-musician role of the strolling minstrel and social-critic role of the court jester into one persona. Beatrice Otto points out that this overlap between the two has historical precedent: Watt, the lute player for King Henry VII (reigned 1485–1509), is also called a "fole" (fool) in the king's account book. Otto writes: "There was common ground in the duties of minstrels and jesters – both provided entertainment at banquets and festivals. The medieval minstrel may also have shared the jester's paradoxical privilege of being able to judge those he served, and many minstrels composed songs of derision about unpopular matters."[9]

Anderson differs from his peers in folk and rock music in the manner of his vocal delivery during concerts. He doesn't project the earnest, everyman persona of musicians like Pete Seeger. His inclination toward sardonic humor and sarcasm is akin to the type of social critique a fool or court jester would revel in, and this is apparent on *Thick as a Brick*. Although Anderson is very serious about his musical performance on stage and expects perfection from his bandmates, he is also aware of his role as an entertainer. In between songs he engages in much stage banter, making ribald jokes about himself, his fellow musicians, or society in general, and offering snide remarks about the concert venue or technical difficulties with equipment. This playful banter creates a rapport with the audience and demonstrates how Anderson appropriates certain performance conventions of minstrels and jesters into Jethro Tull's concerts. When the band performed *Thick as a Brick* and *A Passion Play* in concert, they added some surreal comedy bits, making each show unpredictable and somewhat improvised.

The electric folk bands and musicians in general show a close affinity with the medieval strolling minstrels. They learn their craft "on the road," picking up techniques, influences, and ideas from other musicians they play with. They are more in the oral music tradition than the written music tradition (although many folk musicians can read musical notation). Lastly, they are primarily self-taught musicians who foster their love of early music outside of academia and music conservatories.

ALBUM COVERS

Jethro Tull's interest in the Middle Ages did not find its way onto their album covers until after *Thick as a Brick*, although the inside gatefold of *Aqualung* consists of a painting of the group inside a Gothic cathedral. *Living in the Past* mimics the bulk and grandeur of an illuminated manuscript with its thick front and back panels. The cover to *Minstrel in the Gallery* is a painting depicting courtly entertainment in the main hall of a castle or banqueting house. The group of players in the minstrels' gallery on the front cover is mirrored on the back with a photograph showing the band in the balcony of the radio station in Monte Carlo where they recorded the album. Later album covers, such as those for *The Broadsword and the Beast* (1982), *Crest of a Knave,* and *The Jethro Tull Christmas Album,* show the band's continuing fascination with early British history.

MUSICAL MEDIEVALISM

Beginning with their second album, *Stand Up,* Anderson shifted Jethro Tull away from the electric blues influences that dominated their first album, *This Was,* and adopted elements from a number of sources, including medieval/Renaissance minstrel music and late-1960s acoustic folk music.[10] In fact, it could be said that Anderson and the band embarked on this traditionalist tack just weeks after the release of *This Was* on October 18, 1968. Their British single "Love Story/Christmas Song" was recorded and released in November 1968.[11] The B-side, "Christmas Song," with Anderson playing the mandolin and tin whistle for the first time, has a distinctive medieval/Renaissance character that is far removed from the blues. By the years 1971–1972, when *Aqualung* and *Thick as a Brick* were released, this influence was an integral part of Jethro Tull's music. Anderson said in a 1982 interview of the band's movement away from the blues: "I quickly became dissatisfied with what we were doing. I found it hard to go onstage and convincingly be a polite shade of black. What really got me was that I was singing something that was essentially stolen. And it wasn't just stealing music, it was stealing somebody's emotions and point of view, almost pretending to have an awareness of what it means to be black."[12]

Anderson's increasing use of the flute and acoustic guitar from *Stand Up* onward summons up resonances with the medieval strolling minstrels, troubadours, and trouvères who commonly accompanied themselves on the flute, recorder, and lute. The flute is one of the oldest and most widespread of all musical instruments. There is nothing particularly "medieval" or "English" about it, and the recorder was used more often by strolling minstrels.[13] Yet with flute in hand, Anderson became quite clever at embodying the persona of a medieval English strolling minstrel. Anderson did not study early music firsthand, however.

He picked up influences from Roy Harper, John Renbourn, and Bert Jansch, three British acoustic guitarists who blended folk music and early music.

In this period Anderson also changed the way he played and composed for the flute. He abandoned the electric-blues-guitar-derived flute lines he played on *This Was* for lines reminiscent of medieval and Renaissance music. For instance, in "My Sunday Feeling," the first song on *This Was*, Anderson employs the blues progression and the call-and-response verse form, commonly used by blues musicians such as Muddy Waters and B. B. King, in which the singer sings a line and then "responds" to it with a riff on harmonica or guitar. The opening section (Vocal 1) of *Thick as a Brick* uses the same convention of call and response, yet the blues influence has all but vanished. The flute melody's lilting dotted eighth notes, ascending contours, and bright F Mixolydian mode contrast with the dark, heavy, descending contours of "My Sunday Feeling." Edward Macan sees this shift away from the blues as a major trend in late 1960s progressive rock: "While modality and the I-IV-V blues progression coexisted uneasily in British rock during the early days of psychedelia, by the late 1960s progressive rock musicians had largely abandoned the rigid framework of the blues progression in favor of modality's greater flexibility."[14] Regarding his flute playing, Anderson often sang through the flute on Jethro Tull's blues-influenced songs. This technique gave the instrument more of a thick, heavy, electric guitar timbre. However, on much of *Thick as a Brick* and *A Passion Play*, he plays with a pure, clear tone.

Anderson's movement away from electric blues is also evident in his use of the acoustic guitar (and other acoustic plucked instruments), creating associations with the troubadours' and trouvères' use of the lute in secular medieval song. On *This Was* Anderson sings, plays the flute and harmonica, and dabbles on the piano, but on *Stand Up* he adds four more instruments to his recorded repertoire: acoustic guitar, balalaika, bouzouki, and mandolin. Anderson writes:

> When Mick [Abrahams] left the band in December of '68 to be replaced by Martin Barre, it offered me the chance to broaden my flute playing by moving out of the blues form and towards the use of a more eclectic mix of influences, some half-formed from childhood memories, some, more recently adopted from Classical music, Asian music and the more adventurous peer group

progressive pop and rock work of the time. Curiously, Mick's departure also re-awakened the guitar player in me; not only acoustic and electric guitars but mandolin, bouzouki, balalaika and almost anything with strings (and frets) attached![15]

From *Stand Up* on, Anderson makes the acoustic guitar (and other acoustic plucked instruments) an essential element in the band's music and begins to develop a characteristic style as identifiable as his singing and flute playing. In fact, on *Thick as a Brick* he plays five acoustic instruments (acoustic guitar, flute, soprano saxophone, violin, and trumpet), and they are the foil, or counterbalance, to the electric instruments. Although Anderson never recorded on the lute, guitarist Martin Barre plays it in Vocal 11 ("The poet and the wise man . . . ") of *Thick as a Brick*. The use of medieval instruments by the band members becomes more pronounced during the tour for 1977's *Songs from the Wood:* on the song "Velvet Green" Martin Barre plays the lute, keyboardist David Palmer plays portative organ, and drummer Barrie Barlow plays the nakers and tabor. Finally, Anderson's playing technique on both flute and acoustic plucked instruments is replete with trills, turns, mordents, and other ornamentation found in lute and keyboard music from the medieval to the Baroque periods.

Two other examples from *Aqualung* are worthy of note as evidence of musical medievalism in early Jethro Tull. The first is the "chant" section in "My God." In the middle of a song attacking the "bloody church of England," Anderson obviously mimics plainchant and the serene character of medieval sacred music in general. Second, the recorders in "Mother Goose" – combined with the lyrical allusions to nursery rhymes – give the song its medieval/Renaissance feel.

THE MEDIEVAL *LAI* AND JETHRO TULL'S LONG SONGS

A second musical factor, besides instrumentation, that shows Jethro Tull moving away from the blues is their adoption of a wider variety of song forms. Although song forms are covered more fully in chapters 4 and 7, I focus now on one form that both *Thick as a Brick* and *A Passion Play* resemble: the medieval *lai*.[16] Although its origins are obscure, most medieval scholars believe the *lai* began as an extended poetic form in the late twelfth century. The French poet Marie de France is the first poet of definitive authorship of the form. She wrote her *lais* in Anglo-Norman, a dialect of Old French, and the subject matter was predominantly courtly love. Beginning in the early thirteenth century, the form was used by the trouvères and troubadours, who expanded and diversified it, added music, and made it variable in length depending on the number of stanzas. The *lai* would later be taken up by Guillaume de Machaut, who regularized the form into twelve stanzas. Machaut added a feature to his *lais* that the two Jethro Tull albums also have: the last stanza repeats material from the first stanza, rounding off the form and bringing it to a satisfying conclusion. Unlike the motet or the mass, which were cultivated by composers throughout the Renaissance and Baroque eras and beyond, the *lai* was abandoned after Machaut. Consequently, it is an unadulterated example of large-scale medieval song form.

The structure of the lyrics and music of the two Jethro Tull albums shows many similarities to the forms of the *lais* written by the trouvères and troubadours of the thirteenth century, and to Machaut's *lais* from the late fourteenth century. Concerning the former, Christopher Page writes: "For the troubadours and trouvères a *lai* was a specific lyric form, of most ambitious design, in which each subdivision of the text had its own metric form and musical setting."[17] Similarly, *Thick as a Brick* and *A Passion Play* are "of most ambitious design," and most of the vocal sections have their own metric form and musical setting. Concerning Machaut's *lais*, Richard H. Hoppin writes: "It is obvious that the poetic structure of the *lai* must determine the larger aspects of its musical form. The different stanzaic forms require different music, and only the last stanza can, and does, repeat the melody of the first."[18] *Thick as a Brick* and *A Passion Play* match this description. Expanding on this, Isabelle Ragnard writes: "The absence of a refrain, a relatively unconstraining framework for the versification, requires that the poet 'invent' the form [of the music] as he goes along, just as he freely invents his poetic material."[19] This is true of *Thick as a Brick* in that Anderson wrote the lyrics first, shaping the music to fit the varying structures of the lyrical stanzas.[20] This is not true of *A Passion Play*, since much of the music was composed before the lyrics (more on this in chapters 6 and 7).

But were Anderson and the band modeling their two albums on the form of the medieval *lai*? No. Were they even aware of the form? Perhaps. My purpose in pointing out the similarities between the forms of the *lai* and the two albums is not to show that Anderson knew of the form and tried to emulate it, but that his compositional thought process was comparable to that of a medieval composer writing a *lai*. In a 1977 article from *Creem* magazine, he said that he does not get his musical ideas from listening to or studying music, but from an emotional response to what he calls "folk memory." When asked by rock journalist Eric "Air-Wreck" Genheimer, "Have you always liked traditional English folk music, or did you pick it up recently by listening to old recordings or something?" Anderson replied:

> No, I don't listen to anything. I hate that approach, personally speaking. The academic delving and the subtle sharpness of traditional English music is a relatively sterile intellectual exercise. I believe first and foremost in a folk memory. I'm of particularly mixed origin; my mother is English, my father is Scottish. So you have the peculiar sort of mixture of origins in me. But I do believe in a folk memory or something which is at once Anglo-Saxon and Celtic mixed together from way back a long, long time ago and I believe that we retain something of, certainly not the academic wherewithal to put that type of music together, but something of the emotional response to that music.[21]

The clever use of early musical and cultural tropes in Jethro Tull's oeuvre, which I've only provided the most obvious examples of in this chapter, made me skeptical about this comment. Since the interview occurred thirty-five years ago, I asked Anderson in 2012 about his knowledge of early music. Again he was modest and unassuming about his talents: "As far as medieval music, Renaissance music, Baroque music, I actually have no real knowledge of that music other than little snippets of things I have heard. I'm just someone who picks up little elements of things and tries to utilize them. I'm not a musician who's studied the disciplines of music-making in the conventional sense. I don't read or write music. My knowledge is extremely limited."[22] Referring to the more overt early music references in Jethro Tull's albums *Songs from the Wood*, *Heavy Horses*, and *Stormwatch*, Anderson said in a 1993 *Rolling Stone* interview: "Looking back on some of that stuff, it was a bit self-conscious in its acknowledgment of formal historical references from English, Irish, Scottish and European folds. As with the blues, it's best when it just oozes out of you when you're trying to write a song."[23] The medievalism in Jethro Tull seems to come from this "oozing," this emotional response to folk memory, rather than any conscious effort to recreate it. While it is unlikely that Anderson was familiar with the medieval *lai* as a musical form and explicitly tried to model it when he was writing *Thick as a Brick* and *A Passion Play*, it is possible that a modern songwriter grappling with a large-scale piece can follow similar thought patterns as the trouvères or Machaut and create a comparable structure.[24]

POSTSCRIPT: "WE'LL WAIT IN STONE CIRCLES"

Jethro Tull's interest in the Middle Ages, and ancient British history in general, was such an identifiable characteristic of the band that they became fodder for parody in mainstream rock culture. In the 1984 mockumentary *This Is Spinal Tap*, a fictional band of aging rockers are trying to find a gimmick for their live show that will help rejuvenate their floundering career. Guitarist Nigel Tufnel's stroke-of-genius answer is "Stonehenge." The band agrees to the idea but is subsequently laughed at by the audience because of the silly hooded robes, insipid lyrics, dancing dwarves, and an eighteen-*inch* stage prop of Stonehenge that was supposed to be eighteen *feet*. While this scene clearly parodies the genres of hard rock and heavy metal in general, and their dabblings in ancient history and culture, Jethro Tull may have been a more direct target. In the middle of "Stonehenge" Tufnel plays a jig on mandolin, and the keyboardist takes up the tune with a flute-like setting on his keyboard. Jethro Tull employs the jig often in their music, and Anderson is closely identified with the mandolin and the flute. More tellingly, the band released their video *Slipstream* in 1981, which contains a music video for the song "Dun Ringill" (from their 1979 album, *Stormwatch*).[25] The video shows Anderson lip-synching to the song – about the Iron Age standing stones of Dun Ringill on the Isle of Skye – while sitting on a rocky promontory near the white cliffs of Dover (an iconic image, like Stonehenge, of "ancient" England). Although Black Sabbath had a song called "Stonehenge" on their 1983 *Born Again* album and created an actual Stonehenge stage prop for the live show, Jethro Tull's song and video most likely were also sources of inspiration for the *Spinal Tap* parody.

THREE

Geared toward the Exceptional Rather than the Average: The Album Cover and Lyrics of *Thick as a Brick*

JUST AS THE MUSIC OF *THICK AS A BRICK* WAS INSPIRED BY THE broadened possibilities and creative atmosphere of rock music in the late 1960s and early 1970s, so was its album cover. The album cover became a wildly creative art form during this period, and browsing the stacks in the rock section of a used record store even today can be quite an adventure. One may find the psychedelic ambigram on the Grateful Dead's *American Beauty* (1970), the working zipper of the Rolling Stones' *Sticky Fingers* (1971), the rotating wheel of *Led Zeppelin III* (1970), or the stark, enigmatic whiteness of the Beatles' *White Album* (1968). Some record covers were designed to be simulacra of physical objects and were "interactive," almost like origami puzzles. Jefferson Airplane's *Long John Silver* (1972) can be folded into a cigar box. Alice Cooper's *School's Out* (1972) folds out into a school desk. Bob Marley and the Wailers' *Catch a Fire* (1973) resembles a Zippo lighter with a "lid" that flips open revealing the record. Isaac Hayes's *Black Moses* (1971) folds out into the shape of a cross and shows the singer attired in robe and sandals. Jethro Tull's *Thick as a Brick* not only looks like a newspaper, it actually *is* a newspaper, the *St. Cleve Chronicle & Linwell Advertiser*. Once you open the gatefold and unfold the bottom section, you realize you're holding a full-size twelve-page newspaper filled with dozens of inane, preposterous stories and advertisements plus the lyrics (supposedly written by an eight-year-old boy genius), a mock review of the album, a crossword puzzle, and a naughty connect-the-dots puzzle. Although some of these album cover designs were nothing more than kitsch, they show how malleable and expressive the medium of the long-playing disc could be in terms of packaging.

THE SIGNIFICANCE OF ALBUM COVERS

It is difficult these days to appreciate the visual impact and selling power that an album cover had in the 1950s through the 1980s. Roger Dean, who created many album covers for Yes (among other bands), said, "I bought the Grateful Dead album *Aoxomoxoa* [1969] a year before I could afford a record player simply for Rick Griffin's cover."[1] The compact disc, with its small size and uncompromising plastic jewel case, is not much of an attention grabber – although designs for CD box sets can be just as diverse and creative as LPs were. A downloadable MP3 file can come with a wide array of online visual and textual material, but alas, this is a medium with no physicality.

Album covers did for musicians in previous decades what music videos and online websites do for artists now: attract attention to the artist and their music. Some record covers, like *Whipped Cream & Other Delights* by Herb Alpert's Tijuana Brass (1965), attracted attention to themselves because of their sexual content. Some attracted attention because of their artistic merit, aesthetic beauty, or their shock value. Some albums, like *Trout Mask Replica* by Captain Beefheart & His Magic Band (1969), attracted attention simply because they were odd. *Thick as a Brick* fits into this last category; it is definitely odd.

Although album covers have been creative in terms of design, graphics, illustration, and photography since the inception of the long-playing record in the late 1940s, the musicians back then were given limited input. Many record labels had an identifiable style that was developed by art departments with graphic designers. Often these graphic designers fitted the liner notes, song lyrics, and photographs or drawings of the musicians into a standard template. This changed in the late 1960s and early 1970s when the musicians themselves began to consider the album packaging as a vital avenue of expression. Steve Jones and Martin Sorger write: "As the market for rock music grew, recording artists gained more leverage, and clauses for artistic control began appearing in contracts, including control over packaging. Spearheading the trend were the Beatles."[2]

In his article on the album covers of the Beatles, Ian Inglis points out four functions of the album cover.[3] The first is to protect the record from damage, the second is to advertise the recording, the third is to provide accompanying materials to the recording, and the last is to be a work of art that can be appreciated in and of itself. Virtually all album covers accomplish the first three of Inglis's functions, but fewer accomplish the fourth. The Beatles paved the way for rock musicians who saw the album cover both as a work of art and as an integral part of the album. The cover of *Sgt. Pepper's Lonely Hearts Club Band* was especially influential in this regard. The rise of psychedelic art, innovations in graphic design and printing technology, and the creative freedom that record companies granted artists in this period all produced an expansive environment for album cover design. As Jones and Sorger say, "The cover and the record together acted as a kind of complete audio-visual experience."[4] Joni Mitchell is in a class by herself in turning the LP into a multivalent medium of self-expression. Beginning with her first album, *Song to a Seagull* (1968), she augmented her roles as principal songwriter, lyricist, and performer by painting the art for many of her album covers. Similarly, *Thick as a Brick* qualifies as an album cover that is a work of art unto itself.

Some of the more literarily inclined songwriters in the rock era went beyond composing lyrics and had their writing experiments spill over onto the album packaging. For example, Bob Dylan included extra poems/lyrics titled "Some other kinds of songs ... Poems by Bob Dylan" on the back of his 1964 album, *Another Side of Bob Dylan*. Jim Morrison included his poem "The Celebration of the Lizard" on the inside gatefold of the Doors' *Waiting for the Sun* (1968).[5] In addition to the lyrics (printed on the two record sleeves), Peter Gabriel included a prose story on the inside gatefold of Genesis' *The Lamb Lies Down on Broadway* (1974). In essence, the story of *The Lamb* is told twice, first in the lyrics and second in the prose story. *Thick as a Brick* is also a unique literary experiment, with the members of the band writing all the material for the twelve-page newspaper.

THE MAKING OF THE *ST. CLEVE CHRONICLE*

Concerning the time and effort the band put into the design of the album cover, Anderson said this in an interview from 1979: "All of that album cover... and I've said this before and it's absolutely true, took longer to put together than the album. I'm not suggesting it's any more important, but it took a long time to write all of that. I did, I suppose, more than half of it; Jeffrey [Hammond] did quite a lot and John Evans did a bit, and it was put together, put into columns and laid out, by Royston Eldridge at Chrysalis."[6] A closer look at the band's activities in late 1971 and early 1972 shows the breakneck speed at which both the music and album cover were created. During a break in the American leg of the *Aqualung* tour in August 1971, Jethro Tull began work on the music at Morgan Studios in London.[7] After finishing the tour on November 18, 1971, they continued the process of writing, arranging, and rehearsing at the Rolling Stones' rehearsal studio in Bermondsey.[8] They completed the recording and mixing again at Morgan Studios in December.[9] In two interviews Anderson says it took approximately one month to make the record (two weeks to write, arrange, and rehearse the music and then ten days to two weeks to record).[10] In another interview Anderson says the process took a little over six weeks.[11] Regardless of which account is correct, the band had the music recorded by the end of December 1971. One month to a little over six weeks is an incredibly short period of time to produce a piece of music of such complexity. The band and Royston Eldridge then must have spent all of January and February writing and designing the newspaper, since the album was released in the United Kingdom on March 10, 1972. To complicate matters, the band started another tour on January 6, 1972, so it appears that they wrote the material for the newspaper while they were traveling throughout Scandinavia and Western Europe playing concerts almost every night. Regarding this, Jeffrey Hammond says: "I just remember doing a lot of recording into a Dictaphone... or a small tape recorder, and tapes got sent off to various secretaries to type up. But most of it was giggling, I think, and laughing at some of the more immature sections of it."[12]

Royston Eldridge was uniquely qualified to take on such an unusual project. Before being hired by Chrysalis Records, he worked as a rock journalist for the popular British music periodicals *Melody Maker* and *Sounds* and also for a small-town newspaper. As David Rees puts it, "He had the possibly unique experience of leaving a newspaper to work for a record company only to find one of his first tasks was to compile a newspaper!"¹³ Eldridge gives his story on designing the cover for *Thick as a Brick* in the *Jethro Tull: Classic Artists* documentary:

> When the group had the idea to do it like a newspaper, I was the obvious mug to help them put it together. It was a pretty complex thing, actually. I'd hate to try to do it now. I don't think you could do it nowadays. There were enormous problems with how you put it together to keep the record safe, who was going to print it. Some of the paper was too thin and tore too easily. We had problems with retailers making sure it fit into the racks. Everything in the paper, the whole twelve pages from births, deaths, marriages, sport reports (the weirdest sports you ever heard of), it was all written by the group. Every photograph features either friends of the group, members of the road crew, even a review of the album inside. [Manager] Terry Ellis, for instance, he's featured in a photograph. [Producer] Robin Black is the roller-skating champion. Every small ad had some relevance.¹⁴

From just a cursory glance at the newspaper, one recognizes that the packaging of the album is intended to be satirical. In fact, the album is a spoof of concept albums. While Jethro Tull were obviously inspired by the grand concepts and new frontiers that rock bands were exploring in the late 1960s and early 1970s, they also found it to be a great opportunity for parody. (This topic will be discussed later in this chapter on the lyrics and in chapter 8 on the group's peculiar brand of humor.)

Jethro Tull was not the first, nor the last, to make the cover of an album look like a newspaper. The Dave Brubeck Quartet (*Dave Brubeck at Storyville: 1954*) and Elvis Presley (*Elvis Sails!*) were the first to use this trope in the 1950s. Artists like Pete Seeger (*Gazette Vol. 2*), Jefferson Airplane (*Volunteers*), and the Four Seasons (*The Genuine Imitation Life Gazette*) used it in the 1960s. John Lennon's overtly political album *Some Time in New York City*, with the lyrics to the songs printed in vertical columns on the cover, was released in June 1972, just months after *Thick as a Brick*. Guns N' Roses used the format for their *G N' R Lies* album (1988). Yet none of these albums approach the expansiveness, depth, or the comic absurdity of the *Thick as a Brick* newspaper, the front page of which is shown in figure 3.1.

CONTENT OF THE NEWSPAPER

The *St. Cleve Chronicle & Linwell Advertiser* contains more than sixty articles; over thirty pictures, drawings, and illustrations; as well as puzzles,

3.1. Cover of *Thick as a Brick*

comic strips, classified ads, television and radio listings, advertisements, and a horoscope. The articles consist of local news stories, editorials, advice columns, and sports reports, most of which display the band's absurd sense of humor. While many of the articles are inane and preposterous ("Mongrel Dog Soils Actor's Foot" on page 1 and "Magistrate Fines Himself" on page 3), several have a serious tone. For instance, "Do Not See Me Rabbit" on page 9 tells the story of a World War II Royal Air Force pilot who was shot down over London by a German Me-109 fighter in the summer of 1940.

Several of the articles address the controversy surrounding Gerald "Little Milton" Bostock, the supposed author of the "epic poem" *Thick as a Brick,* and Jethro Tull's musical interpretation of it. "Judges Disqualify 'Little Milton' in Last Minute Rumpus" on the front page reports that Bostock's reading of his poem on BBC television caused protests from viewers who felt that the work "was a product of an 'extremely unwholesome attitude towards life, his God and Country.'" Just below this, another article, titled "Little Milton in School-Girl Pregnancy Row," states that a fourteen-year-old girl, Julia Fealey, accused the eight-year-old Bostock of impregnating her. On page 3 "Major Beat Group Records Gerald's Poem" reports that "one-legged pop flautist Ian Anderson . . . was so enthused by [*Thick as a Brick*] he wrote forty-five minutes of pop music to go with it." On page 5 the article "Chrysalis and Bostock Firm Foundation Deal" reports that a special royalty on all sales of *Thick as a Brick* will go toward a fund called the "Bostock Foundation" to assist young boys and girls in the literary arts. The article also says that Bostock has signed with Chrysalis Records to be the first participant in a series of spoken-word recordings. Page 7 contains the full text of the poem with the preface: "We print here, for all to read, Gerald Bostock's controversial poem 'Thick as a Brick' which caused so much controversy." All of these articles contribute to the "concept" of *Thick as a Brick:* Jethro Tull putting to music a controversial poem written by a marginalized and misunderstood boy genius. This is undoubtedly one of the strangest concepts for a concept album.

Most of the material in the newspaper is simply the reporting of everyday life in a supposed small town in the county of Somerset in the southwest of England. It is evident that the band had great fun writing and designing it. There is an obituary on page 2 with the names of the recently deceased being "Bury," "Graves," "Hurse," and "Stiff." Page 4 contains a hilariously bad poem, "Ode to a Nose," submitted by a reader. A column about pets on page 5 is written by a "motoring correspondent" who describes animals in terms of vehicles. In the "Weekend Radio" listings on page 7, this curious entry appears: "Serious Music, Delirius D. Rivel, Myart, Randelsson, Sherbet, Gettitonmann, Rightonmann, Lisp and Ibetyoure Boredwith-Thisky," obviously puns on composers' last names. In the classified ads on page 9, we find this: "Brick urgently required. Must be thick and well kept." There are ridiculous references to stuffed penguins, rabbits, and non-rabbits throughout the newspaper. This type of absurd humor was greatly influenced by *Monty Python's Flying Circus*.

There are many subtle references to band members and people associated with Jethro Tull scattered throughout the newspaper. The mock review of the album on page 7 is credited to one Julian Stone-Mason B.A., whose first name contains "Ian," and Anderson has admitted he wrote it himself.[15] In the classified ads on page 10, there is an ad for Royston Estate Agency Ltd. with its address as 44 Eldridge Street, an obvious reference to Royston Eldridge. Eldridge's name also appears in an ad on page 11 and in a picture caption on page 12. John Covach points out that in the article "Visiting Prof. Gives Talk" on page 5, the professor's name, Andrew Jorgensen, contains "Anderson." In the article "Man Threw Bottle" on page 2, we learn that the man who threw the bottle at Jorgensen while he was giving his talk was Albert Innes, which contains "Ian."[16] On page 11 there is coverage of the St. Clevians' favorite local sport, "fennel." A photograph shows a player, Max Quad (probably bassist Jeffrey Hammond), being restrained by an umpire (Ian Anderson) after attacking another player, the Rev. John Smythe-Liphook (probably guitarist Martin Barre), who is lying limp on the field. This type of absurdist sports humor reminds one of the "Upper Class Twit of the Year," "Silly Olympics," and "The Philosophers' Football Match" sketches from *Monty Python's Flying Circus*.

Though there appears to be little thematic connection between the music and lyrics of *Thick as a Brick* and *A Passion Play*, other than that they both contain one conceptual, album-length composition, there are obvious associations between the two album covers. The cover for *A Passion Play* is a gatefold with the lyrics printed on the inside. Glued to the inside spine is a playbill for a performance of *A Passion Play* at "The Linwell Theatre" on Parrish Street by the Linwell Players. The *Thick as a Brick* newspaper is called the *St. Cleve Chronicle & Linwell Advertiser.* It appears that Linwell is a neighboring village to St. Cleve in the band's fictional world. Parrish Street is also mentioned many times in the *St. Cleve Chronicle.* Two of the members of the Linwell Players in *A Passion Play* are Max Quad (Jeffrey Hammond) and John Tetrad (Barrie Barlow). In the coverage of the fennel game on pages 11 and 12 of the *St. Cleve Chronicle,* two of the players are named Max Quad and John Tetrad (again Jeffrey Hammond and Barrie Barlow). It seems that these gentlemen lead busy lives, playing fennel by day and doing a bit of acting in the evenings. It's obvious that the band intended no deep connection between the two album covers and were just having some fun.[17]

THE LP DILEMMA

Extremely long progressive rock songs from the 1970s such as *Thick as a Brick* and *A Passion Play* presuppose a certain style of listening that is not in vogue today: listening at home, on a hi-fi stereo system, without any distractions, to the entire long-playing (LP) record, with the album cover in hand. Few of these qualifiers play a central role in the listening habits of the average rock fan today. As a result, the experience of listening to albums like these today is quite different from what it was when they were released. Jim Curtis writes: "The aural complexity of the Beatles' *White Album,* and the imagistic density of Dylan's *Blonde on Blonde* ma[ke] for frustrating listening in a car. Stoplights, street signs, and exit ramps distract one's attention from the intense involvement which the music demand[s]."[18] Modern-day music fans prefer the portability and accessibility of CD and MP3 players and eschew the large stereo systems that graced most homes in the 1970s. The long-playing record, then the primary format for commercial sound recordings, is one of the least portable media in the history of recorded sound. This was a major reason for the LP's demise. Today, listening to music is just one element in a mobile, faster-paced, multitasking world. Most people listen to music while they are walking, exercising, dancing, driving, riding mass transportation, and working. *Thick as a Brick* and *A Passion Play*, with their lengthy and continuous music, were designed to be consumed in their entirety with the full attention of the listener. As Lester Bangs wrote of *Thick as a Brick*, "You had to take the whole pie at once or not at all."[19] Today's listeners may find this hard to swallow, since they are used to downloading short individual songs rather than entire albums.[20] Album packaging also played a huge role in defining listening habits in the 1970s. The extravagance and creativity of record covers with their expansive gatefold designs encouraged the listener to closely study the lyrics and visual elements, as if one were reading a book. John Covach writes: "The *St. Cleve Chronicle* is densely packed with references that bear upon the lyrics to *Thick as a Brick*. . . . [T]he album packaging is almost as important in figuring out the themes addressed in the lyrics as the lyrics themselves; and this creates a crucial interdependence between the music, lyrics, and packaging that was unprecedented in its day."[21] Yet, remarkably, *Thick as a Brick* and *A Passion Play* have aged well despite being created for a listening audience that is vastly different from audiences today.

Thick as a Brick is one of those albums for which one must have both the original LP and the CD (either the 1997 remaster or the 2012 remix) to fully appreciate. The listener needs the original LP, since the newspaper provides the satirical foundation for the concept and is one of the most innovative and entertaining record covers ever conceived in the rock era. Also, the cover cannot be faithfully reproduced in the CD or MP3 format. On the other hand, the listener needs the remastered or remixed CD or MP3 for the vast improvement in clarity and sound quality, which reveals additional timbres and layers in the music. If one has difficulty procuring the original LP through online record retailers, in a library, or in a used record store, there are page-by-page scans of the newspaper available for viewing online.[22] In 2012 Anderson released remixed CD and LP editions of *Thick as a Brick* with the complete newspaper, essentially solving the dilemma. (See the epilogue for more information on these releases.)

THE LYRICS OF *THICK AS A BRICK*

Thick as a Brick and *A Passion Play* bring us face-to-face with that nebulous concept known as the concept album. Marianne Tatom Letts devotes much of the first chapter of her book *Radiohead and the Resistant Concept Album* to the subject and shows just how many different approaches bands took to this musical idiom. Several of Jethro Tull's albums could be considered concept albums, in that the lyrics involve a specific topic or theme. *Too Old to Rock 'n' Roll, Too Young to Die!* is probably the best example in that it is a song cycle that tells the story of an aging rocker who finds, many years after his heyday, that he is popular again. Many Jethro Tull albums have songs with a specific theme in their lyrics but also include songs that have little or nothing to do with that theme. Some that fall into this category are *Aqualung* (organized religion), *Songs from the Wood* (English folklore), *Stormwatch* (the forces of nature over man), and A (cold war paranoia). *Thick as a Brick* and *A Passion Play* are concept albums that fall into a slightly different category in that their music is unified, being one continuous song, yet their lyrics are oblique and difficult to grasp, which clouds the "concept." In 1976, when asked by an interviewer, "How did the conception for *Thick as a Brick* start?" Anderson replied:

> It wasn't a conception really, just the act of writing a song thinking about what I might have been, what I began life as being, what kind of childhood images moved me – dealt with in a very oblique fashion, because I'm not setting out to create a threadbare tale of emotional woe or to even delineate emotional happenings. I'm just creating a background lyrical summation of a lot of things I feel about being a contemporary child in this age and the problems that one has – the problems of being precocious beyond one's age or having interests beyond one's age, and to some extent being ruled in a kind of heavy-handed, unexplained fashion by father-figures.[23]

Anderson muses on several specific themes in the lyrics, yet he never intended them to be easily digestible or unified, describing them as "very oblique." He speaks of the lyrics being about "childhood images," and this is reflected in the fragmentary and episodic nature of the many sections of the lyrics. This steers listeners away from thinking he has created a linear story line with a plot, or a "tale of emotional woe." Above all, Anderson obliges the listener not to take the lyrics too seriously. In interviews he often brings up the humor of *Monty Python's Flying Circus* as a way of describing the satirical and absurd aspects of not only the album's lyrics but also its music, packaging, and stage show. In an interview on the remastered CD of *Thick as a Brick* from 1997, Anderson says:

> [*Thick as a Brick*] came about primarily because the thing we had done a year before, which was the *Aqualung* album, had generally been perceived as a concept album, whereas to me it was just a bunch of songs, as I've always said. So the first thing about *Thick as a Brick* was, let's come up with something which is the mother of all concept albums, and really is a mind-boggler in terms of what was then relatively complex music, and also lyrically was complex, confusing, and above all a bit of a spoof. It was quite deliberately, but in a nice way, tongue-in-cheek, and meant to send up ourselves, the music critics and the audience perhaps, but not necessarily in that order! This was the period of *Monty Python's Flying Circus* and a very British kind of a humor, which was not terribly well understood by the Japanese or the Americans when we finally went out to perform *Thick as a Brick* in concert. But they sat politely, if a little confused, through the whole thing and came back next time for more, so it can't have gone too far amiss.[24]

SALIENT THEMES IN THE LYRICS

Anderson treads a fine line between seriousness and spoof in *Thick as a Brick*. The lyrics delve into serious matters, yet they are presented as if they were an "epic poem" written by an eight-year-old schoolboy, Gerald "Little Milton" Bostock, and Jethro Tull has set the poem to music. Concerning the creation of Gerald Bostock, Anderson says: "He's the little figure that I'm sort of saying is me as a little lad, who was supposed to have everything going for him, a really quite precocious little lad, very bright, very clever, read books, and knew a lot of things at an early age, but was well into opting out of that and making his own way ... a sort of exaggerated version of me as a similarly-aged child."[25] On the concept of the album, Anderson says: "*Thick as a Brick* was tongue in cheek, what with the album's pretense that the lyrics had been written by a 12-year-old school boy named Gerald Bostock.[26] At the same time, the album expressed some serious sentiments about English society, as well as some rather serious music writing. But it was also meant to be a bit of fun."[27] Some Jethro Tull fans have done a thorough line-by-line analysis of the

3.2. Comic on p. 7 of the *St. Cleve Chronicle*

lyrics. While these analyses give insight into what certain sections or phrases are about, these all-encompassing interpretations tend to be overly serious, contrived, and tedious, and do not take into account the fact that Anderson never intended them to be taken too seriously. (I provide no overall interpretation and limit my comments to a few themes in the lyrics based on Anderson's own thoughts about them. The complete lyrics to the piece can be found in appendix 1.)

In the above quote, Anderson mentions that the lyrics express some "serious sentiments about English society." One of the important issues in the lyrics is how modern educational institutions breed an attitude of conformity among children and consequently marginalize gifted children. A key phrase concerning this is "we will be geared toward the average rather than the exceptional." This is spoken by bassist Jeffrey Hammond during Instr. 11 (3:06 side 2).[28] The phrase also appears in a three-panel comic strip titled "Prof. Panglos and Rabbit" underneath the lyrics on page 7 of the *St. Cleve Chronicle,* shown in figure 3.2.

The first two panels of the strip show the professor feeding a cat and a rabbit their dinner – from a laboratory test tube. The cat, who has been properly conditioned by Prof. Panglos, readily eats his "din dins," but the rabbit, an exceptionally free-thinking rabbit, is suspicious of what the professor is trying to feed him. The last panel shows the rabbit by himself saying, "I'm geared toward the average rather than the exceptional." "Pangloss" is the name of the tutor in Voltaire's satirical novel *Candide,* first published in 1759. Throughout the novel, Pangloss, who is a devotee of philosopher Gottfried Leibniz and his views on optimism, tries to convince the young Candide that everything is fine and that he lives in the "best possible of worlds." For instance, Pangloss unfeelingly believes that "individual misfortunes are for the general good: the more individual misfortunes there are, the more everything is as it ought to be."[29] Candide has trouble fitting the tragedies he sees in his own life and in others' into Pangloss's simplistic rubric and ultimately begins to think for himself. Perhaps Pangloss is used in the comic strip to represent the "wise men" who "don't know how it feels to be thick as a brick" referred to in the lyrics (in lines 7–8 from Vocal 1).

The apprehension that the rabbit feels about being "geared toward the average rather than the exceptional" is also satirically addressed in the article "New School Plans" on page 8 of the newspaper, shown in figure 3.3. The article reports on a new educational system that would give its students, according to chairman Sir Robert Sidcastle, "a sense of academic equality and a group identity which would relieve the crushing burden of individual aspiration and frustration during school life." Sir Sidcastle further states that the academic standard would be "geared toward the average rather than the exceptional." Anderson elaborates on this:

> The phrase "thick as a brick" is a North English colloquial term meaning "stupid." Like the religious themes on *Aqualung,* the theme of *Thick as a Brick* came out of my adolescent feelings about society and how it tries to bend you away from your will and toward its will, as if you're not bright enough to make your own choices. I wasn't a precocious child, but I knew how it felt to be one of the more academically gifted people; I knew what it felt like to be ostracized, despised and feared by the rank and file, who weren't terribly bright. Nobody likes the clever kids. So the album came to represent the gulf between growing up clever and the social discrepancy that results from that: the fact that you were really disliked by some of the kids.[30]

Anderson expresses a similar sentiment in "Too Many Too," an outtake from *The Broadsword and the Beast* sessions: "Too many equal and average children who will all grow up the same."[31] Roger Waters of Pink Floyd also addresses this topic in "The Happiest Days of Our Lives" and "Another Brick in the Wall, Part 2" from the 1979 album *The Wall,* and conveys it powerfully in the 1982 movie with schoolchildren on a conveyor belt falling into a meat grinder.

New School Plans

The new Educational system around which Harrowditch Comprehensive School will be built was discussed at a Founder Fathers meeting on Monday. Over 200 people were present as chairman, Sir Robert Sidcastle outlined the new system in a frank talk with parents.

He told them that it was the aim of the new school to provide its pupils "with a sense of academic equality and a group identity which would relieve the crushing burden of individual aspiration and frustration during school life". The academic standard would depend, he said, on the child who is rather slower to learn than the unduly gifted ones. "We will be geared toward the average rather than the exceptional," said 'Sir Sid', "but we believe that the true group-learning experience will be invaluable in the later adjustments to future urban society."

3.3. Article on p. 8 of the *St. Cleve Chronicle*

Along the same lines, the lyrics and newspaper express the importance of individuality and free thinking and address how those with political power can stifle the voice of the poor and undereducated. Anderson says:

> In the case of *Thick as a Brick,* it started off from one line. The concept, or concepts, expressed in the music, or in the lyrics, is that everyone's right. And the necessity, I think, should be apparent for everyone to decide, to make their own judgment on things in their own way, regardless of age or experience, or even intelligence. We have at one end of the scale ... the intellectual society ... who are necessarily making judgments on people on the other end of the scale who may be ... thick as a brick. "Your wise men don't know how it feels to be thick as a brick." How the hell can they decide for the man in the street what he should want?[32]

John Covach points out that this theme of individualism is reiterated and championed in the article titled "Visiting Prof. Gives Talk" on page 5 of the *St. Cleve Chronicle*.[33] The article reports that the visiting professor to St. Cleve, Andrew Jorgensen, believes that "man must learn to assume individual identity as opposed to the collective super-society style of life" and "man must learn to function as an independent observer of mass-behavior and develop the right of each individual to intellectual freedom on the particular level he is personally capable."

The last theme worth noting is the lampooning of the British upper class that comes through in many places in the lyrics, especially in Vocal 7

("I see you shuffle in the courtroom"). These satirical passages, along with the absurd stories in the newspaper, deflate the serious tone of the weightier themes in the lyrics and exhibit Anderson's biting wit and eye for caricature. Although the lyrics to *Thick as a Brick* are oblique and obscure, a clearer view of what the album is "about" can be obtained when they are considered in conjunction with Anderson's interviews and certain sections of the *St. Cleve Chronicle*.

GRAMMATICAL TRANSGRESSIONS IN THE LYRICS

The lyrics to *Thick as a Brick* break several basic rules of English grammar and composition. While this is common in rock lyrics, and actually laudable, this is rarely the case with Anderson, who is one of the more sophisticated lyricists from the rock era. If one were to judge Anderson's lyric writing ability on *Thick as a Brick* alone, one could well criticize him as being a pretentious writer who is meddling with literary genres beyond his capacity. Yet with a songwriting career that has spanned forty-five years and three hundred songs, he deserves more than that, and *Thick as a Brick* deserves more than just a cursory critique of its adherence to the established rules of grammar and storytelling. Anderson breaks these rules on purpose. This is alluded to in the article "Judges Disqualify 'Little Milton' in Last Minute Rumpus" on the front page of the *St. Cleve Chronicle*. The article notes that some viewers who watched Gerald Bostock recite his poem on a BBC 2 program "felt that it was not one poem but a series of separate poems put together merely to appear impressive." Since Anderson conceived of the lyrics as being the musings of an eight-year-old boy, it's only natural that they would have some grammatical inconsistencies.

The first problem in understanding the lyrics is their shifting narrative mode. It is difficult to grasp who is addressing whom throughout much of the lyrics, because the viewpoint shifts arbitrarily between the first-, second-, and third-person point of view, both singular and plural. For example, Vocal 1 is in the first-person singular ("I," "my") and addresses the second-person plural ("you," "your," "yourselves"). Suddenly in Vocal 2 the music switches from a folk style to a rock style, and the viewpoint switches to first-person plural ("we") and addresses the third-person singular ("a son," "him"). Then in Vocal 3 the first and second persons are abandoned in favor of just the third person. This section is simply the description of characters ("Poet," "painter," "soldier") in a setting from the vantage point of an omniscient observer, and the lyrics have little connection with the first two vocal sections. These shifts in narrative mode give the lyrics a fragmented point of view and contribute to their obliqueness.

A second difficulty is the introduction of many characters throughout the course of the lyrics, but there is confusion as to who the characters really are. Vocal 1 seems to be addressing modern society at large and accuses the "wise men" of being unsympathetic to those who are "thick as a brick" (the lower classes and the undereducated). Vocal 2 presents a child ("a son is born") who will be socially engineered into one of these unfeeling wise men. Vocal 3 describes a setting with a host of characters: the poet, the painter, the infantry, the do-er, the thinker, the master of the house, the soldier. The "youngest of the family" mentioned here may be the son from Vocal 2, but this is unclear. Some of these characters are mentioned later in the lyrics and some are not. It appears that many of the characters in the text are not treated as characters in a story line, but are used simply to create imagery or to portray a setting. Thus, it is difficult to get engrossed with, or invested in, the lyrics because of the lack of a central protagonist (such as Ray Lomas, Tommy, Rael, or Pink[34]).

Third, like the music, some sections of the lyrics are well formed and can stand alone, while other sections seem fragmentary and transitory. For instance, when one reads sections like Vocals 1, 3, and 7 out of the context of the lyrics as a whole, they still retain some degree of coherency. But the majority of the vocal sections make little sense at all when considered by themselves. Again, this gives the lyrics an overall feeling of obliqueness and fragmentation.

Fourth, as mentioned earlier, the lyrics do not adhere to a linear story line and have abrupt narrative shifts that seem to have no apparent purpose or meaning. The word "LATER" appears in three places in capital letters to show there is an obvious break in time and place in the narrative. In addition, the lyrics are printed in the newspaper as if they were an article, obscuring the overall form, scansion, and rhyme schemes. Also, the lyrics are broken up into twenty-three separate paragraphs that

THICK AS A BRICK
By Gerald "Little Milton" Bostock

We print here, for all to read, Gerald Bostock's controversial poem "Thick as a Brick" which caused so much contoversy —Ed

Really don't mind if you sit this one out.

My words but a whisper—your deafness a SHOUT. I may make you feel but I can't make you think. Your sperm's in the gutter—your love's in the sink. So you ride yourselves over the fields and/you make all your animal deals and/ your wise men don't know how it feels to be thick as a brick. And the sand-castle virtues are all swept away in/the tidal destruction/ the moral melee. The elastic retreat rings the close of play as the last wave uncovers the newfangled way. But your new shoes are worn at the heels and/your suntan does rapidly peel and/your wise men don't know how it feels to be thick as a brick.

And the love that I feel is so far away: I'm a bad dream that I just had today—and you/shake your head and/say it's a shame.

Spin me back down the years and the days of my youth. Draw the lace and black curtains and shut out the whole truth. Spin me down the long ages: let them sing the song.

See there! A son is born—and we pronounce him fit to fight. There are black-heads on his shoulders, and he pees himself in the night. We'll/make a man of him / put him to a trade/ teach him/to play Monopoly and/how to sing in the rain.

The Poet and the painter casting shadows on the water—as the sun plays on the infantry returning from the sea. The do-er and the thinker: no allowance for the other—as the failing light illuminates the mercenary's creed. The home fire burning: the kettle almost boiling—but the master of the house is far away. The horses stamping—their warm breath clouding in the sharp and frosty morning of the day. And the poet lifts his pen while the soldier sheaths his sword.

And the youngest of the family is moving with authority. Building castles by the sea, he dares the tardy tide to wash them all aside.

The cattle quietly grazing at the grass down by the river where the swelling mountain water moves onward to the sea: the builder of the castles renews the age-old purpose and contemplates the milking girl whose offer is his need. The young men of the household have/all gone into service and/are not to be expected for a year. The innocent young master—thoughts moving ever faster—has formed the plan to change the man he seems. And the poet sheaths his pen while the soldier lifts his sword.

And the oldest of the family is moving with authority. Coming from across the sea, he challenges the son who puts him to the run.

What do you do when/the old man's gone—do you want to be him? and/your real self sings the song. Do you want to free him? No one to help you get up steam—and the whirlpool turns you 'way off-beam.

LATER.
I've come down from the upper class to mend your rotten ways. My father was a man-of-power whom everyone obeyed. So come on all you criminals! I've got to put you straight just like I did with my old man—twenty years too late. Your bread and water's going cold. Your hair is short and neat. I'll judge you all and make

3.4. *(left and facing)* Lyrics to *Thick as a Brick* from the *St. Cleve Chronicle*

do not correspond with the fourteen vocal sections (see figure 3.4). All of these factors make the lyrics cryptic and mysterious, and cajole the listener into delving more deeply into them to find their meaning. Undoubtedly this was part of the spoof: a search for profundity when there is none. To try to resolve the problems in the lyrics would be a tedious task indeed and would take away from the enjoyment of the piece as a damn sure that no-one judges me.

You curl your toes in fun as you smile at everyone—you meet the stares. You're unaware that your doings aren't done. And you laugh most ruthlessly as you tell us what not to be. But how are we supposed to see where we should run? I see you shuffle in the courtroom with/your rings upon your fingers/your downy little sidies and/your silver-buckle shoes. Playing at the hard-case, you follow the example of the comic-paper idol who lets you bend the rules.

So!
Come on ye childhood heroes! Won't you rise up from the pages of your comic-books?/your super-crooks/and show us all the way. Well! Make your will and testament. Won't you? Join your local government. We'll have superman for president/let Robin save the day.

You put your bet on number one and it comes up every time. The other kids have all backed down and they put you first in line. And so you finally ask yourself just how big you are—and you take your place in a wiser world of bigger motor cars. And you wonder who to call on.

So! Where the hell was Biggles when you needed him last Saturday? And where are all the Sportsmen who always pulled you through? They're all resting down in Cornwall —writing up their memoirs for a paper-back edition of the Boy Scout Manual.

LATER.
See there! A man is born—and we pronounce him fit for peace. There's a load lifted from his shoulders with the discovery of his disease.

We'll/take the child from him/ put it to the test/teach it/to be a wise man/how to fool the rest.

QUOTE
We will be geared toward the average rather than the exceptional/ God is an overwhelming responsibility/ we walked through the maternity ward and saw 218 babies wearing nylons/ cats are on the upgrade/ upgrade?

LATER
In the clear white circles of morning wonder, I take my place with the lord of the hills. And the blue-eyed soldiers stand slightly discoloured (in neat little rows) sporting canvas frills. With their jock-straps pinching, they slouch to attention, while queueing for sarnies at the office canteen. Saying—how's your grannie and/ good old Ernie: he coughed up a tenner on a premium bond win.
The legends (worded in the ancient tribal hymn) lie cradled in the seagull's call. And all the promises they made are ground beneath the sadist's fall. The poet and the wise man stand behind the gun, and signal for the crack of dawn. Light the sun.

Do you believe in the day? Do you? Believe in the day! The Dawn Creation of the Kings has begun. Soft Venus (lonely maiden) brings the ageless one.

Do you believe in the day? The fading hero has returned to the night—and fully pregnant with the day, wise men endorse the poet's sight.

Do you believe in the day? Do you? Believe in the day!

Let me tell you the tales of your life of/ the cut and the thrust of the knife/ the tireless oppression/ the wisdom instilled/ the desire to kill or be

killed. Let me sing of the losers who lie in the street as the last bus goes by. The pavements are empty: the gutters run red—while the fool toasts his god in the sky. So come all ye young men who are building castles! Kindly state the time of the year and join your voices in a hellish chorus. Mark the precise nature of your fear. Let me help you to pick up your dead as the sins of the fathers are fed with/ the blood of the fools and/ the thoughts of the wise and/ from the pun under your bed. Let me make you a present of song as/ the wise man breaks wind and is gone while/ the fool with the hour-glass is cooking his goose and/ the nursery rhyme winds along.
So! Come all ye young men who are building castles! Kindly state the time of the year and join your voices in a hellish chorus. Mark the precise nature of your fear. See! The summer lightning casts its bolts upon you and the hour of judgement draweth near. Would you be/ the fool stood in his suit of armour or/ the wiser man who rushes clear. So! Come on ye childhood heroes! Won't your rise up from the pages of your comic-books?/ your super-crooks/and show us all the way. Well! Make your will and testament. Won't you? Join your local government. We'll have superman for president/ let Robin save the day. So! Where the hell was Biggles when you needed Him last Saturday? And where are all the Sportsmen who always pulled you through? They're all resting down in Cornwall—writing up their memoirs for a paper-back edition of the Boy Scout Manual.

OF COURSE
So you ride yourselves over the fields and/ you make all your animal deals and/ your wise men don't know how it feels to be thick as a brick.

spoof of concept albums. As cited in a previous quote, Anderson and the band deliberately sought to conjure up a "mind-boggler" to "send up ourselves, the music critics and the audience."

The narrative transgressions in the lyrics are disconcerting only when one divorces the lyrics from the music and tries to analyze them as if they were poetry, prose, or a short story. The music provides the continuity, structure, and unity that is lacking in the lyrics in two ways. First, the instrumental passages give the lyrics continuity by smoothing out the abrupt shifts in the narrative. Second, the repetition of music and text grants the piece a tighter structure and greater unity. (Both of these elements are examined below and also in the section on the instrumental passages in chapter 5.)

The instrumental passages in *Thick as a Brick* effectively smooth out the abrupt shifts in the narrative. If the lyrics were sung straight through, the disjointed flow of images and shifts in narrative voice would render them incoherent. The instrumental passages, with their forays into virtuosic soloing and ensemble playing, temporarily shift the listener's attention away from the lyrics. In some instances they function as scenery changes do between acts in a play, transporting the listener from the setting of one vocal section to the setting of the next. The nineteen instrumental passages in *Thick as a Brick* allow the listener to forgive the "transgressions" that the narrative commits and to follow the lyrics as if they were meant to convey a story, even though they don't. This interdependence between the lyrics and music is reflected in Anderson's organic writing style. When I asked Anderson the proverbial question, "Which came first, the lyrics or the music?" he responded:

> With *Thick as a Brick*, the lyrics and music were largely growing organically together. The lyrics were coming at the same time, or just before, the music. I don't usually write the words first and the music second. I try to get them both together. Writing words is a musical experience, because as soon as you write words, you imply rhythm, you imply some form. You have a cadence just speaking the words. Melodies will begin to suggest themselves as soon as you read those words off a piece of paper, or these days, off a computer screen. The music comes very quickly. I never have a problem writing music. The lyrics are more thoughtful. If I can get on a roll with writing lyrics, the music can follow on right away and it seems to write itself.[35]

TEXTUAL REPETITION IN *THICK AS A BRICK*

The second way that the music of *Thick as a Brick* provides the unity that is lacking in the lyrics is repetition. The manner in which a piece of music uses repetition, in either its words or its music, largely determines its shape and scope. In most popular and rock music it is common to find whole blocks of lyrics repeated verbatim at regular intervals. This is the case with verse-chorus form, where the chorus repeats the same lyrics each time it comes around. *Thick as a Brick* uses repetition, but in unorthodox ways. There are five sections in the piece where lyrics are repeated, but mostly in fragments or with variations, and the repetitions occur at irregular intervals. A perusal of the form of the lyrics (shown in appendix 1) will aid the reader in seeing these instances of repetition.

First, lines 5–8 from Vocal 1 (0:38 side 1) are repeated verbatim at the end in Vocal 14 (20:32 side 2). This repetition gives the piece an arch form, ending it with the same material with which it began. Anderson sings the lines in Vocal 14 with a world-weariness in his voice, expressing his disappointment that nothing has come of his critique of society.

> So you ride yourselves over the fields
> And you make all your animal deals
> And your wise men don't know how it feels
> To be thick as a brick.

Second, the lyrics in Vocal 2 and Vocal 8 are linked thematically and contrast a child with the man he becomes. Vocal 2 occurs near the beginning of side 1 (3:01), and Vocal 8 occurs at the beginning of side 2 (0:48), giving these sections an introductory function.

Vocal 2	Vocal 8
See there! A son is born –	See there! A man is born
And we pronounce him fit to fight.	And we pronounce him fit for peace.
There are black-heads on his shoulders,	There's a load lifted from his shoulders
And he pees himself in the night.	With the discovery of his disease.
We'll make a man of him	We'll take the child from him
Put him to a trade	Put it to the test
Teach him to play Monopoly	Teach it to be a wise man
And how to sing in the rain.	How to fool the rest.

Third, in Vocal 3 Parts 1 and 2 (6:08 and 9:20 side 1), there is a contrast made between the poet and the soldier and their respective "weapons" (pen and sword), and a contrast between a son ("the youngest of the family") and a father ("the oldest of the family").

Vocal 3 Part 1	Vocal 3 Part 2
And the poet lifts his pen	And the poet sheaths his pen
While the soldier sheaths his sword.	While the soldier lifts his sword.
And the youngest of the family	And the oldest of the family
Is moving with authority.	Is moving with authority.
Building castles by the sea,	Coming from across the sea,
He dares the tardy tide	He challenges the son
To wash them all aside.	Who puts him to the run

Fourth, the lyrics of Vocal 7 Part 2 ("So! Come on ye childhood heroes!" 18:39 side 1) and Vocal 7 Part 4 ("So! Where the hell was Biggles" 20:00

side 1) are repeated verbatim in Vocal 13 Parts 1 and 2 (18:08 and 18:52 side 2). These sections appear near the ends of sides 1 and 2, giving them a concluding function.

Vocal 7 Part 2 and Vocal 13 Part 1

So! Come on ye childhood heroes!
Won't you rise up from the pages
Of your comic-books? your super-crooks
And show us all the way.

Well! Make your will and testament.
Won't you? Join your local government.
We'll have superman for president
Let Robin save the day.

Vocal 7 Part 4 and Vocal 13 Part 2

So! Where the hell was Biggles
When you needed Him last Saturday?
And where are all the Sportsmen
Who always pulled you through?

They're all resting down in Cornwall
Writing up their memoirs
For a paper-back edition
Of the Boy Scout Manual.

Fifth and last, the lyrics of Vocal 12 Part 2 ("So come all ye young men" 14:49 side 2) are repeated in Vocal 12 Part 4 (17:13 side 2). These sections function as a chorus would in verse-chorus form.

So come all ye young men who are building castles!
Kindly state the time of the year
And join your voices in a hellish chorus.
Mark the precise nature of your fear.

While one can find plenty of loose thematic connections throughout the lyrics, these five occurrences are the most obvious use of textual repetition in *Thick as a Brick*.

POSTSCRIPT: THE ECCENTRIC JETHRO TULL

Although the lyrics, music, and packaging of *Thick as a Brick* can be confusing, the album does possess a peculiar charm. One might regard the album as bizarre and eccentric, but this adds to its appeal. Stephen Akey writes of the lyrics to *Thick as a Brick:* "The sheer Englishness of it fascinates. Its references to 'downy little sidies' and 'queueing for sarnies' and 'coughing up tenners' constitute a poetry of the exotic. Given the homogeneity of so much Anglo-American rock (not to mention Jethro Tull's immense popularity in the United States at the time), I can only admire the otherness of *Thick as a Brick,* the sense it gives of being a report from a unique culture."[36] Indeed, the lyrics – as well as the music, the album packaging, and the live show – mark Jethro Tull as quintessential English eccentrics. The late 1960s and early 1970s can be called the great age of the English rock eccentrics. John Lennon of the Beatles, Syd Barrett of Pink Floyd, and Robert Fripp of King Crimson had the mystique of alchemists as they used the recording studio as their laboratory to shape psychedelic visions into other-worldly sounds. Glam rock was born in the United Kingdom in this period, and David Bowie and Freddie Mercury defined the image of the outlandish, mercurial rock icon. Speaking of Peter Gabriel of Genesis, Kari Kallioniemi writes, "the new English rock-star attacked the puritan side of Victorian tradition but embraced its eccentric Englishness."[37] Jethro Tull began fostering their own brand of eccentricity as early as their first album, *This Was:* the cover shows the band members – then in their early twenties – dressed as rickety old codgers. Like Peter Gabriel of Genesis, Anderson relished in creating images of English eccentricity in his lyrics and in his appearance onstage. His stage garb, especially from the late 1960s to the late 1970s, shows him scouring British society for caricature:

1969–1971	Tramp in a ragged greatcoat
1969–1976	Mad minstrel flutist or court jester
1977	Woodsman or lumberjack
1978	Country squire
1979	Tartan-clad Scotsman

It was not only Anderson who embodied the eccentric; keyboardist John Evans dressed in a clown suit, bassist Jeffrey Hammond wore a black-and-white zebra suit (with matching bass guitar), drummer Barrie Barlow wore a kilt, and guitarist Martin Barre wore a glittering silver suit.

Chris Riley, who played guitar in the John Evan Band (the band that later would become Jethro Tull), told Tull biographer Martin Webb: "Ian, John, and Jeffrey suffered from varying forms of eccentricity. Ian was later always described as eccentric, but in my view the eccentric was Jeff – a true eccentric. I think Ian nurtured his and worked on it a bit, it was an image thing, whereas Jeff was genuine. In tiers of eccentricity I would have put it Jeffrey, John, and Ian."[38] This eccentricity is germane to the lyrical ideas in *Thick as a Brick,* which stress the importance of individual expression as a foil against the homogeny and hegemony of mass society. Writing in 1859, John Stuart Mill cautions, "In this age, the mere example of non-conformity, the mere refusal to bend the knee to custom, is itself a service. Precisely because the tyranny of opinion is such as to make eccentricity a reproach, it is desirable, in order to break through that tyranny, that people should be eccentric. Eccentricity has always abounded when and where strength of character has abounded. That so few now dare to be eccentric marks the chief danger of the time."[39] Jethro Tull responds to the danger of normalcy in dress, lyrics, musicality, and performance. Warning against hegemony, the band is clearly geared toward the exceptional rather than the average.

FOUR

The Music of *Thick as a Brick:*
Form and Thematic Development

BEFORE EXAMINING THE FORM AND THEMATIC DEVELOPMENT of *Thick as a Brick*, it would be helpful to read a portion of the first review of the album, which warns the listener that the structure of the work may seem a bit odd: "One doubts at times the validity of what appears to be an expanding theme throughout the two continuous sides of this record but the result is at worst entertaining and at least aesthetically palatable. Poor, or perhaps naïve taste is responsible for some of the ugly changes of time signature and banal instrumental passages linking the main sections but ability in this direction should come with maturity."[1] This review isn't from *Rolling Stone* or *Melody Maker*, the leading music periodicals when the album was released. Beating the critics at their own game, Ian Anderson wrote this tongue-in-cheek review himself and included it on the album on page 7 of the *St. Cleve Chronicle*. Although Anderson (under the pseudonym Julian Stone-Mason B.A.) writes that *Thick as a Brick* shows "naïve taste," this is a piece of music whose form shows a great deal of "maturity." The form of *Thick as a Brick* is one of its most distinctive features, and a close examination lends insight into the originality of the piece.

As with most music, an appreciation of the musical content of *Thick as a Brick* cannot be fully grasped by using only one method of analysis. What John J. Sheinbaum concludes about the Yes song "Roundabout" is also true of *Thick as a Brick*: "Interpreting 'Roundabout' *solely* as a rock song misses much of the detail that invites consideration alongside the art-music tradition, but at the same time, to describe the song as if it were merely a piece *of* that tradition also misses much of the detail essential for understanding the song in terms of its background as rock music."[2] *Thick as a Brick* is essentially an album of rock music, but it is more accurately described as a convergence between the worlds of rock, folk, and classical music, exhibiting both the common ground and the tension between these three styles. It is a composite of the defining features of these three styles of music. In a nutshell, it has the loud intensity of rock music, the lyrical introspection of folk music, and approaches the compositional depth of classical music. My analysis of *Thick as a Brick*'s form draws parallels to large-scale forms found in classical music simply because, being forty-three minutes of continuous music, it is far more complex than the common song forms of much rock and folk (such as strophic, AABA, and verse-chorus; see "Common Popular Music Forms" below). Yet *Thick as a Brick*'s large-scale form is constructed from the building blocks of these same small-scale forms, so a consideration of them is just as necessary.

In the past twenty years, several scholars have convincingly compared large-scale forms in progressive rock pieces to various large-scale forms in classical music.[3] These scholars have shown that bands like Yes and Genesis blended rock with classical music not simply at a surface level (overdubbing a string arrangement), but at a deep structural level. In considering the form of *Thick as a Brick*, David Nicholls states that it is "at once [a] song cycle, multi-movement suite, and symphonic poem, yet succeeds brilliantly at transcending all of these supposed models in creating a seamless musical, textural, and pictorial *Gesamtkunstwerk*."[4] I would add that *Thick as a Brick* also resembles theme and variations form and the medieval *lai*, as discussed in chapter 2. But Anderson is quite candid, and comic, in admitting that he followed none of these models: "I remember in an act of extreme bluffing on a daily basis, coming in saying 'OK right, next piece of music we have today, to add on to the rest of the stuff ... is such and such,' and I had only written it that morning. I would come in the next day and pretend it was all part of some master plan, some grand scheme, whereas, in fact, of course, I was only making it up as I went along."[5] Although the aforementioned classical forms are useful in showing the expansive scope of *Thick as a Brick*, they don't adequately describe the form of this piece. My approach, which follows below, shows how the small-scale popular music forms of strophic, AABA, and verse-chorus were used to construct the large-scale form.

THE ROLE OF FORM IN POPULAR MUSIC

Listeners of popular, folk, or rock music are more often drawn to a song's melody, lyrics, or performance than they are to a song's form. The major reason for this is that these styles of music usually are made from small-scale forms that are easily discernible and don't bring attention to themselves. Small-scale forms carry within them an inherent series of expectations that are subconsciously ingrained into a musical culture. Everyone seems to know that when they hear a verse and a chorus, another verse and chorus will usually follow. We take note of a song's form only when these expectations are altered, or denied, and it is easy for an audience to lose interest in a piece of music when it does not deliver what is expected from it. A piece like *Thick as a Brick* alters and denies expectations so many times that once the listener gets past the first ten minutes, he or she has no idea what should be expected next. Its form is not easily discernible, and this can confuse the listener.

To appreciate a work such as this, the listener must recognize that it is drawing on expectations from both the classical and the popular song worlds, from both large-scale and small-scale forms. Anderson himself acknowledges the incongruities between these two worlds in his remarks about performing *Thick as a Brick* in its entirety during Jethro Tull's 1972 tour in support of the album:

> There was a time in my life when I got very upset with the audiences, back in around 1972, when we were performing *Thick as a Brick*. The difficulty then was trying to play the acoustic music that we didn't have to play when we were doing the heavy rock music of the *Aqualung* album. The audience was just about able to cope with the acoustic section in "Aqualung," or in "Wind Up" or "My God," knowing that they were going to get the big rock 'n' roll riff any minute. With *Thick as a Brick* suddenly there was a lot more music . . . The audiences, particularly in America, were not sympathetic to the concert atmosphere that it was necessary to maintain: that they had to be quiet in the quiet places, and could react and jump up and down in the loud bits. In 1992 in almost every country in the world the people have now learned how to respond to that song. Today, as soon as I start playing *Thick as a Brick* there's a great wave of recognition, but then immediately people go quiet.[6]

When Anderson says "concert atmosphere," I presume he means the atmosphere of a classical music concert, where actively listening to the music is paramount. Anderson is hoping the crowd will act as if they are at a classical concert during the softer, acoustic sections – so that they can actually hear what's being played – and act as if they are at a rock concert during the loud electric sections. He is also hoping they will expand their attention spans beyond what they are used to and actively listen to a long and complex piece of music.

These considerations of form would not be so significant if *Thick as a Brick* were successful only with progressive/experimental rock listeners who are attracted to large-scale pieces. The album, however, was very successful as a mainstream rock and pop album, selling millions of copies and, as mentioned earlier, reaching number one on the American *Billboard* 200 Album Chart. This is unusual for several reasons. First, the average music listener rarely encounters a forty-three-minute rock song. Second, it is extraordinary that an album can reach number one with no singles. Additionally, in the review of the album on page 7 of the *St. Cleve Chronicle,* Ian Anderson wrote that the album was "for the underground market" and "not blatantly commercial." So there must be something about the music that was attractive and accessible to the mainstream popular music audience. I believe the small-scale popular, folk, and rock song forms (strophic, AABA, and verse-chorus) embedded within the large-scale form were a major factor in making *Thick as a Brick* accessible.

To explore further the significance of the form of *Thick as a Brick,* it would be helpful to consider what philosopher, sociologist, and musicologist Theodor Adorno said about the clash between classical and popular music, especially with regard to their forms. Although Richard Middleton successfully pointed out several flaws in Adorno's negative assessment of popular music, Adorno's critique is still useful in showing some incongruities between classical and popular music forms, and how *Thick as a Brick* successfully integrates their polarities.[7] Adorno argued that popular music in the twentieth century was deficient because its forms were too predictable and turned people from active listeners into passive listeners. He wrote: "The whole structure of popular music is standardized, even where the attempt is made to circumvent standardization. Standardization extends from the most general features to the most specific ones . . . The composition hears for the listener. This is how popular music divests the listener of his spontaneity and promotes conditioned reflexes... The schematic build-up dictates the way in which he must listen while, at the same time, it makes any effort in listening unnecessary."[8] Adorno felt that this standardization turned music from being a creative activity into a commercial activity, and that the writing and recording of popular music was just another enterprise of mass production in which mediocre musical ideas were plugged into preexisting forms. Conversely, he praised the unique, "one-off" structures that classical composers created that gave free rein to their musical ideas. Adorno died in 1969, and one wonders what he would have thought of the progressive and experimental rock bands of the late 1960s and early 1970s. Perhaps *Thick as a Brick* would have tickled his fancy, since it succeeds in the areas where he says popular music fails. Its structure is not standardized, neither in its general features nor in its specific ones. The composition does not "hear" for the listener, but expects effort and active listening from the listener. Speaking of *A Passion Play,* Anderson states:

> I like an album that's difficult to listen to. I like to have to sit down and really work into the music. A listener should make that effort. I don't like music that kind of unconsciously gets your foot tapping. That's Musak [sic]. I could write that kind of music, but it's just too easy. That's using music as a tactical weapon to sell records. I think it's important for the listener to feel that an effort has been made, that he has actually contributed in some way to the enjoyment for the music. The only tricks that I use when I play are used to try and help the audience want to make the effort. I admit to doing that. I try to entice the audience into wanting to listen.[9]

Thick as a Brick gives the listener the best of both worlds. Its unpredictable form provides the listener with a unique musical experience, yet it is built with the materials familiar to everyone, the *bricks* of the popular song forms.

COMMON POPULAR MUSIC FORMS

Before exploring the diversity of song forms in the vocal sections of *Thick as a Brick,* the following section provides a brief overview of common forms from which practically all pop and rock songs are constructed. Understanding the different song forms and how they are utilized in *Thick as a Brick* gives a deeper appreciation of its complexity and subtlety. The most prevalent forms in popular and rock music from the post–

World War II era to the early 1970s are strophic, AABA, verse-chorus, and compound form (which combines elements from more than one form).[10] To these must be added through-composed form, though it is rarely encountered. None of these categories are mutually exclusive, as many songs from the rock era exhibit characteristics from more than one category. Anderson composed songs in all of these forms – usually with alterations – up to and including *Thick as a Brick*.

Strophic form is the most basic of the song forms, because it doesn't contain any of the contrasting sections found in the other forms. It consists of a variable number of lyric stanzas, each sung with relatively the same melody over the same harmonic progression. It was used often by folk and blues musicians such as Woody Guthrie, Muddy Waters, and Bob Dylan. Examples include Dylan's "Blowin' in the Wind" and "The Sound of Silence" by Simon and Garfunkel. Jethro Tull's "My Sunday Feeling" and "Locomotive Breath" are strophic forms.

The AABA form was used extensively by composers in the Tin Pan Alley tradition of American popular song, which lasted from the late nineteenth century into the 1950s. The form then became prominent in rock music. Each of the four sections is usually eight bars long, giving it its other common name, thirty-two-bar form. The first two A sections have the same melody and chord progression, the B section – also called the bridge or middle eight – presents new material, and the last A section repeats the first melody and chord progression, bringing the song to its conclusion. Judy Garland's version of "Over the Rainbow" by Harold Arlen and E. Y. Harburg uses this form. "Yesterday" and "Hey Jude" by the Beatles are in AABA form but with some alterations (such as a repeat of the B and final A sections). Jethro Tull's "Hymn 43" is based on this form, with its B section extended by a guitar solo and a repeat of the B section lyrics. The first three minutes of *Thick as a Brick* (Vocal 1) approximate this form with extended AAB sections and a truncated and altered final A section.

The verse-chorus form is similar to AABA form in that it presents two different sections of music, but it is different in that the emphasis is placed on the chorus. Although many songs in strophic or AABA form have what sounds like a chorus at the end of each A section, the refrain, or "tag," is not distinctive enough to be considered a separate section in itself. For instance, Dylan's "Blowin' in the Wind" has a refrain at the end of each stanza ("The answer my friend . . . "), but it is not different enough from the material in the stanza to be thought of as a chorus. The same is true of the refrain of Vocal 1 of *Thick as a Brick* ("So you ride yourselves over the fields . . . "). A third example of this is the Beatles' "I Want to Hold Your Hand," which is considered by John Covach and Walter Everett to be an AABA form rather than verse-chorus.[11] On the other hand, Beatle songs like "Penny Lane" and "All You Need Is Love" have an obvious distinction between verse and chorus and thus are clearly in this form. Several of Jethro Tull's songs fit this form (e.g., "Bungle in the Jungle"), as Anderson was never averse to a big chorus or a catchy "hook."

In through-composed form, each line, stanza, or small group of stanzas is given different music. Rather than fitting the words into a preexisting structure, the shape and flow of the lyrics determine the musical structure. Examples in rock music of this form are rare, because repetition and easily discernible structures (AABA, verse-chorus) are easier for a listener to digest. The Doors' "The Soft Parade" and several Frank Zappa pieces would qualify. Jethro Tull's "Cheap Day Return," a short acoustic piece on *Aqualung,* as well as the instrumental "By Kind Permission Of" from *Living in the Past* have little or no repetition of musical material and therefore fit into this category. *Thick as a Brick* could be considered to be through-composed, yet, because it has sections that repeat, it is closer to compound form.

Compound, or sectional, form combines elements from more than one song form. For example, Queen's "Bohemian Rhapsody" and Led Zeppelin's "Stairway to Heaven" combine strophic with through-composed form. Meatloaf's "Paradise by the Dashboard Light" combines strophic and verse-chorus with through-composed form. Instead of each line or stanza receiving a different musical treatment (like through-composed form), stanzas are grouped into larger sections with each of these larger sections given a different treatment. Many of the large-scale pieces by the progressive rock bands fall into this category, beginning quietly and slowly and building to a grand climax. A popular compound form is verse-chorus-bridge, which is a combination of AABA and verse-chorus. A bridge (the B section of an AABA form) is included after the second chorus of verse-chorus form, creating an ABABCB structure.

U2's "Beautiful Day" is in this form, with the C section, or bridge, occurring at the lyrics "See the world in green and blue." By the time *Aqualung* was in the works, Anderson was writing songs with compound forms, such as "Aqualung" and "My God."

SONGS FORMS IN *THICK AS A BRICK*

Jethro Tull's first four albums exhibit a wide variety of song forms, using all the above forms. The same is true for *Thick as a Brick*. Yet the form of each of the vocal sections, let alone the piece as a whole, cannot be gleaned from a cursory glance at the lyrics the way they are presented in the original album packaging. Gerald Bostock's poem (actually Anderson's) is printed on page 7 in the *St. Cleve Chronicle* as if it were a newspaper article, with narrow columns, slashes in odd places, and verses grouped in irregular sections (see figure 3.4). Yet if one arranges the lyrics according to their rhyme schemes and musical scansion, the separation between, and forms of, the vocal sections become clearer (see appendix 1). While many of the vocal sections in the piece do not adhere strictly to the common popular song forms discussed above, table 4.1 shows which ones they most closely resemble.

Anderson wrote the lyrics before the music, so the form of the lyrics played a large part in determining the form of the music.[12] The form of *Thick as a Brick* is composed of fourteen vocal sections interspersed with nineteen instrumental passages, each of which is between one to five minutes in duration. (To differentiate between the vocal sections in the course of the analysis, I have labeled them "Vocal 1," "Vocal 2," etc.) These vocal sections are linked seamlessly together by the composed or improvisatory instrumental passages (labeled "Instr. 1," "Instr. 2," etc. in table 4.2), with some of the vocal sections having instrumental passages within them. No two vocal or instrumental passages are exactly the same, which gives the piece a great musical diversity. At the same time, melodies from both the vocal and instrumental passages return later in the music in altered forms, which gives the piece coherency. Table 4.2 shows how *Thick as a Brick* breaks down into its vocal and instrumental sections and includes timings,[13] meters, pitch centers,[14] and the first line of each section's lyrics.

FORM AND THEMATIC DEVELOPMENT OF *THICK AS A BRICK*

Table 4.1. Song forms in *Thick as a Brick*

SECTION	SONG FORM	LYRICS
Vocal 1	AABA (last "A" section is altered)	"Really don't mind..."
Vocal 2	Through-composed	"See there! A son is born..."
Vocal 3 Part 1	Verse-chorus	"The Poet and the painter..."
Vocal 3 Part 2	Verse-chorus	"The cattle quietly grazing..."
Vocal 4	Through-composed	"What do you do..."
Vocal 5 Part 1	Strophic	"I've come down..."
Vocal 5 Part 2	Strophic	"Your bread and water's..."
Vocal 6	Through-composed	"You curl your toes in fun..."
Vocal 7 Part 1	1st "A" of AABA	"I see you shuffle..."
Vocal 7 Part 2	2nd "A" of AABA	"So! Come on ye childhood..."
Vocal 7 Part 3	"B" of AABA	"You put your bet on..."
Vocal 7 Part 4	Last "A" of AABA	"So! Where the hell was Biggles"
Vocal 8	Through-composed	"See there! A man is born..."
Vocal 9	Strophic	"In the clear white circles..."
Vocal 10	Through-composed	"The legends worded..."
Vocal 11	Strophic	"The poet and the wise man..."
Vocal 12 Part 1	1st verse of verse-chorus	"Let me tell you the tales..."
Vocal 12 Part 2	1st chorus of verse-chorus	"So come all ye young men..."
Vocal 12 Part 3	2nd verse of verse-chorus	"Let me help you to pick up..."
Vocal 12 Part 4	2nd chorus of verse-chorus	"So! come all ye young men..."
Vocal 13 Part 1	Reprise of Vocal 7 Part 2 (2nd "A" of AABA)	"So! Come on ye childhood..."
Vocal 13 Part 2	Reprise of Vocal 7 Part 4 (Last "A" of AABA)	"So! Where the hell was Biggles"
Vocal 14	Reprise of lines 5–8 of Vocal 1	"So you ride yourselves..."

Table 4.1 shows that Vocals 1, 3, 5, 7, 9, and 11–13 approximate well-known popular and rock song forms: AABA, verse-chorus, and strophic. If any of these sections were extracted from *Thick as a Brick*, they would almost sound as if they were complete songs. In contrast to this, Vocals 2, 4, 6, 8, and 10 can be considered to be through-composed. All five of them have melodic lines that either do not repeat or repeat only once. They are also short in duration, with most of them having six or fewer lines of text and singing that lasts less than one minute. Three of the five are accompanied by ostinati and wander away from their tonic area. Because of these features, they sound open-ended, fragmentary, and transitional when compared to the other sections, which are longer,

Table 4.2. Large-scale form of *Thick as a Brick*

SIDE 1

SECTION	TIMING	METER	PITCH CENTER	LYRICS
Vocal 1	0:00–3:01	$\frac{12}{8}$	F	"Really don't mind…"
Vocal 2	3:01–3:36	$\frac{5}{4}$	C Dorian	"See there! A son is born…"
Instr. 1	3:36–5:01	$\frac{5}{4}, \frac{4}{4}$		
	5:01–6:08	$\frac{4}{4}$	G Aeolian	
Vocal 3 Part 1	6:08–7:15	$\frac{4}{4}$		"The Poet and the painter…"
Instr. 2	7:15–9:20	$\frac{4}{4}$		
Vocal 3 Part 2	9:20–10:30	$\frac{4}{4}$		"The cattle quietly grazing…"
Instr. 3	10:30–11:19	$\frac{4}{4}, \frac{6}{8}$		
Vocal 4	11:19–11:52	$\frac{6}{8}$	D Mixolydian	"What do you do…"
Instr. 4	11:52–12:31	$\frac{4}{4}$	B Aeolian	
	12:31–13:16	$\frac{12}{8}$	D	
Vocal 5 Part 1	13:16–14:13	$\frac{12}{8}$		"I've come down…"
Instr. 5	14:13–15:26	$\frac{12}{8}$		
Vocal 5 Part 2	15:26–15:54	$\frac{12}{8}$		"Your bread and water's…"
Instr. 6	15:54–16:24	$\frac{12}{8}$		
	16:24–16:35	$\frac{12}{8}$	F	
Vocal 6	16:35–17:06	$\frac{6}{8}$		"You curl your toes in fun…"
Instr. 7	17:06–17:26	$\frac{6}{8}$		
	17:26–17:41	$\frac{4}{4}$		
Vocal 7 Part 1	17:41–18:08	$\frac{4}{4}$		"I see you shuffle…"
Instr. 8	18:08–18:39	$\frac{4}{4}$		
Vocal 7 Part 2	18:39–19:06	$\frac{4}{4}$		"So! Come on ye childhood…"
Vocal 7 Part 3	19:06–19:29	$\frac{4}{4}$	G Aeolian	"You put your bet on…"
Instr. 9	19:29–20:00	$\frac{4}{4}$	F	
Vocal 7 Part 4	20:00–20:25	$\frac{4}{4}$		"So! Where the hell was Biggles"
Instr. 10	20:25–21:11	$\frac{4}{4}, \frac{6}{8}$		
	21:11–22:07	free	C Dorian	
	22:07–22:43	free		

repeat lyrics or music, have stronger melodic material, and, because of their forms, sound more like "songs." Of the through-composed vocal sections, Anderson comments: "Sometimes I thought I'd do a section, a little moment that serves as punctuation in the greater scheme of things, a one-off, a little splash of color somewhere on the canvas that doesn't have to be repeated or reused anywhere else."[15] The pattern of alternating between popular song forms and transitional, through-composed sec-

Table 4.2. (cont.) **Large-scale form of *Thick as a Brick***

SIDE 2

SECTION	TIMING	METER	PITCH CENTER	LYRICS
Instr. 10	0:00–0:48	free, 6/8	C♯	
Vocal 8	0:48–1:24	6/8	C Dorian	"See there! A man is born…"
Instr. 11	1:24–2:58	6/8	G	
	2:58–4:04	free		"We will be geared toward…"
Vocal 9	4:04–5:12	12/8	F	"In the clear white circles…"
Instr. 12	5:12–5:59	6/8, 12/8	C Dorian	
Vocal 10	5:59–6:29	4/4	G Aeolian	"The legends worded…"
Vocal 11	6:29–10:57	4/4		"The poet and the wise man…"
Instr. 13	10:57–12:37	4/4		
	12:37–13:11	4/4	C Dorian	
Vocal 12 Part 1	13:11–13:47	4/4		"Let me tell you the tales…"
Instr. 14	13:47–14:49	mixed		
Vocal 12 Part 2	14:49–15:03	4/4	D Aeolian	"So come all ye young men…"
Instr. 15	15:03–16:07	mixed		
Vocal 12 Part 3	16:07–16:43	4/4	C Dorian	"Let me help you to pick up…"
Instr. 16	16:43–17:13	mixed		
Vocal 12 Part 4	17:13–17:44	4/4	D Aeolian	"So! come all ye young men…"
Instr. 17	17:44–17:58	4/4		
	17:58–18:08	4/4	F	
Vocal 13 Part 1	18:08–18:31	4/4		"So! Come on ye childhood…"
Instr. 18	18:31–18:52	4/4, 7/8, 9/8	C Dorian	
Vocal 13 Part 2	18:52–19:21	4/4	F	"So! Where the hell was Biggles"
Instr. 19	19:21–19:41	4/4	G Aeolian	
	19:41–20:26	6/8	C Dorian	
Vocal 14	20:26–20:54	12/8	F	"So you ride yourselves…"

tions is consistent until Vocal 11; there are no through-composed vocal sections after this. Vocal 12 repeats material, Vocal 13 brings back lyrics and melodies heard in previous sections (Vocal 7 Parts 2 and 4), and Vocal 14 is a reprise of the refrain (lines 5–8) of Vocal 1. Bringing back familiar material cues the listener that the end of the piece is near and gives it a satisfying conclusion.

Thus, the vocal sections maintain a balance between familiar popular song forms, which provide recognition because material is repeated, and through-composed sections, which bring new material to the ear.

The former provide moments of stasis like an aria, while the latter keep the music moving forward like a recitative. If all the vocal sections were in one form, the predictable pattern might bore the listener after five or ten minutes. Yet if no material was repeated, or could be recognized as popular song forms, the listener may also lose interest because the music would appear long-winded and formless. Further, if too many tight-knit forms such as verse-chorus and AABA were used, the piece would sound like a series of songs strung together (a medley) rather than a continuous flow of music. If too many through-composed, open-ended forms were used, then the piece would sound like it was wandering aimlessly.

Adding to the musical variety in the piece, the sections that resemble common song forms (Vocals 1, 3, 5, 7, 9, and 11–13) are treated in a number of different ways, especially through the placement of instrumental passages (see table 4.2). Vocals 5, 9, and 11 are in strophic form, but Vocal 5 is distinctive in that it has an instrumental passage embedded within it. Vocals 1 and 7 are in AABA form, yet the sections of Vocal 7 are broken up with two instrumental passages, one after the first "A" section and one after the "B" section. So not only does the piece as a whole have a variety of song forms, but also each of the songs forms are altered and expanded in different ways.

Although table 4.2 shows how *Thick as a Brick* is constructed from numerous short vocal sections and instrumental passages, it is difficult to truly summarize the song's form. Another way of grasping its form is to view it as a series of larger chunks of music with climaxes. Large-scale works in classical music have the scope and scale to build to multiple peaks, but it is the rare rock song that has them. Both *Thick as a Brick* and *A Passion Play* have them in abundance. It is challenging enough for a rock band to write a satisfying climax to a large-scale song, but it is even more difficult to convincingly build to multiple climaxes and to bring the music back to a state of tranquility after them. Unlike songs like Led Zeppelin's "Stairway to Heaven" and Lynyrd Skynyrd's "Free Bird," which slowly and gradually build to their grand finales, the climaxes on the two Jethro Tull albums come in waves, or cycles. Several elements of the band's style facilitate this. First, the frequent changes in tempo, meter, and key/mode area provide opportunities for the band to either build up to climaxes or taper off from them. Second, the use

Table 4.3. Multiple climaxes in *Thick as a Brick*

CYCLE	BUILDUP	CLIMAX	TIMING
1	Vocal 1 to Instr. 1	Organ and electric guitar solos, unison machine-gun rhythms	0:00–5:01 side 1
2	Instr. 1 to Instr. 2	Double-tracked electric guitar solo	5:01–9:17 side 1
3	Vocal 3 Part 2 to Vocal 7 Part 4	Last stanza of Vocal 7 Part 4	9:17–20:25 side 1
4	Instr. 10 to Instr. 11	Second occurrence of driving $_8^6$ rhythm during Barlow's drum solo	20:25 side 1–2:58 side 2
5	Instr. 11 to Instr. 13	Pounding unison rhythm	2:58–12:33 side 2
6	Instr. 13 to Vocal 14	Sustained climax until the end	12:33–20:26 side 2

of acoustic and electric instruments (alone or in combinations) gives their music a broad dynamic range, from a soft, solitary acoustic guitar to the full band playing *fortissimo*. Lastly, changes in texture, especially homophony turning into polyphony, create density and intensity. In some sections the instruments and vocals are double-tracked and electronically manipulated to create denser timbres. Table 4.3 shows how *Thick as a Brick* can be heard as a series of six cycles in which groups of vocal and instrumental sections build up to climaxes and then subside. While what constitutes a "climax" is somewhat imprecise and subjective, this method does provide a way to grasp the flow of the large-scale form.

The album has two musical peaks in its first nine minutes, both consisting of instrumental soloing. In the first cycle the acoustic Vocal 1 gives way to the electric Vocal 2, then to soloing in Instr. 1 by Evans on organ and Barre on electric guitar (3:36–4:24 side 1). After the solos, and a short acoustic guitar passage, more tension is generated by machine-gun rhythms played in unison by the entire band (4:37–5:00 side 1). A V-I cadence on bass guitar (D to G) releases the tension and guides the music into the pastoral soundscape of Vocal 3 Part 1. The second, and greater, climax is Barre's electric guitar solo in Instr. 2 (7:15–9:15 side 1) after the first verse and chorus of Vocal 3. This is an unusual place for a climax; a guitar solo like this usually comes after the second chorus in verse-chorus form rather than the first. The double-tracked soloing here by Barre is magnificent, and the rest of the band augments it with a degree of collective improvisation. This level of soloing wasn't possible in Instr. 1, since the rigidity of the $\frac{5}{4}$ meter reins in the intensity of the playing. The band is able to quickly and convincingly calm down enough after the solo so that Vocal 3 Part 2 matches the tranquility of Vocal 3 Part 1.

The third climax is in a vocal section (Vocal 7 Part 4) and has a long, eleven-minute buildup. While the first two cycles are short and build from soft acoustic sections to loud electric sections, this one has less extreme contrasts in dynamics and a mixture of acoustic and electric instruments throughout. The music begins to reach a peak with the martial rhythms in Instr. 8 (18:19–18:39 side 1) and climaxes with the double-tracked vocals in Vocal 7 Part 4.

The fourth cycle has less of an organic flow than the first three, being a series of diverse styles of music. It begins with Instr. 10, which consists of a double-tracked flute solo (the denouement of the third cycle), three strident chords treated heavily with reverb and echo, swirling electronic effects, and more of the strident chords at the beginning of side 2. Vocal 8 (0:48 side 2) then starts with passionate fury before Barlow plays a frenetic drum solo in Instr. 11 (1:32 side 2). The climax is reached when the full band in unison interrupts Barlow's solo for a second time (2:53 side 2). After this the music eventually disintegrates into silence.

The calming presence of the acoustic guitar in Vocal 9 after the chaotic playing in Instr. 11 signals the beginning of the fifth cycle. The trajectory of this buildup resembles that of the first two, in which soft acoustic music (Vocals 9, 10, and 11) gives way to a forceful instrumental passage (the incessant march in Instr. 13, which the band plays in unison). The peak is reached at 12:01–12:33 side 2, with Barre bending notes and Barlow pounding out the rhythm on his low tom-toms.

The sixth and last cycle is loud and electric throughout, yet it still builds up tension and excitement multiple times until the end. The climaxes here are not achieved through shifts in tempo, dynamics, or instrumentation (as they were in the first five cycles), but by key/mode changes and the return of previous vocal sections and motives. The sixth cycle begins to build up with the four parts of Vocal 12 (verse-chorus form), which have three instrumental passages interspersed between them. They are all equally boisterous, yet the music reaches another level with the modulation from D to F in Instr. 17 (17:58 side 2) and the reprise of the lyrics and melody of Vocal 7 in Vocal 13. A final climax is reached at the end of

Instr. 19 (20:25 side 2), where the band halts on three climactic chords, and Anderson's acoustic guitar and vocal bring the piece to an end in Vocal 14.

As table 4.3 shows, the climaxes in *Thick as a Brick* are achieved in a variety of ways. The most obvious type is when a soloist reaches a peak in expression and execution with the rest of band accompanying at full volume and intensity. This occurs in Instrs. 1 and 2, the climaxes of the first two cycles. A second type is when the entire band is hammering out a rhythm in unison, which occurs at the end of the first, fourth, fifth, and sixth cycles. Yet a climax isn't defined simply as a section where the music is the loudest and most intense. The climax of the entire album is the return of Vocal 1 at the end ("So you ride yourselves over the fields . . ."), which is sung quietly by Anderson accompanied only with his acoustic guitar. The tonal return to F and the melodic and motivic return of familiar material create a climactic moment. Conversely, some loud sections create great tension yet do not feel "climactic," such as the echo-laden passage in Instr. 10 (21:11–22:07 side 1). Some climaxes have long buildups (the third, fifth, and sixth cycles) while others have little or no buildup (the first, second, and fourth).

Curiously, *Thick as a Brick* has convincing climaxes without the help of, even in spite of, the lyrics. Since the lyrics do not tell a coherent story, they do not dictate the buildups and climaxes of the cycles. The band achieves moments of great musical import simply through instrumental playing and Anderson's ardent vocal delivery. Two of the climaxes occur with the lyrics "They're all resting down in Cornwall / Writing up their memoirs / For a paper-back edition / Of the Boy Scout Manual" (the third and sixth cycles). These are hardly soul-stirring words when read on the page, but when Anderson sings them with the band playing at full force, they do sound climactic. Of course, this may be part of the spoof of concept albums that the band intended with *Thick as a Brick:* creating a grand musical climax with arcane and obtuse lyrics.

Thick as a Brick combines small-scale and large-scale forms, effectively marrying influences from both popular and classical music. The variety of song forms, the integration of instrumental passages, and the buildups to multiple climaxes make it a unique work that is more than just a medley of tunes or a conventional-length song that has been inordinately stretched out.

REPETITION AND THEMATIC DEVELOPMENT

In the post–World War II era, popular music has been governed by certain practical conventions that have established its boundaries. For example, a popular song usually lasts less than five minutes. Also, a popular song has no more than six different main sections of music (an introduction, verses, choruses, a bridge, an instrumental solo, a coda). Lastly, a popular song contains a fair amount of repetition, in both the lyrics and music. *Thick as a Brick* is one of the few songs to gain mainstream success while radically breaking these three conventions. It lasts for forty-three minutes, it has well over twenty-five different sections of music (counting the instrumental passages), and it uses repetition in ways that popular music normally does not. This section examines how *Thick as a Brick* uses repetition in both orthodox and unorthodox ways.

In any piece of music, too much repetition tends to bore a listener; familiarity breeds contempt. Yet unfamiliarity often breeds just as much contempt. Music that continually presents new material keeps the listener at a distance, because she or he has nothing recognizable to grasp. The music seems to be wandering aimlessly with no sense of "home." Hence, the ways in which a piece of music employs repetition and presents new, contrasting material largely determine its shape and scope and how it is perceived by the listener. A comparison between how repetition is used in popular music and classical music is helpful in understanding how it is employed in *Thick as a Brick*. In most popular and rock music it is common to find whole blocks of music repeated at regular intervals, often verbatim. For example, in a typical verse-chorus song, the verses repeat the same music (with different words) at least twice and the chorus repeats the same music and words at least three times. Popular songs often reiterate instrumental riffs and end with a fadeout that continually repeats the chorus. In some songs a guitar riff is repeated throughout a song, such as in "(I Can't Get No) Satisfaction" and "The Last Time" by the Rolling Stones.

The exact repetition that is found in popular music is similar to the repeat in binary dance form in the Baroque period (although the performer has the freedom to embellish the material) and the repeat of the exposition in sonata form in the early Classical period. Although this gives the music symmetry and accessibility, it stymies the forward movement, organic shape, and progressive intensity that composers with more Romantic sensibilities – such as Beethoven – sought. Following the lead of Haydn, Mozart, and Beethoven, composers in the early nineteenth century began to eschew exact repetition in favor of through-composition and thematic development.[16] In the Romantic period, Brahms's developing variation, Liszt's thematic transformation, and Wagner's manipulation of leitmotifs became new compositional models that later composers adopted to avoid exact repetition of musical material.[17] Richard Middleton writes that with composers like Beethoven, repetition "tends to be absorbed into an irregularly shaped, prose-like discourse."[18] Middleton's use of the phrase "irregularly shaped, prose-like discourse" is an excellent description of both the lyrics and music of *Thick as a Brick* and describes well the way its use of repetition mirrors that of the Romantic composers. While the music of TAAB does not approach the complexity and subtlety found in the works of these composers, nevertheless the use of these advanced compositional techniques gives the piece a depth not normally found in popular music. Yet, as stated previously, TAAB also contains exact repetition that characterizes popular music and certain forms from Baroque and Classical-era music (binary dance and sonata). The use of these different types of repetition breaks the piece out of the common popular music forms, creates a balance between new material and repeated material, and helps to sustain the listener's interest for the length of its forty-three minutes.

At least four progressive rock scholars have pointed out the connections between large-scale progressive rock pieces and the programmatic works of the Romantic composers, especially the symphonic poem.[19] In program music the form of a work is dictated by a poetic or other extra-musical idea the composer conveys through music, rather than the common forms such sonata, rondo, or minuet and trio. Thematic development and the manipulation of leitmotifs play a large role in giving unity and shape to a piece of music that eschews exact repetition and the Classical-era forms. The symphonic poems of Franz Liszt were some of the first manifestations of this Romantic paradigm, and Richard Wagner brought it to a fuller fruition with leitmotif manipulation in his music dramas. In its use of thematic development, *Thick as a Brick* bears resemblances to Liszt's symphonic poems but is even closer to a work he began composing before any of his symphonic poems, his Piano Concerto no. 2 in A major. The concerto has six sections, but they are merged together into one continuous movement through the development of several themes. Detlef Altenberg writes that both of Liszt's piano concertos had "enormous significance for Liszt's compositional development, being preparations for such techniques of the symphonic poem as thematic transformation and the compression of several movements in one."[20] Just as Liszt united the distinct movements of a concerto into one extended, organic piece, Jethro Tull took the distinct song forms of popular, folk, and rock music and fused them into one extended, organic rock song.

MUSICAL REPETITION IN *THICK AS A BRICK*

Reiterating Richard Middleton's quote, the repetition in *Thick as a Brick* "tends to be absorbed into an irregularly shaped, prose-like discourse."[21] Both the music and the lyrics are treated in this fashion. In a 1972 interview during the tour to promote *Thick as a Brick,* Anderson commented: "I don't want to get caught up in... the commercial aspects of repetition. I don't really like repetition unless it serves a very definite purpose musically within the context of a whole piece. [Speaking of *TAAB*]: If you look at that record... there is some repetition, but not a great deal."[22] Doane Perry, Jethro Tull's drummer for more than two decades, echoes this in speaking of form in the band's music:

> The song forms [in Jethro Tull's music] didn't really traditionally adhere to what is known as "AABA" song form. It was more linear, and you had parts that didn't really repeat at predictable places; and, when they did repeat, they often repeated with a great deal of change. So it was more like classical music in that way... There would be certain familiar motifs that would appear here and there. The idea was to try to create an evolving series of parts that didn't necessarily have to be repeated the way you would predictably hear music performed in a more pop format.[23]

There are three ways in which musical repetition is employed in *Thick as a Brick,* the first being the repetition of musical material within the sections that resemble popular song forms (such as the three A sec-

Table 4.4. Vocal sections of *Thick as a Brick* with local repetition

SECTION	TIMING	SONG FORM	COMMENTARY
Vocal 1	0:00–3:01 side 1	AABA	The first two A sections have the same melody and chord progression. The last A section has a different melody but a similar acoustic guitar accompaniment.
Vocal 3 Parts 1 and 2	6:08–10:30 side 1	Verse-chorus	The verses and choruses each have the same melody, chord progression, and instrumentation.
Vocal 5	13:16–15:54 side 1	Strophic	Each line of text has the same melody, chord progression, and instrumentation.
Vocal 7 Parts 1 to 4	17:41–20:25 side 1	AABA	The three A sections have the same melody and chord progression.
Vocal 9	4:04–5:12 side 2	Strophic	Both stanzas have the same melody, chord progression, and instrumentation.
Vocal 11	6:29–10:57 side 2	Strophic	The three stanzas have roughly the same melody, chord progression, and instrumentation.
Vocal 12 Parts 1 to 4	13:11–17:44 side 2	Verse-chorus	The verses and choruses each have the same melody, chord progression, and instrumentation.

tions in AABA having the same, or similar, music). This will be referred to as "local" repetition. The second is the return of a block of music later in the work, with only slight variations. This is commonly known as a "reprise," which the Beatles employed on *Sgt. Pepper's Lonely Hearts Club Band*. The third is thematic development of short vocal and instrumental motives, which composers from the Romantic era brought to perfection. What follows is not a comprehensive analysis of repetition and thematic development in *Thick as a Brick*, but a study of the most prominent instances in the work.

In *Thick as a Brick* there are seven occurrences of local repetition, the repeat of musical material within the sections that resemble the forms of popular songs (see table 4.4). The "Commentary" column explains which elements in the music are repeated. These sections sound tight-knit and self-contained, and they adhere closely to common popular music forms, largely because of their use of local repetition. Because of this, two sections of *TAAB* were extracted and turned into coherent

Example 4.1. *Thick as a Brick,* melody in first A section of Vocal 1, 0:11 side 1

Example 4.2. *Thick as a Brick,* melody in second A section of Vocal 1, 1:00 side 1

"singles" (although no singles were taken from the album when it was released in 1972). Vocal 1 appears as "Thick as a Brick Edit #1" on Jethro Tull's first greatest hits album *M.U. The Best of Jethro Tull* from 1976. Vocal 5 appears as "Thick as a Brick Edit #4" on *Repeat: The Best of Jethro Tull Vol. 2* from 1977. Vocal 1 has become quite popular as a Jethro Tull "single" with much rotation on American classic rock stations to the present day.

Yet in almost all of these seven sections, exact repetition is avoided by changes in the melody or instrumentation. For instance, in the first A section of Vocal 1, Anderson plays the theme in example 4.1 on the flute after singing each line. In the second A section a different theme, shown in example 4.2, is played by the electric guitar, piano, bass.[24] Further, the refrains of the A sections ("So you ride yourselves . . . ") have different instrumentation. The accompaniment in the first refrain is just acoustic guitar and flute. In the second refrain, piano, electric guitar, bass, and drums are added.

The second type of repetition used in *Thick as a Brick* is the reprise of sections, or blocks, of music later in the work with only slight variations. This type of repetition helps to bookend the piece by bringing back on side 2 something easily recognizable from side 1. There are two instances of this type of repetition. First, Vocal 13 Parts 1 and 2 (18:08 and 18:52 side 2) bring back the lyrics and melody of Vocal 7 Parts 2 and 4 (18:39 and 20:00 side 1) with slight changes in the instrumentation. This reprise of both lyrics and music near the end acts as a cue to the listener that the piece is drawing to its conclusion. Second, Vocal 14 (20:26 side 2) brings back the melody, instrumentation, and lines 5–8 of Vocal 1 (0:38 side 1). This short reprise provides a satisfying conclusion to the piece by ending it with the same music with which it began.

The third type of repetition found in *Thick as a Brick* is the development or transformation of vocal and instrumental motives. As Anderson said in 1972, "*Thick as a Brick* isn't a lyrical concept built around any one theme. It's a musical concept: all sorts of musical lines keep reappearing all the way through, sometimes in different keys or in different time signatures."[25] Elaborating on this in 2012, Anderson said:

> "There was a deliberate attempt to make use of themes, to revisit them, to develop them. It was done consciously, but without a master plan. There was no attempt to sketch everything out beforehand and say, 'This is the beginning, the middle, and the end,' and, 'We'll use this again here and this again there.' It was very much just sequential. So when it felt right for something to make a reappearance, then it made its reappearance. It was whimsical and spontaneous."[26]

It is in this category that TAAB goes beyond the conventional types of repetition found in popular, folk, and rock music by employing more sophisticated and subtle compositional techniques found in classical music. Active and concentrated listening is required to hear how these motives are developed throughout the piece. Although TAAB can be enjoyed without delving deeply into the music, the piece grows richer with every listen, because there is much to find if one looks below the surface. It is here that Anderson's views on active listening (quoted in full previously) are most pertinent: "I like to have to sit down and really work into the music. I think it's important for the listener to feel that an effort has been made, that he has actually contributed in some way to the enjoyment for the music. I try to entice the audience into wanting to listen."[27] The following seven motives are developed thematically in *Thick as a Brick*. All of these themes are short and somewhat fragmentary, thus they lend themselves well to melodic, harmonic, rhythmic, and instrumental variation.

MOTIVE 1

Motive 1 is the opening guitar pattern heard at the beginning of *Thick as a Brick*; it appears eight times in the piece (see example 4.3 and its

Table 4.5. Appearances of *Thick as a Brick* Motive 1

SECTION	TIMING	METER	PITCH CENTER	INSTRUMENTATION
Vocal 1	0:00 side 1	12/8	F	Acoustic guitar
Instr. 6	16:24 side 1	12/8	F	Acoustic guitar
Vocal 7 Part 1	17:41 side 1	4/4, 12/8	F	Acoustic guitar with different picking pattern
Vocal 9	4:04 side 2	6/8 or 12/8	F	Acoustic guitar with new vocal melody
Instr. 12	5:47 side 2	12/8	C Dorian	Acoustic guitar
Instr. 18	18:42 side 2	7/8 and 9/8	C Dorian	Bass, electric guitar, organ
Instr. 19	19:41 side 2	6/8	C Dorian	Bass, electric guitar, organ
Vocal 14	20:26 side 2	12/8	F	Acoustic guitar

appearances in table 4.5). Although this motive sounds melodically similar every time it appears and is played almost exclusively on acoustic guitar, the band finds ways to alter it through its metrical ambiguity. This opening guitar pattern is in 12/8 meter, a compound meter that is easily manipulated into sounding like other compound or simple meters, depending on how the twelve notes are grouped or which subdivisions of the beat are accented. This meter can easily be heard in 6/8 or 4/4, with two or four primary beats per measure, and this is how the band varies the motive.

Example 4.3. *Thick as a Brick,* Motive 1

When the guitar pattern returns for the first time near the end of Instr. 6 (16:24 side 1), it is again in 12/8 meter, with the notes in four groups of three. Anderson reinforces this by strumming the four primary beats of 4/4 time before the entrance of the familiar picking pattern. Immediately after this, at the beginning of Vocal 6 (16:35), drummer Barrie Barlow subtly suggests 6/8 meter using his hi-hat and, a little later, his splash cymbal. This hi-hat rhythm will return and be the foundation

Table 4.6. Metrical progression from 16:18–17:41, side 1

SECTION	TIMING	EVENT
Instr. 6	16:18	Anderson strums in $\frac{4}{4}$
Instr. 6	16:24	Anderson picks in $\frac{12}{8}$
Vocal 6	16:35	Barlow plays hi-hat and splash cymbal in $\frac{6}{8}$
Instr. 7	17:15	Barlow stops; Anderson strums in $\frac{6}{8}$
Instr. 7	17:26	Anderson continues strumming but switches to $\frac{4}{4}$
Instr. 7	17:31	Evans plays Motive 3 on organ in $\frac{4}{4}$ but hints at $\frac{12}{8}$
Vocal 7	17:41	Anderson picks in $\frac{4}{4}$ but hints at $\frac{12}{8}$

of Barlow's drum solo in Instr. 11. Meanwhile, Anderson continues accenting the four primary beats of his $\frac{12}{8}$ pattern. After Barlow drops out at 17:15, Anderson surrenders his $\frac{12}{8}$ picking pattern and consents to the $\frac{6}{8}$ meter using simple strumming. Then, convinced that Barlow is through pestering him with $\frac{6}{8}$ meter, Anderson surreptitiously morphs his strumming back to $\frac{4}{4}$ meter at 17:26. A few seconds later, John Evans begins playing a variation of Motive 3 (see below) on the organ that suggests a $\frac{12}{8}$ feel. Anderson picks up on this and begins playing a variation on the opening picking pattern that, while still in $\frac{4}{4}$, also suggests $\frac{12}{8}$ because of the four dotted eighth notes in Evans's organ theme. Thus, in the span of a minute and a half of music, Anderson, Barlow, and Evans play with the metrical ambiguity inherent in the $\frac{12}{8}$ guitar pattern by first imposing $\frac{6}{8}$ onto $\frac{12}{8}$, adopting $\frac{6}{8}$ entirely, switching from $\frac{6}{8}$ to $\frac{4}{4}$, then returning to $\frac{12}{8}$ by implying it within the $\frac{4}{4}$ meter. (Table 4.6 summarizes this metrical progression.)

The opening guitar pattern returns again at Vocal 9 (4:04 side 2) in its original form, but Anderson soon alters it and sings a new melody over it, giving the section a different character. This appearance is particularly refreshing because it brings order to the music after the drum solo and chaotic playing in Instr. 11. Next, the motive appears briefly in Instr. 12 (5:47 side 2) in C Dorian, vanishing as quickly as it is noticed. The next two appearances of Motive 1 (in Instrs. 18 and 19) are discussed in the section on Motive 2 below, since the two motives are closely related. The last appearance of the motive is in its original $\frac{12}{8}$ form, ending the piece in Vocal 14 (20:26 side 2).

MOTIVE 2

Motive 2 is a *moto perpetuo* theme appearing first in Vocal 2 accompanying the lyrics "See there! A son is born – " (see example 4.4). As table 4.7 shows, it appears four times.

After its initial appearance in $\frac{5}{4}$ meter near the beginning of side 1 (Vocal 2), this motive returns near the beginning of side 2 (Vocal 8; see example 4.5). The motive has been altered and extended from ten to twelve notes, and drummer Barlow gives it a swinging $\frac{6}{8}$ feel. The note values are also changed (diminuted) from eighth into sixteenth notes.

Example 4.4. *Thick as a Brick*, Motive 2

Example 4.5. *Thick as a Brick*, Motive 2 in $\frac{6}{8}$ meter, 0:48 side 2

Table 4.7. Appearances of *Thick as a Brick* Motive 2

SECTION	TIMING	METER	PITCH CENTER	INSTRUMENTATION
Vocal 2	3:04 side 1	$\frac{5}{4}$	C Dorian	Bass, electric guitar
Vocal 8	0:48 side 2	$\frac{6}{8}$	C Dorian	Bass, electric guitar
Instr. 18	18:42 side 2	$\frac{7}{8}$ and $\frac{9}{8}$	C Dorian	Bass, electric guitar, organ
Instr. 19	19:41 side 2	$\frac{6}{8}$	C Dorian	Bass, electric guitar, organ

This variation of Motive 2 bears a striking resemblance to Motive 1, the opening $\frac{12}{8}$ guitar pattern (more on this below). The motive appears for a third time in its most sophisticated form in Instr. 18, where it is treated in a *fortspinnung* manner. Grove Music Online defines this term as "a short idea or motif [that] is 'spun out' into an entire phrase or period by such techniques as sequential treatment, intervallic transformation and even mere repetition."[28]

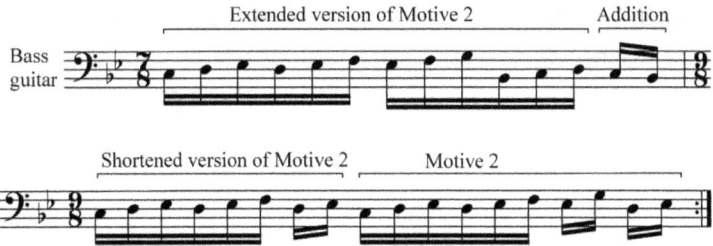

Example 4.6. *Thick as a Brick*, Motive 2 *fortspinnung* passage, 18:42 side 2

Shown in example 4.6, the motive is spun out using repetition, and the meter is changed yet again to ⅞ and ⁹⁄₈. This extraordinary passage first presents the extended ⁶⁄₈ version of Motive 2 (example 4.5), heard in Vocal 8. Two sixteenth notes have been added to the end (C and B♭) to round out the phrase and create a ⅞ bar. The ⁹⁄₈ bar that follows contains two phrases, the first being a shortened version of Motive 2 (example 4.4) with two notes, E and G, taken out. The second phrase is Motive 2 in its original form. In both of the phrases in the ⁹⁄₈ bar, the notes' values have been diminuted from eighth notes to sixteenth notes.

The motive's fourth and final appearance is a minute later in Instr. 19. In this section it is heard initially in its ⁶⁄₈ guise, as in Vocal 8 (example 4.5). Then it is truncated to six notes and interrupted three times by a string orchestra playing Motive 4 (see below, example 4.10). After the three string orchestra interludes, the motive continues uninterrupted in the form it took in Vocal 8. As mentioned earlier, this ⁶⁄₈ version of Motive 2 bears a striking resemblance to Motive 1, the opening ¹²⁄₈ guitar pattern. This suggests a strong connection between Motive 1 (in ¹²⁄₈) and Motive 2 (in ⁵⁄₄), with the ⁶⁄₈ meter version in Vocal 8 being the link between the two. When Motive 2 is changed from ⁵⁄₄ to ⁶⁄₈ in Vocal 8, it comes closer to the structure and feel of Motive 1, whose ¹²⁄₈ meter has already been tinged with ⁶⁄₈ connotations. Yet it is difficult to hear the similarity between the two motives when they are presented in their original forms at the beginning of *Thick as a Brick*. The ¹²⁄₈ meter of Vocal 1 and ⁵⁄₄ meter of Vocal 2 are in fact presented as contrasting sections, the first having mostly acoustic instruments, soft dynamics, and played in a folk style in F; the second having electric instruments, loud dynamics, and played in a rock style in C Dorian. They don't begin to congeal until the $\frac{6}{8}$ meter of Vocal 8. In essence, the first appearance of Motive 2 can be thought of as a variation on Motive 1, since both of them have a continuous, *moto perpetuo* nature.

MOTIVE 3

Motive 3, in example 4.7 and table 4.8, is first heard on electric guitar and flute in Instr. 2 and appears four times. The first two appearances of this motive come at the beginning (7:15 side 1) and the end (9:04 side 1) of Barre's electric guitar solo in Instr. 2. It reappears in Instr. 7 (17:31 side 1) in a high register on Evans's organ and its melody is slightly altered (see example 4.8). It is then played dozens of times on the organ throughout the next three and a half minutes in altered melodic and rhythmic forms, in different octaves, and in different organ settings. It comes back for the last time near the end in Instr. 19 (19:21 side 2), where it is taken up again by the electric guitar and flute.

Example 4.7. *Thick as a Brick,* Motive 3

Example 4.8. *Thick as a Brick,* Motive 3 on organ, 17:31 side 1

Table 4.8. Appearances of *Thick as a Brick* Motive 3

SECTION	TIMING	METER	PITCH CENTER	INSTRUMENTATION
Instr. 2	7:15 side 1	$\frac{4}{4}$	G Aeolian	Electric guitar and flute
Instr. 2	9:04 side 1	$\frac{4}{4}$	G Aeolian	Electric guitar and flute
Instr. 7 through Instr. 10	17:31–21:09 side 1	$\frac{4}{4}$	F	Organ
Instr. 19	19:21 side 2	$\frac{4}{4}$	G Aeolian	Electric guitar and flute

Example 4.9. *Thick as a Brick,* Motive 4, 11:23 side 1

MOTIVE 4

Motive 4, shown in example 4.9, is presented first on organ, electric guitar, and bass in Vocal 4 (11:23 side 1) accompanying the line "Do you want to be him?"

The motive returns over thirty minutes later played by the string orchestra in Instr. 19 (19:46 side 2) with the first cell inverted, making all four of them ascending. The motive is used three times in quick succession to interrupt the $_8^6$ version of Motive 2 (example 4.5), which is truncated to its first six notes. The first violins ornament the motive with countermelodies in its second and third appearances, as shown in example 4.10.

MOTIVE 5

This motive, shown in example 4.11, is heard first in the voice and glockenspiel in Vocal 6 at the line "You curl your toes in fun" (16:35 side 1). The descending phrase in the third measure of this melody is a diminution of example 4.2, from which it most likely was derived. The motive is heard again on the flute and tubular bells in Instr. 11 (a fifth higher starting on G) over Barrie Barlow's drum solo (1:41 and 2:09 side 2).

MOTIVE 6

Motive 6, in example 4.12 and table 4.9, is a descending theme that appears six times. It is first played by Evans on the Hammond organ in a semi-improvisational fashion with no definite pulse or meter. I have transcribed it in $_8^6$, since it is in that meter in all subsequent appearances. This motive provides continuity between the two sides of the LP (or the two tracks on the CD), since it appears both at the end of side 1 and the beginning of side 2. Three reverb-laden chords on electric guitar and

Example 4.10. *Thick as a Brick,* Motive 2 interrupted by Motive 4, 19:46 side 2

swirling wind sounds also help to provide continuity. Yet the second appearance of the motive at the beginning of side 2 is heard not on the organ, but on the flute and soprano saxophone (0:12 side 2). Also present here are punctuating, staccato figures by these same two instruments that imply a $\frac{6}{8}$ feel, foreshadowing the $\frac{6}{8}$ meter of Vocal 8, which begins at 0:48 side 2. The motive's third appearance occurs just as Vocal 8 ends with Martin Barre playing a version of the theme on electric guitar in Instr. 11 (1:23 side 2). The theme is heard twice more in this section on organ, electric guitar, and bass, interrupting Barlow's drum solos at 1:54 and 2:53.

Example 4.11. *Thick as a Brick,* Motive 5, 16:35 side 1

Example 4.12. *Thick as a Brick,* Motive 6

Table 4.9. Appearances of *Thick as a Brick* Motive 6

SECTION	TIMING	METER	PITCH CENTER	INSTRUMENTATION
Instr. 10	21:26 side 1	Free	C Dorian	Organ
Instr. 10	0:12 side 2	$\frac{6}{8}$	C♯	Flute and soprano saxophone
Instr. 11	1:23, 1:54, 2:53 side 2	$\frac{6}{8}$	G	Organ, electric guitar, bass
Instr. 19	20:04 side 2	$\frac{6}{8}$	C Dorian	Organ and soprano saxophone

In its last appearance much later in Instr. 19 (20:04 side 2), the theme is played by the organ and the soprano saxophone. Also present are the punctuating, staccato figures on flute and soprano saxophone that accompanied the motive's second appearance at the beginning of side 2.

Example 4.13. *Thick as a Brick,* Motive 6 layered onto Motive 2, 20:04 side 2

This last appearance is significant because it is layered on top of Motive 2 (played by the organ, electric guitar, and bass). Yet this is the version of Motive 2 that has been transformed to ⁶⁄₈ meter and is twelve notes long (example 4.5) instead of the original ten in ⁵⁄₄ meter. Because of this, the two motives lock perfectly in sync with each other in ⁶⁄₈. They also accompany each other well because they are in contrary motion: Motive 2 is an ascending theme, while Motive 6 is a descending theme. This layering of the two themes (example 4.13) creates an electrifying climax to the piece and makes the sudden reappearance of Motive 1 at the end all the more striking.

MOTIVE 7

Motive 7 (example 4.14) has two sections, the A section being a dotted-eighth-note motive and the B section being a descending sequential melody. The A section alone is first heard on flute and organ punctuating the end of an ascending melody in Instr. 13 (12:37 side 2). The A and B sections are presented together at 12:48 side 2. This motive has a ubiquitous presence in Vocal 12 Parts 1 and 3 and in Instrs. 13, 14, 15, and 16. In these four and a half minutes of music (12:37–17:10 side 2), it is heard dozens of times, sometimes with altered melodies and rhythms in both the A and B sections. Sometimes the A section appears alone and is repeated at different dynamic levels. Sometimes the B section is fragmented or sequenced downward. We hear the motive for the last time in Instr. 18 (18:33 side 2) played by the organ and electric guitar with the rhythm of the A section evened out and the B section augmented (note values doubled).

Example 4.14. *Thick as a Brick*, Motive 7

CONCLUSIONS ON THEMATIC DEVELOPMENT

In Instr. 19 (19:21–20:26 side 2) Motives 1, 2, 3, 4, and 6 return in quick succession either fused together, pitted against one another, or layered on top of one another. First to appear in this section is Motive 3 at 19:21. Then Motives 1 and 2, presented at the beginning of the piece as contrasting themes, are fused into a single driving *moto perpetuo* theme at 19:41 only to be interrupted three times by the string orchestra playing Motive 4 at 19:46, 19:51, and 19:57. After these interruptions the *moto perpetuo* gets going again with Motive 6 layered on top of it in contrary motion (20:05). After a grand climax on three chords, the band cuts out, leaving Motive 1 to finish the piece where it began. Tables 4.10 and 4.11 indicate where in the music the motives occur throughout *Thick as a Brick*. The numbers above the lines indicate the motives, while the numbers below the lines indicate the timings for sides 1 and 2. The motives emerge at a leisurely pace in the first forty minutes of the work and are packed more densely at the end.

Table 4.10. Appearances of all *Thick as a Brick* Motives throughout side 1

1	2		3	3
0:00	2:30	5:00	7:30	10:00
4		1 5	3 1	6
10:01	12:30	15:00	17:30	22:43

Table 4.11. Appearances of all *Thick as a Brick* Motives throughout side 2

6 2	6 5 6 5 6	1	1	
0:00	2:30	5:00	7:30	10:00
	7			3 1+2 4 1+2+6 1
10:01	12:30	15:00	17:30	20:54

This final flurry of motives is a technique that Richard Wagner used to perfection to bring acts, whole music dramas, and even the entire Ring cycle to a climactic end. Wagner took the wealth of leitmotifs built up in the first three music dramas of *Der Ring des Nibelungen* (*Das Rheingold, Die Walküre,* and *Siegfried*) and packed them all into *Götterdämmerung* with wild abandon. In *Götterdämmerung* the leitmotifs are altered so far beyond their original forms and come at the listener in such profusion that it is virtually impossible to keep track of them. A similar technique on a much smaller scale is happening in the last minute and a half of *Thick as a Brick* and shows how dedicated the band was to the craft of musical composition, something rarely found in such depth in rock music.

This section on thematic development highlights a conundrum that is characteristic of much of the best progressive rock music: the seemingly incongruous blend of composition and improvisation. Although the bulk of this chapter so far has shown how compositionally dense the music is, *Thick as a Brick* still sounds somewhat improvisational and spontaneous. In the "Discography" section of Jethro Tull's official website, we read this baffling sentence about the album: "Indeed, several segments were recorded in just one improvisational take."[29] In the interview that is included as a bonus track on the remastered CD, Anderson, Barre, and Hammond say it took only eight to ten days to record the backing tracks, with many of them being first takes.[30] In fact, Ian Anderson said this in 1974: "The things that appeared most calculated on my albums were figured out on the spot."[31] Skeptical of this comment, I asked Anderson to elaborate. He responded: "I think on my feet when I'm working on music and music arrangements. Sometimes the guys think I've got it all worked out in my head. I'm just making it up as we go along. It comes into my head and I say 'play these notes.' But other times there is more collaboration in the fine-tuning of people's individual parts in the context of an arranged piece."[32] *Thick as a Brick* displays a wealth of compositional depth, yet the music was written, arranged, rehearsed, and recorded in less than two months while the band was finishing up the *Aqualung* tour. Additionally, only keyboardists John Evans and David Palmer, who arranged the string orchestra parts in Instr. 19, had classical training. The rest of the band members, including Ian Anderson, are essentially self-taught musicians who cannot read nor write musical notation with any fluency.

To sum up this section on repetition and thematic development in *Thick as a Brick*, I would like to draw an analogy to "organic form" in literary theory. In the late eighteenth century, literary critics such as August Wilhelm Schlegel and Samuel Taylor Coleridge propounded that literature was being shackled by its own stagnant forms and that new paradigms were needed. Their ideas about "open-ended form" and "organic form" became central themes in Romanticism. These new ideas about form had their origins in literary theory but then spread throughout all the arts, especially music. Influenced by the theories of Schlegel, Coleridge wrote in a lecture he gave on Shakespeare: "The form is mechanic when on any given material we impress a predetermined form, not necessarily arising out of the properties of the material – as when to a mass of wet clay we give whatever shape we wish it to retain when hardened. The organic form, on the other hand, is innate; it shapes as it develops itself from within, and the fullness of its development is one and the same with the perfection of its outward form."[33] Similarly, Anderson describes the compositional process of *Thick as a Brick* as a spontaneous, organic process. His rambling, stream-of-consciousness description is itself spontaneous and organic:

> I really wasn't aware if it had been done before or not. [Writing an album consisting of one long song] ... Every day we just went in and a new bit of music came on and we said rather than stop there, let's just join it together with that little bit you were playing yesterday, whatever that was. That was a great bit, just to kind of tail out of this and bring us into that. Or we could use that idea we used before and make that a link sequence. Every day ... we would add another three or four minutes worth of real-time musical arrangement to the stew ... The good thing about *Thick as a Brick*, in the making of it, was that it was relatively spontaneous. I would write a piece of music in the morning, go in to rehearsals ... and we would work on that during the day, tie it into what we had been working on the previous day, and then have a run-through of everything to date. So we built up the album day by day. Each day I would come in with a new piece. I was reacting to what I had done the day before and it was built up in a very organic way.[34]

Thick as a Brick succeeds as an "organic form" because its composition and final form were not governed by the "laws" that govern popular music forms. It presents a large amount of continually new musical material yet contains just enough repetition and thematic development to prevent it from sounding incoherent, or as if it were wandering aimlessly. This balance of new musical material, repetition, and thematic development in both lyrics and music was a hallmark of the progressive rock style and created an audience that appreciated large-scale pieces of rock music.

FIVE

The Music of *Thick as a Brick:*
Other Features

THIS CHAPTER CONTINUES THE STUDY OF *THICK AS A BRICK*'S music, focusing on its stylistic diversity, instrumental passages, instrumentation, and harmony. As with many large-scale progressive rock songs, *Thick as a Brick* is a stylistically diverse and restless piece of music, with unrelenting shifts in musical style, meter, key area, tempo, texture, dynamics, instrumentation, and mood. The listener's interest is maintained throughout the piece because there is always some new and unexpected turn in the music that continually propels it forward. Speaking of certain songs on the *Aqualung* album, Anderson said: "Even within the context of an individual song I still like the idea that you can have perhaps a loud riff to start the thing off, and then it goes into a gentle acoustic passage, and then it does some other big stuff and then it changes tempo and feel and goes off into something else, round the houses, a couple of guitar solos, whatever, and back to something else. I like that in music."[1] Yet the stylistic diversity on *Thick as a Brick* is not the type that is found on Frank Zappa and the Mothers of Invention's *Freak Out!* (1966) or the Beatles' *White Album* (1968), where the songs overtly adopt or parody several different styles of music (dance hall, doo-wop, surf music, psychedelia, novelty songs, sound collage, etc.). Albums such as these are like musical quilts in which separate squares made from different fabrics are patched together with the seams showing. *Thick as a Brick* is an organic and blended album, as if it were a tapestry woven on a loom. It contains stylistic changes, yet they are smoothed over with a wealth of transitional material. Using the metaphor of a chef, Anderson says: "You have to find things that complement each other, you have to find the right flavors, the right colors, the right textures and you have to put those things together and blend them and coax them into something that is a satisfying and pleasing mixture. That's what making eclectic music is all about."[2]

A major reason why *Thick as a Brick* succeeds as a large-scale composition is that it takes the listener on a journey. Peter Gabriel speaks of the Genesis song "Stagnation" from their second album, *Trespass* (1970), as being a "journey song," which "went through a series of landscapes." He continues: "I think some of my favorite pieces of music are when I, as a listener, get taken into different worlds made out of sound."[3] This is characteristic of early 1970s rock music, especially progressive rock. The music of Yes is evocative in this manner, and this quality is accentuated by Roger Dean's cover art, which portrays fantastical imaginary landscapes. Although not associated with progressive rock, pianist Keith Jarrett pursued this idea in his improvisatory solo piano concerts and even wrote in the liner notes of his massive set *The Sun Bear Concerts* (1976), "think of your ears as eyes." Both *Thick as a Brick* and *A Passion Play* have this same quality and are journeys through diverse styles of music. In an interview from 2000, Anderson said:

> I like singing songs that put people in a landscape. I have a picture in my head for each song that I write, and it's a framed, still image. My early training as a painter and drafter, I think, produced in me a way of writing music and lyrics that illustrate visual ideas. I try to bring some maturity to the thing I've been doing for most of my career, writing songs that tell people a story, not in the temporal sense, but a story they make up to fit the picture I suggest to them. It's like sending people a postcard.[4]

Along with the music, certain sections of the lyrics of *Thick as a Brick* contain striking imagery, creating a picture in the mind's eye as one listens. Vocals 3, 9, and 11 are evocative in this way, with their depictions of "people in a landscape."

While many styles of music can be heard in *Thick as a Brick*, the principal styles in the piece are rock and folk. This practice of shifting between rock and folk styles is a distinctive element in Jethro Tull's music and was first employed on their second album, *Stand Up*. At this early stage, most of their songs were in either a rock or folk style and rarely contained both styles within the same song. By their fourth album, *Aqualung*, the band was deftly shifting between the two styles within songs, often creating two distinct moods or viewpoints. *Thick as a Brick* can be seen as an album-length employment of this practice, with its musical dialogue between, as Allan Moore puts it, "lyrical folk introspection and hard rock declamation."[5]

The influence of classical music also plays a large role in *Thick as a Brick*. I discussed previously that this influence is mainly felt in the large-scale form of the work and in its use of thematic development. Yet the passages for string orchestra in Instr. 19 (19:46, 19:51, and 19:57 side 2) play a huge role in bringing the piece to its boisterous climax. On the use of classical instruments in Jethro Tull's music, Anderson says this:

> I know a lot of people don't like the idea of strings muscling their way into the rock format, and they can be dreadfully slushy and overly romantic, but I do have a love for acoustic instruments. I also love loud electric guitar playing and heavy drumming and bass playing, but the idea of the two being somehow successfully wed together has always and continues to appeal to me. We have stayed with that idea almost from the word go, and we've continued to use strings where we feel that it works.[6]

Along with shifts in musical style, *Thick as a Brick* contains frequent shifts in meter, texture, tempo, and dynamics, which I will discuss below, devoting a paragraph for each.

Besides the obvious use of unusual meters in *Thick as a Brick* (such as the brash $\frac{3}{4}$ sections of Vocal 2 and Instr. 1), there are many examples of the band's penchant for playing much more subtle metrical games. As discussed in the section on form, the band subtly manipulates the $\frac{12}{8}$ meter of Motive 1 in several ways, morphing it into a straight $\frac{4}{4}$ or a swinging $\frac{6}{8}$. This fluidity of meter is a hallmark of progressive rock, especially with drummers such as Barrie Barlow, Phil Collins of Genesis, Bill Bruford of Yes and King Crimson, and Neil Peart of Rush. Instr. 10, which is in $\frac{4}{4}$, features two momentary forays into $\frac{6}{8}$ meter (20:52, 21:01 side 1). The band accomplishes this by dropping a beat from the $\frac{4}{4}$ meter for two measures and giving the two resulting $\frac{3}{4}$ bars a $\frac{6}{8}$ feel by Barlow's accenting beats 3 and 6. Instr. 14 (14:33 side 2) and Instr. 16 (16:58 side 2) each contain passages that have consecutive measures of $\frac{5}{4}$, $\frac{3}{4}$, and $\frac{6}{4}$. In Instr. 15 (15:32 side 2) a march theme is given quirky accents mainly by the swooping timpani, making it alternate between $\frac{3}{4}$ and $\frac{5}{4}$. Lastly, the most outrageous meter games are played in Instr. 18 (18:42 side 2) in the *fortspinnung* passage (see example 4.6). In the span of ten seconds, the band rushes through measures of $\frac{7}{8}$, $\frac{9}{8}$, $\frac{7}{8}$, and $\frac{9}{8}$, dropping only the vaguest hints at where the bars lines are. Only through repeated listenings can one discover the meters used.

Textural contrast is a central element of the soundscape of *Thick as a Brick* and takes many forms throughout the piece. The prevailing texture in TAAB, as in most popular and rock music, is melody-dominated homophony, in which a single melodic line (whether in a vocal section or instrumental passage) is supported by a chord progression provided by the rest of the band. Yet the type of homophony employed by progressive rock bands like Jethro Tull borders on polyphony, in which two or more melodic lines of equal importance are heard. While Anderson's voice and flute, Barre's guitar, and Evans's organ are the primary melodic voices in the music, Hammond's bass playing and Barlow's drumming also contribute many melodic ideas to the texture. This creates a wide variety of voices all competing for the melodic material. The typical *modus operandi* within most progressive rock bands is not just to complement each other, but to compete with each other! The band not only employs a wide variety of textures in TAAB, but they also pit the textures against one another. One specific type of textural contrast is homorhythmic playing (where two or more voices play the same rhythm) versus polyrhythmic playing. Instr. 2 is a perfect illustration of this. This section commences with the entire band playing Motive 3 (7:15–7:26 side 1). Then begins a passage where Martin Barre plays a guitar solo with a different but complementary overdubbed solo while the flute, organ, bass, and drums play their own semi-improvisatory parts. This creates a dense six-voice texture (7:26–9:03). At 9:04 the instruments again congeal into a single entity playing Motive 3. It is like a beam of white light revealing its spectrum of colors and then enfolding them back up, as portrayed on the cover of Pink Floyd's *Dark Side of the Moon*.

Thick as a Brick contains several shifts in tempo, many of which occur during the most overt changes in mood or musical style. For instance, the switch from the acoustic folk of Vocal 1 to the hard rock of Vocal 2 (3:01 side 1) includes the quickening of the tempo. Although shifts in meter are frequent, the tempo remains relatively moderate throughout side 1. Side 2 features more noticeable shifts in tempo, with the bustling $\frac{6}{8}$ rhythm of Vocal 8 (0:48 side 2), the funereal pace of Vocal 11 (6:29 side 2), and the breakneck speed of the *fortspinnung* passage in Instr. 18 (18:42 side 2).

While Jethro Tull seldom uses the extreme contrasts in dynamics that King Crimson does in pieces like "Larks' Tongue in Aspic Part 1" (1973), they do use dynamics as an effective expressive device in *Thick as a Brick*. Some of the most noticeable contrasts in dynamics occur when there is an abrupt switch from an acoustic folk section to an electric rock section or vice versa. There are three times when the band drops out and only the organ is present: at 10:45, 11:59, and 15:54 on side 1. Instr. 13 (10:57–12:37 side 2) features a gradual crescendo that lasts a minute and a half and sounds as if a distant army is slowly approaching. This is something that is rarely found in most rock music but is quite common in progressive rock, such as the gradual crescendo of the staccato riff near the beginning of "Watcher of the Skies" from the Genesis album *Foxtrot* (1972). As a last example, Motive 7 is played many times at different dynamic levels. The most obvious occurrence of this is the use of terraced dynamics, where the flute and organ play the motive *piano*, then the band as a whole echoes playing it *forte* (Instr. 13, 13:08 side 2).

Yet for all its eclecticism and stylistic diversity, there is never a doubt that *Thick as a Brick* is essentially a rock album. Although it is abstruse, theatrical, and intellectual like much of progressive rock, it is still straightforward. It is refined, yet it never ceases to be raw.

INSTRUMENTAL PASSAGES

While *Thick as a Brick* is full of memorable vocal melodies, it is in the instrumental passages that the compositional brilliance of the band really shines. Although they are short – most are under two minutes – the nineteen instrumental passages are often more musically adventurous than the vocal sections because of their through-composed forms, diversity in instrumentation, wealth of melodic and rhythmic inventiveness, and display of the musicians' virtuosity. I asked Anderson if these passages arose out of improvisations, or if they were carefully composed, and he responded: "In most cases there were key elements and key melodies going on, as opposed to obviously improvisational sections: organ solos, guitar solos, flute solos. But the areas that are what I would call 'part writing,' that are the more evolved, more melodic, with unisons and harmonies, they were mostly written by me. There would be a degree of collaboration with band members. It was fairly fluid. If someone came up with a good idea, we'd use it."[7] These passages serve different functions musically and can be placed into four categories: some function as transitions from one vocal section to the next, some feature virtuosic soloing by individual band members or the band collectively, some provide stark contrasts and take the music in new directions, and some repeat and reinforce the musical material found in the previous vocal section. Almost all of the instrumental passages fall into more than one of these categories.

While all the instrumental passages in *Thick as a Brick* can be considered as transitions or bridges between the vocal sections, some are more "transitional" than others in that they perform many of the same functions as the modulating bridge and development sections in classical sonata form. These functions include taking the material of the previous section and destabilizing its key area, fragmenting its melodies into smaller motives and sequencing them, introducing new thematic material and key areas, and changing tempo and meter. For example, Instr. 1 (3:36–6:08 side 1) moves the music from the $\frac{5}{8}$ meter and C Dorian mode of Vocal 2 to the $\frac{4}{4}$ meter and G Aeolian mode of Vocal 3. Instr. 6 (15:54–16:35 side 1) moves the music from the D pitch center of Vocal 5 to the F pitch center of Vocal 6. It also fragments the organ melody that dominates Vocal 5 into a shorter motive, while the acoustic guitar intersperses new material that turns into Motive 1 in Vocal 6. Many of these transitional passages contain subtle shifts in instrumentation with different groupings of instruments trading and sequencing motives. In Instr. 3 (10:45–10:58 side 1) the organ trades an ascending dotted-eighth-note motive with the soprano saxophone and electric guitar. After a few measures, the flute joins the saxophone and electric guitar, playing a related descending motive in triplets.

In a few instances the end of an instrumental passage introduces the next vocal section by presenting an instrumental version of the tune of the vocal section. This occurs in Instr. 1 (5:12 side 1), Instr. 4 (12:31 side

1), Instr. 7 (17:31 side 1), and Instr. 13 (12:47 side 2). Yet the relationship between the instrumental passages and the vocal sections is more complex than just thinking of the instrumental passages as "transitions" and the vocal sections as "tunes." Vocals 4 and 10 sound transitional because they are fragmentary and tonally unstable, while Instrs. 5 and 8 sound like tunes because they have memorable melodies and are tonally stable.

The second category of instrumental passages is soloing, in which the virtuosic abilities of the band members are displayed. All the members of the band except for Jeffrey Hammond on bass have opportunities for improvised solos. Anderson solos on flute in Instrs. 5, 9, and 10, Martin Barre solos on electric guitar in Instrs. 1 and 2, John Evans solos on organ in Instr. 1, and Barrie Barlow solos on drums in Instr. 11. After Barlow's drum solo, the entire band collectively improvises and brings the music to a sputtering standstill. All of the improvised solos appear in the first two-thirds of *Thick as a Brick*, giving this portion a slightly looser feel. The band's compositional inclinations seem to take over after the collective improvisation in Instr. 11, since the music is tightly composed and arranged throughout the rest of the piece.

While much of the music in *Thick as a Brick* is blended into a mellifluous whole, some instrumental passages introduce contrasting material – the third category – with abrupt shifts in style, tempo, dynamics, key, meter, or instrumentation taking the music in new directions. In Instr. 3 (10:45 side 1), Instr. 4 (11:59 side 1), and Instr. 6 (15:54 side 1), all the instruments drop out except for the organ. In Instr. 10 (21:11 side 1), the strict adherence to rhythm and meter that defined the first twenty-one minutes of the music is suddenly abandoned in favor of rising arpeggiated gestures that adhere to no specific meter. Meter and rhythm are downplayed throughout this three-minute section until Vocal 8 bursts in with $\frac{6}{8}$ meter. Instr. 11 is the section that contains the highest degree of stark contrasts, with its drum solo interrupted by Motive 5, abrupt changes in dynamics, including the use of silence, spoken-word passages, and a nod to free jazz. The next instance of contrast appears in Instr. 17 (17:58 side 2), where an abrupt shift to F (the mode/key at the beginning) signals that the piece is drawing to its conclusion. Lastly, the unexpected string orchestra interludes in Instr. 19 (19:46–20:01 side 2) provide a new tone color and hint at the grandeur of symphonic music.

The final category the instrumental passages fall into is repetition. These passages maintain the meter, key area, tempo, and melodic material of the vocal sections they follow. In Instr. 13 (10:57–12:37 side 2) the band takes the martial rhythm from the previous vocal section (Vocal 11) and repeats it incessantly with progressive intensity. The most repetition employed in *Thick as a Brick* occurs from 12:37 to 17:10 on side 2. This is because of the constant presence of Motive 7 in Vocal 12 Parts 1 and 3 and in Instrs. 13, 14, 15, and 16. In these four and a half minutes of music, this motive is heard dozens of times played by different instruments in different registers and at different dynamic levels. A final example of this category is Instrs. 8, 9, and the beginning of 10, which occur within Vocal 7. Since these passages occur *within* a well-defined song form (AABA) and do not link two different vocal sections, there is no need for stark contrast or transition. This would encumber the integrity of the song form. Instead, they simply prolong the material in Vocal 7 with different instrumentation and accentuation, and the near-constant presence of Motive 3 on organ.

If the vocal sections in *Thick as a Brick* are the bricks, then the instrumental passages are the mortar that binds them together. In fact, the musical edifice of *Thick as a Brick* is constructed more out of mortar than brick, since the instrumental passages take up approximately twenty-three minutes of music while the vocal sections take up approximately twenty-one minutes. Many of the climaxes in the piece occur in the instrumental sections. (For a detailed analysis of the passages, see appendix 3.)

INSTRUMENTATION

Thick as a Brick was recorded using seventeen different instruments played by the five members of Jethro Tull. This goes beyond what is found on the group's previous four albums and far beyond most rock albums. This fact is pointed out in the tongue-in-cheek "review" of the album on page 7 of the *St. Cleve Chronicle*:

> Apart from a short orchestral passage, the members of the group played all the instruments themselves. In addition to his usual flute, acoustic guitar and singing roles, Ian Anderson extended his virtuosity to violin, sax and trumpet,

while Martin Barre played a few lines on that delightful mediaeval instrument, the lute, as well as his electric guitar. John Evan played organ, piano and harpsichord, Jeffrey Hammond-Hammond played bass guitar and spoke some words, and new drummer Barriemore Barlow added the timpani and percussion parts.[8]

In addition to the instruments mentioned in the review, John Evans (presumably) created the swirling wind sounds at the end of side 1 and the beginning of side 2 on a synthesizer.[9] David Palmer composed, arranged, and conducted the string orchestra passages in Instr. 19 (19:46–20:01 side 2). Barrie Barlow played the drum kit, timpani, glockenspiel, and tubular bells.

While the organ, flute, electric guitar, bass, drums, and Anderson's voice are the primary instruments on *Thick as a Brick*, the soundscape is in a constant state of motion. It exhibits an abundance of instrumental tone color not often found in rock music. In this regard, the piece resembles a concerto for orchestra in which many different instruments are given solo passages and a variety of tone colors are produced through the groupings of instruments. In some passages the group sounds like a typical 1970s rock band; in others it sounds like an electric folk group; in still others it sounds like a chamber ensemble (especially in some of the instrumental passages, such as Instrs. 3 and 6).

Table 5.1 and the accompanying legend in table 5.2 indicate what instruments the musicians play in all of the vocal and instrumental sections. Each member of the band contributes elements to the instrumentation that make the sound of this album distinctive.

IAN ANDERSON

While Martin Barre's electric guitar dominates much of the music on *Thick as a Brick*, Anderson's acoustic guitar is put to the forefront in Vocals 1, 6, 7, 9, 10, 11, and 14 and in a few of the instrumental passages. Although the acoustic guitar is present in only twelve minutes of the forty-three-minute work, it seems to have much more of a presence in the music, because it is used in the most identifiable vocal sections (Vocals 1 and 14) and because it marks abrupt stylistic shifts in the music (i.e., from rock to folk). After its central role in Vocal 1 (0:00–3:01 side 1) and brief appearance in Instr. 1 (4:24–4:38 side 1), it is absent for almost twelve

Table 5.1. Instrumentation of *Thick as a Brick*

SIDE 1

SECTION	AG	B	D	EG	F	G	H	L	OR	P	SS	ST	SW	SY	TB	TI	TR	VO	VI
Vocal 1	*	*	*	*	*				*	*								*	
Vocal 2		*	*	*					*									*	
Instr. 1	*	*	*	*	*				*	*									
Vocal 3 Part 1		*	*	*					*									*	
Instr. 2		*	*	*	*				*										
Vocal 3 Part 2		*	*	*					*	*								*	
Instr. 3		*	*	*	*				*	*	*								
Vocal 4		*	*	*					*									*	
Instr. 4		*	*	*	*				*	*									
Vocal 5 Part 1		*	*	*	*				*									*	*
Instr. 5		*	*	*	*				*								*		
Vocal 5 Part 2		*	*	*	*				*									*	*
Instr. 6	*		*	*					*										
Vocal 6	*	*	*			*			*									*	
Instr. 7	*	*			*	*			*	*									
Vocal 7 Part 1	*								*									*	
Instr. 8		*	*	*	*				*							*			
Vocal 7 Part 2		*	*	*	*				*									*	
Vocal 7 Part 3		*	*	*	*					*								*	
Instr. 9		*	*	*	*				*										
Vocal 7 Part 4		*	*	*	*				*									*	
Instr. 10	*	*	*	*	*				*	*	*		*						

SIDE 2

SECTION	AG	B	D	EG	F	G	H	L	OR	P	SS	ST	SW	SY	TB	TI	TR	VO	VI
Instr. 10		*	*	*						*			*						
Vocal 8		*	*	*	*				*	*								*	
Instr. 11		*	*	*	*				*			*		*	*				
Vocal 9	*				*													*	
Instr. 12	*	*	*						*	*					*				
Vocal 10	*	*			*				*									*	
Vocal 11	*	*	*	*	*		*	*	*									*	
Instr. 13		*	*	*	*				*										

OTHER FEATURES OF *THICK AS A BRICK*

SECTION	AG	B	D	EG	F	G	H	L	OR	P	SS	ST	SW	SY	TB	TI	TR	VO	VI
Vocal 12 Part 1	*	*	*						*	*								*	
Instr. 14		*	*	*		*			*							*			
Vocal 12 Part 2		*	*						*									*	
Instr. 15		*	*	*	*		*		*							*			
Vocal 12 Part 3		*	*						*	*								*	
Instr. 16		*	*	*					*							*			
Vocal 12 Part 4		*	*						*									*	
Instr. 17		*	*	*	*				*										
Vocal 13 Part 1		*	*	*	*				*	*								*	
Instr. 18		*	*						*										
Vocal 13 Part 2		*	*	*	*				*	*								*	
Instr. 19		*	*	*	*				*	*	*	*							
Vocal 14	*																	*	

Table 5.2. Instrumentation legend of *Thick as a Brick*

ABBR.	INSTRUMENT	MUSICIAN
AG	Acoustic guitar	Ian Anderson
B	Bass guitar	Jeffrey Hammond
D	Drums	Barrie Barlow
EG	Electric guitar	Martin Barre
F	Flute	Ian Anderson
G	Glockenspiel	Barrie Barlow
H	Harpsichord	John Evans
L	Lute	Martin Barre
OR	Organ	John Evans
P	Piano	John Evans
SS	Soprano saxophone	Ian Anderson
ST	String section	Arranged and conducted by David Palmer
SW	Spoken word	Jeffrey Hammond
SY	Synthesizer/Studio effects	John Evans
TB	Tubular bells	Barrie Barlow
TI	Timpani	Barrie Barlow
TR	Trumpet	Ian Anderson
VO	Vocals	Ian Anderson
VI	Violin	Ian Anderson

minutes until Instr. 6 (16:07 side 1), where it reenters for two minutes and shifts the music from a rock style to a folk style. Near the beginning of side 2, after sections of music dominated by electric instruments and a powerful drum solo that slowly disintegrates into silence, the acoustic guitar enters and again grounds the music firmly back in the folk idiom in Vocal 9 (4:04 side 2), where it remains for four minutes. It is again absent for twelve minutes, and the piece rushes on in electric abandon until Vocal 14 (20:26 side 2), the reprise of the opening section, Vocal 1. Again it is the acoustic guitar that marks an abrupt stylistic change from rock to folk music, ending the piece in the style in which it began.

Although Ian Anderson's singing has always been idiosyncratic, his vocal delivery early in his career shows similarities with other late-1960s British rock singers with their American blues affectations and heavy doses of disaffected angst. On *Aqualung* Anderson's singing had reached a new level of sophistication and depth, and this is also apparent on *Thick as a Brick*. Although there is plenty of spleen in his voice when he is singing of the ills of the British class and educational systems (like his inveighing against the Anglican Church on *Aqualung,*) Anderson more often adopts the tone of a storyteller or bard on *Thick as a Brick*. The repeated use of expressions derivative of English folk balladry, such as "Let me tell you . . . " and "Come all ye . . . " (Vocal 12) require a bardic voice to sing them. Edward Macan captures well Anderson's vocal style when he writes: "[Anderson's] reedy, nasal vocal delivery is far more suggestive of folk-rock vocal techniques than of the open, straight head tone favored by most other progressive rock lead vocalists."[10] Anderson seems to have taken care to leave ample sonic space for his vocals on TAAB and seldom sings over the band while it is playing at full force (as he does in "Aqualung," "Hymn 43," and "Wind Up" from *Aqualung*). As mentioned earlier, many of the musical climaxes and *fortissimo* passages in TAAB are in the instrumental sections (Instrs. 1, 2, 8, 11, and 13 to 19) rather than the vocal sections.

Anderson plays most of his flute parts on *Thick as a Brick* with a clear, open tone and rarely sings through the flute while playing or uses his identifiable flutter-tongue technique. An innovative development in his writing for the flute is pairing it with numerous other instruments to produce new textures and timbral effects. Anderson's flute interacts

Table 5.3. Flute paired with other instruments in *Thick as a Brick*

INSTRUMENT	SECTION	TIMING	TEXTURE
Acoustic guitar	Vocal 1	0:11, 0:56, 1:51 side 1	Countermelody
Clean tone electric guitar	Vocal 1	1:56, 2:27 side 1	Harmony and countermelody
Glockenspiel	Vocal 1	2:22 side 1	Unison
Piano	Instr. 1	5:12 side 1	Countermelody
Distorted electric guitar	Instr. 2	7:20, 9:03 side 1	Harmony
Organ	Instr. 3, 4	10:53, 12:47 side 1	Unison, harmony and countermelody
Violin	Instr. 5	14:13 side 1	Countermelody
Trumpet	Instr. 8	18:19 side 1	Octave doubling
Flute duet	Instr. 9, 10	19:29, 20:25 side 1	Two improvised, yet imitative, solos
Soprano saxophone	Instr. 10, 19	0:12, 20:09 side 2	Harmony
Tubular bells	Instr. 11	1:41, 2:09 side 2	Octave doubling
Lute	Vocal 11	6:33 side 2	Harmony
Harpsichord	Instr. 14	14:04 side 2	Unison
Timpani	Instr. 14, 16	14:33, 16:58 side 2	Counterpoint
Voice	Vocal 13, Parts 1 & 2	18:08, 18:52 side 2	Octave doubling

with these instruments in many different ways, doubling them, playing in harmony, playing countermelodies, playing imitative counterpoint, or improvising solos over them. The flute appears in many of the vocal sections and in all but three of the nineteen instrumental sections. Anderson's flute is the musical "changeling" in the work, appearing in a different guise almost every time it appears. Table 5.3 shows the most obvious instances in which the flute is paired with fifteen other instruments. In Vocal 11 and Instr. 13, Anderson alters the tone of the flute by giving it a tremolo effect similar to the guitar and vocal tremolo in Tommy James and the Shondells' 1968 song "Crimson and Clover." This effect was used previously on Martin Barre's guitar in "A New Day Yesterday" and on Anderson's voice on "Look into the Sun," both on *Stand Up*.

The inflated phrase "Ian Anderson extended his virtuosity to violin, sax and trumpet" in Julian Stone-Mason, B.A.'s mock review was probably meant as a joke; Anderson merely dabbles with these instruments on the album. He plays the violin in the manner of a fiddle in the two parts of Vocal 5 and in Instr. 5, which comes between them (13:16–15:40 side 1). The violin doubles much of what John Evans is playing on the organ in this passage. He plays the trumpet briefly in Instr. 8 (18:18–18:39 side 1), augmenting the martial figure played by the flute, bass, and drums. Anderson plays the soprano saxophone in four places, first briefly in Instr. 3 (10:47–11:15 side 1), doubling first Martin Barre's electric guitar and then Anderson's flute. It appears more substantially in Instr. 10 (0:12–0:30 side 2), where, along with the flute, Anderson plays lilting gestures in $\frac{6}{8}$ that emanate out the swirling wind sounds. It appears for a third time in Vocal 8 (0:52–1:32 side 2), where it doubles the vocal along with the organ and flute and then helps to articulate the strident gestures from the electric guitar, bass, organ, and drums. Lastly, he uses the soprano saxophone in Instr. 19 (20:09–20:21 side 2) to augment the organ and flute passages. The use of the soprano saxophone gives these passages attractive tone colors, but the writing is not nearly as idiosyncratic as Anderson's writing for his acoustic guitar, voice, or flute. Although he never recorded with the violin or trumpet after *Thick as a Brick*, he did develop a distinctive voice on the soprano and sopranino saxophones on Jethro Tull's next two albums, *A Passion Play* and *War Child*.

Although Jethro Tull has always been a rock band that uses heavy doses of electricity, Anderson has said in numerous interviews that he regards himself primarily as an acoustic musician. This is well in evidence on *Thick as a Brick*, where all six of his instruments are acoustic. They are the foil against the electric instruments and provide much of the timbral contrast that makes the piece so aurally compelling.

MARTIN BARRE

The material that Anderson and the band wrote for *Thick as a Brick* is less "riff-oriented" than on earlier albums, where songs such as "Aqualung" or "To Cry You a Song" were defined and shaped by their guitar riffs. As a consequence, Martin Barre's role on the album expanded well beyond merely playing the guitar riffs and soloing. He became an integral part of the arranging, and even the writing, of the music. In an interview, Barre said: "*Thick as a Brick* was probably the first album where there was a lot of input from other members. We've always arranged Tull music and within that term 'arranging,' you could say some of it is writing."[11] Barre is present throughout *Thick as a Brick*, sometimes playing riffs and soloing with heavy distortion, sometimes subtly doubling other instruments with a clean tone to provide color and shading. The section where Barre shines the brightest is Instr. 2 (7:27–9:04 side 1), where he plays a guitar solo and then adds a different, but complementary, overdubbed solo (beginning at 7:45). Barre plays the lute alongside Anderson's strumming on acoustic guitar in Vocal 11 (6:29 side 2).

JOHN EVANS

While many of the virtuoso rock keyboard players of the early 1970s, such as Keith Emerson and Rick Wakeman, were drawn to the new Moog and ARP synthesizers, musicians like Jon Lord of Deep Purple and John Evans channeled most of their creativity into an old standby, the Hammond B-3 organ combined with a Leslie rotating speaker. Evans's Hammond organ is the most prominent instrument on *Thick as a Brick*, present in the soundscape for all but approximately five minutes. It takes a central role as a solo instrument in Instr. 1 and is the main accompanimental instrument in Vocals 3, 5, 7, 10, 11 and 12. Evans brings out the versatility of the instrument by creating a multitude of tone colors. For instance, the organ's distorted timbre rivals Barre's electric guitar in Instr. 1 (3:36–4:06 side 1), and a clean timbre evokes a cathedral-like ambience in Instr. 4 (11:59–12:20 side 1).

For most of the five minutes when the organ is not present, Evans is playing either the piano or the harpsichord. It is a credit to his creativity that he was able to write keyboard parts to complement whatever shifts in style the music took, whether it be hard rock (organ in Vocals 2 and 8), folk/pastoral (piano in Vocal 3), dance-like (organ in Vocal 5), free form (organ in Instrs. 10 and 11), or Renaissance/Baroque (harpsichord in Vocal 11 and Instrs. 14 and 15).

JEFFREY HAMMOND

Jeffrey Hammond shows amazing precociousness on *Thick as a Brick*, which is only the second album on which he played bass for Jethro Tull.

Anderson said of Hammond during the *Aqualung* sessions: "We were teaching him to play the bass as we recorded the album ... and therefore [he] relied on just being taught sequentially the notes that he should play, and memorizing it all."[12] In addition to laying the harmonic foundation for the music on *Thick as a Brick,* Hammond plays highly melodic bass lines all though the album, developing the thematic material alongside the flute, guitars, and keyboards. His bass is the driving force in the first appearance of the $\frac{5}{4}$ riff in Vocal 2 (Motive 2), its returns in $\frac{6}{8}$ meter in Vocal 8, and finally the extremely difficult *fortspinnung* passage in Instr. 18 (18:42 side 2). The rapid sixteenth-note runs in this passage are especially difficult to execute on bass guitar because of the thickness of the strings.

BARRIE BARLOW

Like John Evans and Jeffrey Hammond, Barrie Barlow played in the three precursors to Jethro Tull: the Blades, the John Evan Band, and the John Evan Smash. His first recording with the band was *Life is a Long Song*, a five-song British EP recorded in May 1971 and released in autumn of that year. While Barlow's debut on that EP is impressive, his playing on *Thick as a Brick* (recorded just a few months later) is nothing short of phenomenal. His drumming is a central element in defining the stylistic changes, tempo shifts, and meter shifts that characterize the album. Unlike the many laborious drum solos that plagued late-1960s and early 1970s rock – like Iron Butterfly's "In-A-Gadda-Da-Vida," for example – Barlow's solo passage at the beginning of side 2 (Instr. 11) is concise and well integrated into the flow of the music. In a 1990 *Modern Drummer* interview specifically about the drummers of Jethro Tull, Anderson had this to say about Barrie Barlow: "I'm also quite sure albums like *Thick as a Brick* would've been very different-sounding if somebody else had played drums on them other than Barrie Barlow. All the drummers who've played in Jethro Tull have played very firm roles in the way the music's turned out ... [H]e's playing less for the moment and more with a view towards an overall arrangement and a level of detail. He's a more intellectual sort of drummer, like maybe Bill Bruford was with Yes."[13] On *Thick as a Brick* Barlow also plays timpani (Instrs. 11, 14, 15 and 16), glockenspiel (Vocals 1 and 6, Instr. 7), and tubular bells (Instrs. 11 and 12).

DAVID PALMER

Palmer's relationship with Jethro Tull began on their first album, *This Was*, when he arranged the brass and woodwinds on the track "Move On Alone." On *Thick as a Brick* Palmer arranged and conducted the string orchestra interludes in Instr. 19. Palmer joined Jethro Tull in 1976 as a full-time member and played keyboards (mostly portative organ) along with John Evans while continuing to compose orchestral accompaniments to many of their songs. In the 1980s and 1990s Palmer released albums of symphonic arrangements of the music of Jethro Tull, Genesis, Pink Floyd, Yes, Queen, and the Beatles.

HARMONY

While there is nothing strikingly unique about the harmonic language of Ian Anderson's songwriting in the early seventies music of Jethro Tull, it is richer in content and invention than most mainstream rock during this period. Like other British progressive rock bands, Jethro Tull purposefully sought to broaden the harmonic vocabulary of rock music. Although their chord progressions contain many V-I and VII-I cadences, one also finds v-I, IV-I, and other cadences. Chord progressions are almost always colored with modal mixture, inversions, and suspensions. The band's treatment of chords is also broad, embracing the spectrum from brash power chords (Martin Barre's electric guitar), to detailed ostinato picking patterns (Ian Anderson's acoustic guitar), to arpeggiated flourishes (John Evans's piano and organ). The harmonic rhythm is swift and unpredictable, with chord changes often falling into irregular metrical patterns and dictated by the narrative flow of the lyrics.

One harmonic characteristic that stands out in Jethro Tull's music is its modality, which connects it closely with folk music and medieval/Renaissance music. Edward Macan writes: "Progressive rock's modality... stems largely from the folk revival of the 1960s."[14] Similarly, Allan Moore says: "The Mixolydian/Dorian nature of much English traditional song, and its influence on 'folk rock' is widely accepted."[15] Traditional British folk music is constructed from roughly the same modal structures that were used by the troubadours, trouvères, and minstrels from the medieval and Renaissance eras, and Jethro Tull finds much of its musical ancestry here. While some sections of *Thick as a Brick* use common tonal progressions with a clear predominant chord moving to a dominant seventh chord and then to the tonic, most of the harmony in *Thick as a Brick* is governed by modality. This mixing of modal and tonal harmony is illustrated in the three minutes of Vocal 1, which opens the record. The verses ("Really don't mind...") are dominated by the progression F, Cm, B♭, F (I-v-IV-I), which is firmly in the F Mixolydian mode. The minor v chord and IV-I cadence highlight its modal nature. Yet in the refrain of the verses ("So you ride yourselves..."), there is a recurring pattern of B♭, C, F (IV-V-I), which is clearly a tonal progression in F major. The ten-measure B section (bridge) of Vocal 1 ("And the love that I feel...") winds its way through all the degrees of the scale and has both modal and tonal characteristics. The harmonic motion here is I-v-VII-ii-IV-vi-I-III-IV-V-I. The first two-thirds of the progression is modal, since it contains a minor v chord and then a pattern of alternating major and minor chords ascending by seconds to I. Because of this pattern, the movement from vi to I does not feel cadential. As Edward Macan writes, "Modal harmony is more wayward and unpredictable than functional harmony, since the relationship between chords in the modes is more ambiguous and less hierarchically determined than the major/minor system."[16] Yet the last third of the progression gives a strong sense of tonal resolution with its IV-V-I cadence. The F major/F Mixolydian duality is even present in the opening guitar pattern, Motive 1, which contains both an E♮ (leading tone) in the first measure and an E♭ (flattened seventh) in the second measure (see example 4.3).

Table 4.2 lists the mode and key areas of the various sections. As this table shows, I have given many sections only a pitch center (see the fourth column) rather than pinning them down to specific modes or keys. I did this for the sake of clarity and simplicity, since listing all the modes and keys that the piece visits would make the table much longer than it already is. For example, Vocal 1 has sections in F Mixolydian (verses), F major (refrains), and F minor ("Spin me back down the years..."), so I have simply labeled this section as being in "F." Many of the sections listed in the table as Aeolian or Dorian modes could also be considered to be in minor pentatonic. While a complete analysis of the harmony

Table 5.4. Chord progressions in the first eleven minutes of *Thick as a Brick*

SECTION	TIMING	PROGRESSION	LYRICS
Vocal 1 Verse	0:08	I-v-IV-I (modal)	"Really don't mind..."
Vocal 1 Refrain	0:38	IV-V-I (tonal)	"So you ride yourselves..."
Vocal 1 Bridge	2:00	I-v-VII-ii-IV-vi-I-III-IV-V-I (modal and tonal)	"And the love that I feel..."
Vocal 2 and Instr. 1	3:01	i-IV-VII-i (modal)	"See there! A son is born..."
Vocal 3	6:08	i-VII-i-VII-IV-V-i (modal and tonal)	"The Poet and the painter..."
Instr. 2	7:15	i-VII-i (modal)	
Vocal 4	11:19	I-VII-IV (modal)	"What do you do..."

of *Thick as a Brick* is well beyond the scope of this book, table 5.4 shows the chord progressions of the major sections in the first eleven minutes, providing a snapshot of harmonic movement throughout.

The modes and keys that are used most often in the piece are F major/ F Mixolydian and C Dorian. The sections that are in an acoustic folk vein are mostly in F (Vocals 1, 6, 7, 9, 14, and some of the instrumental passages). The sections that are the darkest and most intense are in C Dorian (Vocals 2, 8, 12, and some of the instrumental passages). "Stormy" is the word that is commonly invoked when speaking of Beethoven's use of C minor, and it is also an apt descriptor of the C Dorian passages in *Thick as a Brick*. These two areas, F and C Dorian, are the two polarities that are pitted against each other. First, the two most noticeable motives (1 and 2) are in these two modes. Second, as mentioned above, F is used most often in the softer, acoustic folk sections, and C Dorian is used in the stormy, hard rock sections.

As discussed previously, the vocal sections alternate between popular song forms (AABA, verse-chorus, strophic) and through-composed (see table 4.1). The sections that are in popular song forms (Vocals 1, 3, 5, etc.) exhibit strong tonal stability because they have chord progressions, melodies, and motives that repeat and reconfirm the key area. The sections that are through-composed (Vocals 2, 4, 6, etc.) have weaker tonal areas because they have less material that repeats and they tend to wander harmonically. For instance, in Vocal 4 a modulation occurs from D Mixolydian to B Aeolian, thus weakening the sense of harmonic stability. In general, the instrumental passages are more harmonically unstable because they are linking passages between the vocal sections. The most harmonically unstable are Instrs. 1, 4, and 12; the last half of Instr. 13; and Instrs. 15 and 19, all of which contain sequences, imitative counterpoint, and modulatory passages.

So after all of this musical analysis, what are we to make of *Thick as a Brick*? It is a combination of rock and folk music augmented with various influences from classical music. Its form is built from a mixture of small-scale popular song forms, and through-composed forms, interspersed with instrumental passages. Its continuous flow of music and use of thematic development give it a large-scale structure that is comparable to that of a symphonic poem. Its instrumental passages serve different functions (transition, soloing, contrast, and repetition) and provide continuity to the work as a whole by smoothing out the disjointed points of view in the lyrics. Its instrumentation incorporates several instruments from outside the rock format, giving it a rich and constantly changing soundscape. Its music overall is quite tuneful and accessible on the surface, yet it possesses a depth that draws the listener deeper into its intricate architecture with every listen.

In short, *Thick as a Brick* is an intoxicating concoction of complex music, strange lyrics, and unusual album design that, amazingly, hit number one on the *Billboard* chart. What is more amazing is that the band's next studio album, *A Passion Play,* also hit the top of the chart. As will be seen in the next chapter, it started out as a disaster.

SIX

The *Château d'Isaster Tapes* and the Album Cover and Lyrics of *A Passion Play*

DURING A BREAK IN THE TOUR FOR *THICK AS A BRICK* IN THE summer of 1972, Jethro Tull began work on the music that would later become *A Passion Play*. From the start, the band intended on writing another concept album. Anderson comments: "[*Thick as a Brick*] was a very successful album, and when it came to the next album I guess we all collectively fell into a trap of thinking, 'Oh shit, maybe we should do this kind of thing again and instead of being silly about it, maybe we should take it seriously.'"[1] Anderson worked on the new music in Montreux, Switzerland, and then moved with the band to the Château d'Hérouville, a castle-turned-recording-studio in the Oise valley northwest of Paris. Although Elton John loved the studio and named his 1972 album *Honky Château* after it, Anderson and the band detested it, referring to it as the "Château d'Isaster." In contrast to the recording of *Thick as a Brick*, which was carried out quickly and without interruption, the new album was plagued with technical difficulties. Bad food and homesickness for England made things even worse for the band. As Anderson says of the Château d'Hérouville: "The equipment was extremely dodgy, everything was going wrong technically every day, and we were really struggling to make this album. We did eventually get three sides of a double album recorded with great difficulty, but then we finally became so disenchanted with it we just jumped on a plane and went back to England. We scrapped the whole thing and started again."[2] Before considering the album cover, lyrics, and music of *A Passion Play*, the lyrics and music from the period at the Château d'Hérouville must be explored. Not only do these recordings contain the origin of some of the ideas on *A Passion Play*, but they are also captivating in and of themselves.

THE LYRICS OF *THE CHÂTEAU D'ISASTER TAPES*

While the lyrics to *A Passion Play* are a finished work, the lyrics to the Château material are the fragments from an unfinished and abandoned concept album and cannot be fit together into any single, coherent theme. In fact, from late 1972 to early 1973 – the period after the completion of the *Thick as a Brick* tour and the release of *A Passion Play* – Anderson was working on four different lyrical strands: the parallels between human and animal behavior, the theater as a conceit for human life, the critique of popular music journalism, and lastly, the lyrics to *A Passion Play*. Some songs that are on Jethro Tull's *War Child* album also fit into these themes.

The first theme that Anderson was musing on in his lyrics from 1972 to 1973 is the parallels between human behavior and animal behavior. In an interview from 1973, Anderson explained his interest in Desmond Morris's 1967 book, *The Naked Ape* and its connection to these lyrical ideas he was formulating: "I'm very interested in animal psychology. Desmond Morris is one of my favourite writers. Maybe one of the greatest disasters of today is that man is too far away from animals and nature."[3] From another interview: "that was at a time when I was writing an album that was exploring people, the human condition, through analogies with the animal kingdom."[4] In his book, Morris describes *Homo sapiens* (the naked ape) strictly in zoological and evolutionary terms. He writes: "I am a zoologist and the naked ape is an animal. He is therefore fair game for my pen and I refuse to avoid him any longer simply because some of his behaviour patterns are rather complex and impressive. My excuse is that, in becoming so erudite, *Homo sapiens* has remained a naked ape nevertheless; in acquiring lofty new motives, he has lost none of his earthly old ones."[5] Anderson's lyrics for the songs in this category, listed in table 6.1, share the same observational stance that Morris takes in his book: however impressive and advanced humans may be, they are still essentially animals. This theme is most obvious in "Look at the Animals," "Law of the Bungle," and "Bungle in the Jungle" from the Château

Table 6.1. Lyrics about the parallels between human and animal behavior

SONG	RECORDING	SUBJECT MATTER
"Animelée"	*The Château d'Isaster Tapes*	No lyrics, but the title is a portmanteau of "animal" and "melee"
"Tiger Toon"	*The Château d'Isaster Tapes*	No lyrics, but the title obviously makes it part of this theme
"Look at the Animals"	*The Château d'Isaster Tapes*	Lyrics about various animals procuring food, eliminating, and copulating, and equating them with humans
"Law of the Bungle"	*The Château d'Isaster Tapes*	Spoken-word satirical portrayal of a businessman as a tiger
"Law of the Bungle Part II"	*The Château d'Isaster Tapes*	No lyrics, but has spoken introduction by Martin Barre, who is "sometimes... an owl." Owl is a character in "The Story of the Hare Who Lost His Spectacles."
"Bungle in the Jungle"	*War Child*	Lyrics describe how modern society follows the law of the jungle
"The Story of the Hare Who Lost His Spectacles"	*A Passion Play*	Spoken-word fable with animal characters
"Sea Lion"	*War Child*	Lyrics about the carelessness and irresponsibility of businessmen, and modern society in general, who "balance the world... like sea lions with a ball at the carnival"

sessions, and in "The Story of the Hare Who Lost His Spectacles" from the *A Passion Play* sessions.[6] This theme first crops up slightly in "Mother Goose" from *Aqualung* and in *Thick as a Brick* ("you make all your animal deals..."). After the Château sessions disintegrated, Anderson seems to have abandoned this theme as the basis for a concept album. Perhaps he thought it wasn't going anywhere or wasn't original enough in that it was too derivative of Morris's book.

The second theme is the use of the theater as a conceit for human life. The lyrics in this category all reiterate in some fashion what the melancholy nobleman Jacques says in Shakespeare's *As You Like It* (act II, scene 7):

> All the world's a stage
> And all the men and women merely players;
> They have their exits and their entrances,
> And one man in his time plays many parts.

Table 6.2. Lyrics about the theater as a conceit for human life

SONG	RECORDING
"Left Right"	*The Château d'Isaster Tapes*
"Solitaire"/"Only Solitaire"	*The Château d'Isaster Tapes* and *War Child*
"Critique Oblique"	*The Château d'Isaster Tapes*
"Scenario/Audition/No Rehearsal"	*The Château d'Isaster Tapes*
"Skating Away on the Thin Ice of the New Day"	*War Child*

Although none of the band members had any formal training or experience in the theater, it is clear they were enamored by it, as evidenced by Jethro Tull's elaborate stage shows. The band has used the conventions of the theater all through their career, something that is discussed in chapter 8 on their concert performances. Table 6.2 shows the songs that use the trope of the theater.

"Left Right" uses metaphors associated with playwriting and the theater to ponder the choices one may make in life. "Solitaire" has a slight relation to this theme in that it begins with a reference to an actor, but the song is more about the third theme, popular music journalism.[7] "Critique Oblique" also has a slight connection, but the lyrics to "Scenario/Audition/No Rehearsal" form the nucleus of this theater theme with its premise that all of us are actors thrust upon the stage of life with no script, no audition, and no rehearsal. We are left to improvise our lives until the theater crumbles to the ground. This extended metaphor has an affinity with some of the ideas of the twentieth-century German philosopher Martin Heidegger. Heidegger uses the ontological concepts of *Dasein* (being-there or existence) and *Geworfenheit* (thrownness) to explain how we are thrown into life with no preparation and with no choice as to when, where, and to whom we are born. The lyrics to "Skating Away on the Thin Ice of the New Day" also address this "thrownness," make mention of "passion play," and end with these lines that align it with the theater theme: "Well, do you ever get the feeling that the story's too damn real and in the present tense? / Or that everybody's on the stage, and it seems like you're the only person sitting in the audience?"[8]

The Château d'Isaster material has many spoken-word passages, which bolsters this theme of life being a play. The songs with spoken-word, or half-spoken/half-sung, passages are "Law of the Bungle," "Law of the Bungle Part II," "Critique Oblique," "Post Last," "Audition," "No Rehearsal," and "Skating Away on the Thin Ice of the New Day." *A Passion Play* also has half-spoken/half-sung passages in Vocal 2 ("Here's your I.D...."), Vocal 5 Part 1 ("And your little sister's..."), Vocal 5 Part 2 ("All of this and some of that's..."), and, of course, "The Story of the Hare Who Lost His Spectacles."[9]

The third theme, the critique of rock music journalism, seems to be a direct result of the critical backlash that the band was receiving in music periodicals from 1972 to late 1973. The theme is found in "Solitaire," "Critique Oblique," and perhaps in "Law of the Bungle," where the tiger can be viewed not only as a businessman but also as a music critic. Anderson makes it clear in *Jethro Tull 25th Complete Lyrics* that the mention of the name "Steve" at the end of "Solitaire" is a reference to Steve Peacock, a music critic who wrote for the British music newspaper *Sounds*.[10] In the March 11, 1972, issue, Peacock wrote a short article titled "Jethro's Hollow Threat" stating that he saw the band twice in three weeks and their act was exactly the same on both occasions. Perhaps Ian was responding to this by taking on the persona of Peacock in "Solitaire," describing Anderson with the lines "and every night his act's the same." This theme was not developed any further and had little effect on what came to be *A Passion Play*.

The fourth and last lyrical strand that Anderson was working on during this period is the actual lyrics to *A Passion Play*. This begs the question: what, if any, are the connections between the Château lyrics and the APP lyrics? The human/animal strand may have led to "The Story of the Hare Who Lost His Spectacles," but Jeffrey Hammond, not Anderson, wrote the fable, so the connection remains unclear. It appears that Anderson shaped the APP lyrics in part from the second theme, since the album portrays human (after)life through the conventions of the theater or a play – that is, a passion play. Much of Vocal 5 Part 1 in APP contains the same, or similar, phrases that are found in the "theater as life" songs such as "Left Right," "Critique Oblique," and "Scenario/Audition/No Rehearsal."

The most difficult aspect of making sense of the Château d'Isaster lyrics is reconciling the two predominant strands: the "human/animal" theme with the "theater as life" theme. Perhaps Anderson was contrasting different ways of observing human behavior, the first in terms of the animal kingdom, the second in terms of the theater. But since the lyrics are merely fragments, it remains a mystery.

THE MUSIC OF *THE CHÂTEAU D'ISASTER TAPES*

The recordings from the band's stay at the Château that were presentable were released on the compilations *20 Years of Jethro Tull* (1988) and *Nightcap* (1993). The former compilation has just the eleven-minute "Scenario/Audition/No Rehearsal," while the latter has that track plus another forty minutes of music. David Rees writes: "During exhaustive searches through hundreds of old studio tapes, Ian Anderson had unearthed the missing parts of the legendary Chateau D'Herouville (Chateau D'Isaster) sessions, and with the unhappy memories of those times now confided to the past, he realized that they were not too bad after all!"[11]

Although Anderson is adamant that *The Château d'Isaster Tapes* are flawed gems, "plagued by clicks, pops and drop-in clunks," to my ears they sound brilliant.[12] The recordings bristle with excitement and energy. The band is playing at their peak, the songwriting is rich in variety, and the sound is dynamic and alive. The Château recordings have a majestic ambience and spaciousness, as if they were recorded in a cathedral-like space. Much like the studio recording of *Thick as a Brick*, there is a spontaneity, a communal "live" feel to this music. In contrast, *A Passion Play* is painstakingly rehearsed (perhaps even over-rehearsed) and sounds as if it is product of the studio, lacking the "live" ambience. *A Passion Play* turned out to be an astounding album, but it sounds a bit flat in comparison to *The Château d'Isaster Tapes*. Even the most tightly composed and finished part of the Château material, "Scenario/Audition/No Rehearsal," has more of a live and spontaneous feeling than *A Passion Play*.

Some of the material from *The Château d'Isaster Tapes* was recycled and reworked for *A Passion Play:* "Tiger Toon," "Law of the Bungle," "Critique Oblique," and "Post Last." "Tiger Toon" and "Law of the Bungle" were used in Instr. 1 of *APP* and function as an overture, or prelude, to the album. "Tiger Toon," with its slow beginning and gradual increase in tempo and intensity, has more grandeur, energy, and swagger than the *APP* overture. Evans plays the harpsichord on the former, but plays a somewhat less dazzling synthesizer on the latter. In addition, Barlow's playing has more drive and swing on "Tiger Toon" than it does in the *APP* overture. The music and some of the lyrics to "Critique Oblique" and "Post Last" were recycled and tightened up to form Vocal 4, Vocal 5 Part 1, Vocal 5 Part 3, and Instrs. 4, 5, 6, and 7 of *APP* (see table 7.3). In much of the Château material, Martin Barre and John Evans play their guitar and organ through heavy distortion. This heaviness is a highlight in the soundscapes of *Aqualung, Thick as a Brick,* and the Château material (where Barre's guitar is really heavy), but it is less apparent on *A Passion Play*. Jethro Tull played some of the material from the Château recordings in their concerts in October and November 1972 during the tour for *Thick as a Brick*. Jon Tiven of *Melody Maker* reported that at Madison Square Garden on November 13 "the band performed several numbers which have not yet been put on disc; they seemed to be quite diverse in nature, ranging from the very complicated melodic and rhythmic transitions which we've been used to from Tull to rather simple, three-chord riffs."[13]

In late March 1973 the band finished up their European tour and retreated to Morgan Studios in London. They wrote, arranged, and recorded *A Passion Play* in a mere seventeen days.[14] According to Anderson:

> It was a case of necessity being the mother of invention. We were committed to a period of recording and some tours coming up. To try to get back and somehow salvage, to raise the sunken ship of the *Château d'Isaster* sessions was too depressing. We had to go on and immediately get cracking on something else. It was a very disciplined period of a couple of weeks at just working hard at it. It's a good way to work, but it was a bit grim and serious, because it had to be done and it had to fit a timetable.[15]

If the whirlwind creation of *Thick as a Brick* in a month and a half is an incredible feat, the creation of *A Passion Play* in a little over two weeks is even more difficult to believe. One might seriously doubt it if the information were not straight from Anderson's mouth, or on the official Jethro Tull website: "With only seventeen days left before the American tour, Ian wrote new material and vastly restructured some of the 'Chateau d'Isaster' ideas and the band recorded the 45-minute album."[16] One gets the impression that Anderson simply reached into his pocket and, behold, there the music was. *A Passion Play* was released on July 6, 1973, in the United Kingdom and on July 23, 1973, in America. My exploration of *A Passion Play* begins here with the album cover and lyrics and continues in chapter 7 with an analysis of the music.

THE ALBUM COVER AND LYRICS OF *A PASSION PLAY*

Compared to the album cover of *Thick as a Brick*, the cover of *A Passion Play* is a letdown; but, honestly, how could the band have topped the originality and cleverness of the *St. Cleve Chronicle*? Jethro Tull further upped the ante against themselves with the cover for *Living in the Past*, a compilation album released in between TAAB and APP, which mixed some of their more popular hits with B-sides and previously unreleased live and studio recordings. This double album has the aura of an ancient codex with its thick front and back panels, its intricate decorative borders, and its general grandiosity. It also contains a booklet with seventeen pages of photos of the band and a list of the musicians and instruments on each song. Jethro Tull reached a plateau in album cover design with TAAB and *Living in the Past*, while APP shows a movement back toward less adventuresome designs and concepts.

The first question that arises from the album cover of *A Passion Play* is how the ballet dancer on the front and back is connected with the concept of the album.[17] The front cover, in black and white (mostly black) shows a recently deceased dancer lying face up on the stage of an empty Baroque theater. The back cover, in bright pink, shows the same dancer alive and full of vigor as she performs an arabesque. These two pictures seem to represent, in condensed form, the journey of Ronnie Pilgrim from death to rebirth in the afterlife, the theme of the album. The film of "The Story of the Hare Who Lost His Spectacles" (shown in the middle of the live performances of APP) features much ballet dancing, and one

6.1. Front cover of *A Passion Play*

of the dancers – the one who says, "Something wonderful is happening!" – appears to be the dancer on the front and back covers of *APP*, shown in figures 6.1 and 6.2.

Upon opening the gatefold of the album, one finds the lyrics printed in blue over a pink background with the Greek theater masks of tragedy and comedy (also in pink). Below the lyrics is a ribbon with "Jethro Tull A Passion Play" embroidered on it (see figure 6.3). A mock theater program is glued to the inside spine, yet reading through the program doesn't unlock many secrets in the music or lyrics and leaves one with a feeling of disappointment, especially in comparison to the sprawling absurdity of the *Thick as a Brick* newspaper. When a listener digs into the *St. Cleve Chronicle*, he or she finds many connections with the themes in

6.2. Back cover of *A Passion Play*

the lyrics. Even though the newspaper is perplexing, it is still entertaining in and of itself. This cannot be said of the mock theater program of *A Passion Play*, shown in figure 6.4. It is clever, but not engaging.

The program lists the eight characters in the play, five of which are the members of Jethro Tull, who are given mock "actor" biographies. The characters have some correlation to the lyrics, but it is not a strong one. The program also indicates the settings of *A Passion Play*'s four acts. They are listed in table 6.3 along with the vocal section and lyrics that begin each one.[18] Though these settings are helpful in piecing together Ronnie Pilgrim's journey through the afterlife, the integration

6.3. Inside gatefold of *A Passion Play*

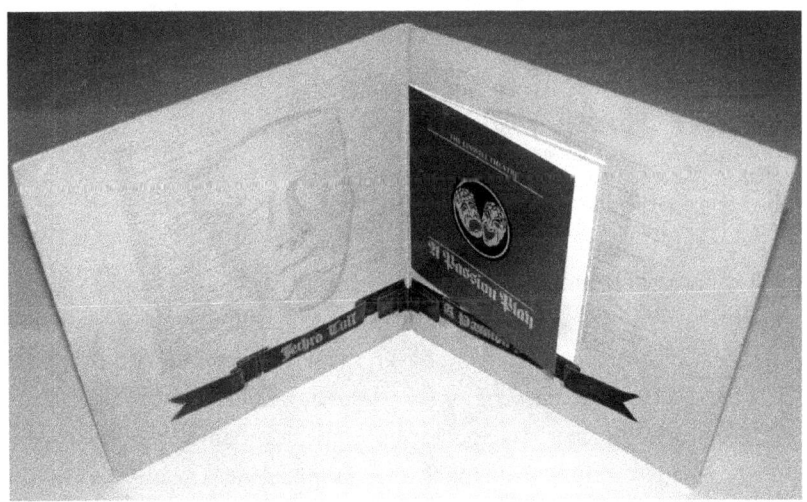

6.4. Inside gatefold of *A Passion Play* with mock theater program

Table 6.3. Settings of the four acts of *A Passion Play*

ACT	SETTING	VOCAL SECTION	LYRICS
Act I	Ronnie Pilgrim's Funeral: a winter's morning in the cemetery	Vocal 1	"'Do you still see me even here?'"
Act II	The Memory Bank: a small but comfortable theater with a cinema screen – the next morning	Vocal 2	"All along the icy wastes…"
Interval	The Story of the Hare Who Lost His Spectacles	Vocal 7	"This is the story of the hare…"
Act III	The business office of G. Oddie and Son – two days later	Vocal 8	"We sleep by the ever-bright hole in the door…"
Act IV	Magus Perdé's drawing room at midnight	Vocal 11?	"Flee the icy Lucifer…"

of the theater program, the album cover, the lyrics, the music, and the concept is not as strong as the integration the band achieved with *Thick as a Brick*.

THE LYRICS TO *A PASSION PLAY*

The lyrics to *A Passion Play*, which can be found in appendix 2, are almost as impenetrable as those for *Thick as a Brick*. In fact, *Creem* rock critic Lester Bangs refused to review the album and asked readers to write in and tell him what it was about.[19] Adding to the difficulty is the picture of a dead ballet dancer on the front cover, the live ballet dancer on the back cover, the mock theater program, and the bewildering fable "The Story of the Hare Who Lost His Spectacles" right in the middle of the music. So it is not just the lyrics and music that are puzzling. The other elements add more levels of complexity and make one wonder how this album sold any copies at all, let alone how it reached number one on the U.S. *Billboard* 200 Album Chart. Jethro Tull's *TAAB* and *APP* are analogous to Bob Dylan's *Highway 61 Revisited* (1965) and *Blonde on Blonde* (1966) in that they present the artist at a peak in popularity, and at a peak in abstruseness! Two reasons why the lyrics of *APP* are not as compelling as those on other Jethro Tull albums is because they were written in a rush and were made to fit music that was already composed. As mentioned previously, some of the *Château d'Isaster* music was reused for APP. On this topic, Anderson says: "With *A Passion Play* the music came first and the lyrics were added on later, which is why I think it's a less successful album... I've done an awful lot of work which I've regretted with a tune first, then trying to find the lyrics and make them fit. It's not something that I think leads to my best work."[20]

Neil Thomason has done an expansive line-by-line analysis of the lyrics to *A Passion Play* on his Ministry of Information website. He sums up well how a listener can approach the lyrics: "The Play works on a number of levels. Two approaches to analysis of The Play are to treat it as a single, cohesive story, or a series of meaningful individual phrases, not necessarily contributing to an overall narrative. The two are not necessarily contradictory, but in practice do tend to be."[21] The first approach benefits the listener by providing him or her with a discernible, linear narrative: the journey of Ronnie Pilgrim through his afterlife. But the narrative is continually interrupted by numerous tangential phrases and allusions – including the lengthy "Story of the Hare Who Lost His Spectacles" – that have little to do with the narrative. The second approach is to abandon the overall concept and simply enjoy the series of disjointed but "meaningful individual phrases," as Thomason puts it. Reading the lyrics in this way makes them comparable to modernist poems such as T. S. Eliot's "The Waste Land" or Ezra Pound's *The Cantos*, where the reader must make connections and fill in the pieces of the puzzle that the author has left out. A detailed analysis of the lyrics to *A Passion Play* is beyond the scope of this book, its focus being musical analysis. Besides, Jan Voorbij and Neil Thomason have already probed the lyrics in great detail on their websites, chasing down references to the "ice-cream lady" and "Magus Perdé" to the farthest footnote in the farthest book.[22]

Although *A Passion Play* has a central protagonist (Ronnie Pilgrim) and a somewhat discernible story line, the lyrics read like a cryptogram. As in *Thick as a Brick*, the text is peppered with an abundance of punctuation, such as ellipses, slashes, and parentheses. Anderson twists idiomatic and clichéd expressions into knots, drops in arcane literary references, and uses elliptical phrases that have little to do with the text that surrounds them. These slippery sayings are lifeless as just words on a page, and they continually derail the narrative, but Anderson's wry and sardonic delivery "sells them." The influence of *Monty Python's Flying Circus* is apparent here, putting nonsense wordplay up front and leaving whatever meanings arise to the listener. Unlike the lyrics to TAAB, end-line rhyming in the APP lyrics is kept to a minimum and there is little adherence to poetic meters. These features, along with the spoken-word passages like "The Story of the Hare Who Lost His Spectacles," give the lyrics a narrative, prose-like shape. Yet there is plenty of internal rhyming, such as is found in the refrain to Vocal 1 ("rush" and "hush").

The lyrics to *A Passion Play* have religious overtones, and Anderson has espoused his universal and inclusive views on religion in numerous interviews. Jethro Tull's most popular album, *Aqualung*, has religion as a major theme, and many of the band's subsequent albums and songs have religious themes. Anderson's second solo album, *Divinities: Twelve Dances with God* (1995), is a musical homage to twelve different religious cultures around the world. In some ways *A Passion Play* is a forerunner to an album like *Divinities* in that the religious beliefs and tropes of several cultures are amalgamated, although Christianity and Buddhism are the two major referents. The lyrics contain many biblical allusions ("the silver cord," "roll the stone away") and references to Christian literature, history, and tradition (Dante's *Inferno*, medieval passion plays). Anderson leaves vague the connection between his lyrics to *A Passion Play* and the actual passion play, the liturgical drama that originated in medieval times depicting the trial, suffering, and death of Jesus Christ. Jethro Tull's passion play is of a secular nature, since there are just a few scattered references to Christ in the lyrics. The primary lyrical matter, the afterlife journey of Ronnie Pilgrim, has little to do with the Christian intermediate state (of which there is little in the Bible) and more to do with *The Tibetan Book of the Dead*. The theme of reincarnation or rebirth is even built into the structure of the music, with the album cyclically beginning and ending with a heartbeat. Anderson says:

> I had some sort of conception of a piece, and what the whole thing was about was the notion of what might happen to you when you die, and the idea that rather than just sort of be allotted a place in a notional heaven or hell, one still had to make a choice, still had to work on towards other levels of post-death options, you know – you were still able to make choices and do one thing or the other

in a post-death experience ... a bit sort of Buddhist in philosophy, I suppose. Anyway, that's what it was about, but deliberately couched in fairly abstract terms and a lot of verbal imagery that I wanted there because I didn't ... I wanted people to listen to it and form their own conclusions about what I was saying ... or what I might be saying.[23]

One mystery that the narrative leaves unresolved is this: what is the nature of Ronnie Pilgrim's existence after his death? His spirit is intact, he is fully conscious, and he is able to describe his surroundings and speak with others he meets. He has use of his senses and some notion of a body, or at least a centralized existence: in Vocal 2 he "step[s] into the viewing room," and in Vocal 11 Part 1 he says, "Twist my right arm in the dark." Yet in other places the lyrics intimate that he has no body. For example, in Vocal 5 Part 2, he's "lost a skin or two." This is one instance in which Anderson uses "abstract terms" to allow listeners to come up with their own conclusions.

In the section on the lyrics to *The Château d'Isaster Tapes* (especially concerning the songs "Skating Away on the Thin Ice of the New Day" and "No Rehearsal"), I pointed out an affinity between the "theater as a conceit for human life" theme and Martin Heidegger's philosophical concepts of *Dasein* (being-there or existence) and *Geworfenheit* (thrownness). This musing on ontology, the study of being, is also quite prominent in the lyrics to APP. Anderson ponders what it may be like to "be" in the afterlife in Vocal 2 ("Here's your I.D. [Ideal for identifying one and all.]"), Vocal 5 Part 2 ("How does it feel to be the play"), Vocal 12 Part 1 ("for those about to BE"), and Vocal 12 Part 2 ("living BE!"). Concurrent with this musing on being is a consideration of nonbeing in Vocal 1 Part 3 ("NO-ONE [but someone to be found]"), Vocal 9 Part 2 ("Where no-one has nothing and nothing is"), and Vocal 11 Part 2 ("half past none"). The connection with *Geworfenheit* is apparent in that Ronnie Pilgrim is thrown into his afterlife with no preparation and spends most of the narrative trying to figure out the contours and boundaries of where he is, who he is, and what will happen to him next.

Although I do provide a summary of the narrative in the following section, the myriad religious and philosophical symbols, references, and themes in the lyrics are beyond the scope of this study. Listeners will find much to explore on the websites developed by Jan Voorbij and Neil

Thomason. In addition, Kevin Holm-Hudson's book *Genesis and The Lamb Lies Down on Broadway* has an excellent analysis (p. 117–30) of the literary allusions in that 1974 album to the Bible, *The Tibetan Book of the Dead*, and the writings of Carl Jung, William James, and Joseph Campbell. Holm-Hudson's conclusions are directly applicable to *A Passion Play*, and the more one listens to the two albums, the more one detects uncanny similarities between their themes, the characters of Ronnie Pilgrim and Rael, and the creative minds of Ian Anderson and Peter Gabriel.

SUMMARY OF RONNIE PILGRIM'S POST-DEATH ADVENTURES

Before the first line in the lyrics to *A Passion Play* is sung, the three-minute instrumental overture begins to unfold the narrative by depicting – with the cessation of a heartbeat – the death of Ronnie Pilgrim. In the three stanzas of Vocal 1, which comprise act I, set in a cemetery, Pilgrim gives his impressions of being a new arrival to the afterlife. The "silver cord" in Vocal 1 Part 1 is a reference to the separation of the soul from the body at death and is analogous to the severing of the umbilical cord at birth, freeing the infant from the mother.[24] Although the concept can be found in many spiritual traditions, the oldest reference to the silver cord seems to be in Ecclesiastes 12:6–7, a book that most biblical scholars believe was written by King Solomon: "Remember him [i.e., your Creator] – before the silver cord is severed, or the golden bowl is broken; before the pitcher is shattered at the spring, or the wheel broken at the well, and the dust returns to the ground it came from, and the spirit returns to God who gave it."[25] The Fulham Road, which runs through London's Fulham and Chelsea districts, is used in the lyrics as a metaphysical thoroughfare where the dead enter the afterlife and are later reborn. Morgan Studios, where *APP* was recorded, is on the Fulham Road, so this was most likely the inspiration for the reference.

Vocal 2, which commences act II, is set in the "Memory Bank." Pilgrim is shown flashbacks of his life on a movie screen and is given an ID. Most of Vocals 3–5 add little to the story, although Vocal 5 Part 2 again speaks of the separation of the soul from the body, and Vocal 5 Part 3 refers to Christ obliquely: "man of passion, rise again." Vocal 6 reprises the refrain of Vocal 1 ("There was a rush...."), bringing the second act to its conclusion. In summary, little happens to Pilgrim on side 1. He dies, he describes his first impressions of the afterlife, and he views his life in flashback. The narrative then takes a detour into the world of fable and fairy tale with "The Story of the Hare Who Lost His Spectacles," which has little to do with what has come before it.

"The Story of the Hare" is described in the mock theater program as an "interval" and functions primarily as a diversion from the heavy subject matter of Pilgrim's journey. Written mostly by Jeffrey Hammond and John Evans, it features the characters of Owl, Kangaroo, Hare, Bee, and Newt, who are musing on a solution to Hare's missing spectacles. It is droll and entertaining and contains some cunning wordplay. Owl is described as sitting on the fence "sc<u>owl</u>ing." Kangaroo is "hopping mad." "Newt k<u>new t</u>oo much." An especially clever bit of wordplay in "The Story of the Hare" is the word charade using the word "kangaroo." A charade, in linguistic terms, is "a set of words formed by respacing but not rearranging the letters of another word, phrase, or sentence."[26] Two examples would be "a <u>daredevil</u> is one who has <u>dared evil</u>," and "If a boy and girl are <u>amiable together,</u> the boy may begin to wonder: <u>"Am I able to get her?"</u>[27] In the story, Kangaroo, who is referred to as the animals' leader, or "guru," declares that Hare is completely helpless and proclaims, "I can't send Hare in search of anything." To this, Newt replies, "You can guru, you can!" with "can guru" being a charade of "kangaroo," though spelled differently. Wordplay occurs in other places as well. In Vocal 11 Anderson squeezes the first four numbers into a short space: "I would give <u>two</u> or <u>three for one</u> of those days that never made impressions on the old score." The wordplay and whimsy here bring to mind the writings of A. A. Milne and Lewis Carroll.

Returning to the main narrative of *A Passion Play* in act III, Vocal 8 finds Pilgrim in the business office of G. Oddie and Son (presumably God and Christ in Heaven) with other post-life sojourners. Vocal 9 is a prelude to a journey through Hell, which is delivered from Satan's perspective in Vocal 10. The "icy Lucifer" is not the devil described in the Bible as the one who "prowls around like a roaring lion looking for someone to devour."[28] It is more like the devil described in Canto 34 of Dante's *Inferno*, encased from the chest down in ice ("Cold is my touch [freezing]" from Vocal 10 Part 1). Like Satan in Milton's *Paradise Lost*, Anderson's Lucifer is *A Passion Play*'s most sharply drawn character. In fact, Lucifer describes himself in the first-person singular (rather than Pilgrim describing him), and this adds to the immediacy of his presence. It is unclear in the lyrics when act IV begins, where the scene changes to "Magus Perdé's drawing room at midnight." Vocal 11 Part 1 returns us from Satan's perspective to the frenetic musings of Pilgrim as he tries to make sense of the metaphysical conundrums confronting him. In Vocal 12 Part 1 until the end of the song, he sees the souls that are about to be reborn and is reincarnated himself. The ending is quite confusing, since three modes of transportation are metaphorically used to bring Pilgrim back to earthly existence in his body: a train (Vocal 11 Part 2), a ferry (Vocal 12 Part 1), and the Fulham Road (Vocal 13). Nevertheless, Pilgrim seems to be reincarnated into his body, since the heartbeat returns at the end and then fades out. Another round of his existence is commenced when the album is played again and the heartbeat at the beginning fades in.

Because the beginning of *A Passion Play* fades in with a heartbeat, this leaves the listener wondering if the piece was intended to be cyclical. The fade out could represent the end of Ronnie Pilgrim's journey through the afterlife, and the fade in at the beginning could represent another life cycle, an example of reincarnation espoused in *The Tibetan Book of the Dead* or in Friedrich Nietzsche's idea of "eternal recurrence." Pink Floyd also used this cyclical technique on their album *The Wall* (1979). The last song on the album ("Outside the Wall") ends with Roger Waters muttering, "Isn't this where..." while the first song on the album ("In the Flesh?") begins with "...we came in?" Although it doesn't trace the life (or afterlife) of a central character like Pilgrim or Pink, *Dark Side of the Moon* (1973) is also cyclical and even uses a heartbeat to join the end of the album to the beginning. Pink Floyd finished recording *Dark Side of the Moon* in January 1973, a month or two before Jethro Tull started recording *A Passion Play*, but there is no evidence to suggest that Tull was influenced by Pink Floyd, or got the idea from them. The heartbeat is a vital element in the music of *A Passion Play* and will be explored further in the section on thematic development in chapter 7.

In March 1998, Mobile Fidelity Sound Labs issued *A Passion Play* as an audiophile 24k Gold CD. This release included subtitles with cues

Table 6.4. Subtitles on the MFSL Gold CD release of *A Passion Play*

SUBTITLE	TIMING	SECTION(S)
Lifebeats	0:00–1:13	Instr. 1
Prelude	1:13–3:28	Instr. 1
The Silver Cord	3:28–7:55	Vocal 1 Parts 1–3, Instr. 2
Re-Assuring Tune	7:55–9:06	Instr. 3
Memory Bank	9:06–13:26	Vocal 2, Instr. 4, Vocal 3
Best Friends	13:26–15:24	Vocal 4, Instr. 5
Critique Oblique	15:24–20:01	Instr. 5, Vocal 5 Parts 1–3, Instr. 6, Instr. 7
Forest Dance #1	20:01–21:36	Vocal 6, Instr. 8
The Story of the Hare Who Lost His Spectacles	0:00–4:19	Vocal 7
Forest Dance #2	4:19–5:30	Instr. 9
The Foot of Our Stairs	5:30–9:48	Vocal 8, Vocal 9 Parts 1–2, Instr. 10
Overseer Overture	9:48–13:49	Vocal 9 Part 2, Vocal 10 Parts 1–2, Intr. 11, Instr. 12
Flight from Lucifer	13:49–17:47	Instr. 12, Vocal 11 Parts 1–2, Instr. 13
10.08 to Paddington	17:47–18:51	Instr. 14
Magus Perdé	18:51–22:45	Instr. 14, Vocal 12 Parts 1–2, Instr. 15
Epilogue	22:45–23:26	Vocal 13, Instr. 16

for each track, listed in the first column of table 6.4. These subtitles give some additional insight into the flow of the narrative, and the official Jethro Tull website states that the subtitles "reflect the original intent of the album."[29] The original album (1973), the original CD releases (1988–1992), and the remastered CD (2003) do not include the subtitles and were cued as either one continuous forty-five-minute track or two tracks with the break coming in the middle of, or just before, "The Story of the Hare Who Lost His Spectacles." The second column of table 6.4 shows roughly the length of each track, and the third column shows how the subtitles correspond with the sections listed in table 7.3, the large-scale form of *APP*.

In summary, the album cover of *A Passion Play* adds a visual element to the music and lends some insight into the lyrics and the concept, but it is not as innovative and engaging as the cover of *Thick as a Brick*. What of the lyrics? Anderson's wordplay and wit draw the listener in, yet the obliqueness of the lyrics keeps the listener at a distance. What makes the album worthwhile, and worthy of close inspection, is its superb music.

SEVEN

The Music of *A Passion Play*

LIKE *THICK AS A BRICK*, *A PASSION PLAY* TAKES THE LISTENER ON a spacious musical journey, although the journey is a bit gloomy because of the subject matter of the lyrics. Yet because of Anderson's wry vocal delivery and the droll and inane "The Story of the Hare Who Lost His Spectacles," the gloominess is not overbearing. The music is rich, layered, and diverse, and a close look at some its features allows one to discover something new with every listen. I begin this chapter by analyzing *A Passion Play*'s overture, explaining how it encapsulates the work as a whole, introduces two of its primary musical motives (Motives 1 and 2), shows the influence of Baroque-era music, and resembles the *Danse Macabre*, the medieval dance of death. I then analyze the work's form, thematic development, instrumental passages, and instrumentation. After this, I discuss the music of "The Story of the Hare Who Lost His Spectacles," and the chapter concludes with some observations on *A Passion Play*'s metrical and harmonic complexities.

OVERTURE

The overture of *A Passion Play* unashamedly lets listeners know what they are in for musically: a work that is as compositionally dense as *Thick as a Brick*. The overture, which comprises the first three and a half minutes of the album, begins and ends with the synthesized approximation of a beating heart. Since the forty-five-minute song as a whole also begins and ends with a heartbeat, the overture encapsulates in miniature the entire work, much like an overture in a Romantic-era opera encapsulates an entire work.

Example 7.1. *A Passion Play*, Overture Theme 1

While the heartbeat and a few studio effects dominate the opening moments of *A Passion Play*, Anderson's soprano saxophone can faintly be heard playing Motive 2 (see example 7.7), the most identifiable melody on the album ("There was a rush . . . "). At 1:13 Anderson on soprano saxophone and Barre on electric guitar play a series of fragmented melodies an octave apart, while the rest of the band lays down a bouncy gigue in $\frac{9}{8}$ meter. At 1:46 Anderson on flute and Evans on synthesizer and organ play a two-measure theme (see Overture Theme 1 in example 7.1) characterized by a quarter-note/eighth-note motive (Motive 1). The two-measure theme is then sequenced twice, with Hammond joining in on bass guitar for the first sequence (1:49). The theme, its two sequences, and some cadential material – which combined take up eight measures – are then repeated with Anderson soloing on flute over the other instruments. The theme, shown in example 7.1, is in G Dorian ending with a half cadence on D.

At 2:08 the band breaks into some rudimentary imitative counterpoint with two instruments, synthesizer and soprano saxophone, taking the lead (Overture Theme 2, example 7.2). Evans's synthesizer (labeled SY) in the left channel and Anderson's soprano saxophone (labeled SS) in the right channel periodically pass variations and inversions of Motive 1 between them.[1] In many instances the soprano saxophone completes a phrase begun by the synthesizer. Electric guitar and organ are also present. An occasional $\frac{12}{8}$ bar is encountered amid the stream of $\frac{9}{8}$ bars, making the gigue sound quirky and off-kilter (see example 7.2).

Overture Theme 2 modulates waywardly to pitch centers that are closely related "geographically" to G, but not closely related functionally

Example 7.2. *A Passion Play*, Overture Theme 2

to it. Since Jethro Tull's music is based more firmly on modal harmony than on functional harmony, these drifting modulations do not seem jarring or errant. The first two measures continue to have G as their tonic pitch (as in example 7.1), but after that the harmonic path twists and turns. The pitch center goes to E (m. 3), then F♯ (m. 8), then G (m. 11), then F (m. 13), and back to G (m. 15). In mm. 15–24 it shifts between G and A. M. 25 brings back the motive in m. 1, m. 26 sequences it up a third, and the passage finally winds down in m. 27 on a B♭ seventh chord. The A♭ on top creates tension and a need to resolve to G, which it does at 2:47 as the theme from Overture Theme 1 returns with Anderson again soloing on flute. At 3:17 the heartbeat returns, descends in pitch, and then stops

Table 7.1. Musical events in the Overture to *A Passion Play*

TIMING	EVENTS
0:00–1:13	Heartbeat (Motive 1) ascends in pitch. Soprano saxophone plays Motive 2 and flourishes of melody. Studio effects
1:13–1:46	Gigue in $\frac{9}{8}$ with electric guitar and soprano saxophone sharing melody
1:46–2:08	Overture Theme 1 in G Dorian on flute, synthesizer, organ, bass, and drums. Anderson solos on flute at the repeat of the theme.
2:08–2:47	Overture Theme 2 with synthesizer and soprano saxophone trading Motive 1. Pitch center twists and turns.
2:47–3:06	Overture Theme 1 returns with Anderson soloing on flute.
3:06–3:17	Whistling and acoustic guitar
3:17–3:28	Heartbeat descends in pitch, slows in tempo, and ceases.

with foreboding finality just as Anderson begins singing the first line of Vocal 1 ("Do you still see me even here?").

The overture is not just an opportunity for the band to show off their compositional and instrumental chops; it also initiates the narrative of the album's concept, the death and afterlife of Ronnie Pilgrim. The initial heartbeat, with its gradual increase in volume and pitch, represents the vitality of life, and the lively gigue in $\frac{9}{8}$ reinforces this vitality with its dance rhythm. The descending pitch, decreasing tempo, and cessation of the heartbeat at the end of the overture (3:17) represents the end of Pilgrim's earthly life. The finality of death is accentuated by the sound of a slamming door at 3:26. Immediately after this Anderson solemnly sings the first line of the lyrics with no instrumental accompaniment, representing the commencement of Pilgrim's afterlife. Anderson's solitary voice, with its rising contour, conjures up mental images of a soul rising out of a body. Table 7.1 summarizes the musical events in this extraordinary overture.

While the early music of Jethro Tull is rife with medieval and Renaissance associations, as explored in chapter 2, this overture shows that there is also an undeniable Baroque quality. The influence of Baroque polyphony, sequential repetition, imitative counterpoint, dances, orchestration, and ornamentation can be heard in many places in the music of *Thick as a Brick* and *A Passion Play*. The $\frac{9}{8}$ gigue in the APP overture sounds very Baroque and shows the uncanny ability that Anderson and the band had for

Example 7.3. Johann Sebastian Bach, *French Suite in E♭ major* BWV *815*, "Gigue"

approximating and appropriating the musical aesthetics of this period. This can be shown with a comparison between the *APP* overture gigue and the B section of the gigue from Bach's French Suite in E♭ major, BWV 815 (see example 7.3). The most obvious similarities are the melodic contours, compound meter, sequencing, and the quarter-note/eighth-note motivic cell in mm. 1, 3, and 7 (compare with Motive 1 in example 7.1), which can be found in many pieces of dance music from the Baroque era.

"Tiger Toon" and "Law of the Bungle" from *The Château d'Isaster Tapes* (on the *Nightcap* CD), from which this section of the *A Passion Play* overture was taken, make this affinity with Baroque aesthetics even clearer, since John Evans plays harpsichord instead of the synthesizer on that recording. While the imitative counterpoint in the *APP* overture is rudimentary, there is a clear intention to bounce Motive 1 from one instrument to another (soprano saxophone and synthesizer in example 7.2) in the Baroque fashion. Even drummer Barlow joins in the counterpoint and plays the rhythm of the theme.

This comparison between the *A Passion Play* overture and a Bach gigue brings up a question: why would Anderson and the members of the band decide to begin a concept album about a man's death, funeral, and afterlife with a bright and bouncy gigue in $\frac{9}{8}$ meter? The mock theater program indicates that the first scene is Ronnie Pilgrim's funeral in

Example 7.4. Hector Berlioz, *Symphonie Fantastique,*
"Dream of a Witches' Sabbath," mm. 21–25

a cemetery. Why not start the album with a Black Sabbath–esque dirge or a funeral procession? Nothing summons up images of funerals and graveyards like the opening of the first song on that band's first album (both called "Black Sabbath") from 1970, which, incidentally, Black Sabbath wrote just months after Tony Iommi's short stint in Jethro Tull in December 1968. But a closer look at the history of music shows how appropriate a gigue is for depicting death. While the overture can be heard as symbolic of life and vitality, as mentioned earlier, it can equally be heard as a dance of death. It has close associations with the *Danse Macabre,* which, according to Oxford Music Online, is "A medieval and Renaissance symbolic representation of death as a skeleton (or a procession of skeletons) leading the living to the grave; in more recent times a dance supposedly performed by skeletons, usually in a graveyard. The 14th-century epidemics of bubonic plague in Europe are generally thought to have influenced the creation of the dance of death."[2]

While the origins of the dance of death lie in medieval and Renaissance culture, it was given a new life, so to speak, in the Romantic era. There are numerous examples of the dance in nineteenth-century music, many of which have as their melodic cell the quarter-note/eighth-note motive that characterizes the *A Passion Play* overture (Motive 1). The final movement of Hector Berlioz's *Symphonie Fantasique* (1830), called "Dream of a Witches' Sabbath," takes place in a graveyard and depicts the opium-induced hallucination of a musician who witnesses his own funeral. The idée fixe (a graceful theme that represents the love interest of the musician and appears in all five movements) is transformed into a grotesque dance in $\frac{6}{8}$ meter (shown in example 7.4).[3] Franz Liszt's *Totentanz* (1849) and Camille Saint-Saëns's *Danse Macabre* (1874) also use the quarter-note/eighth-note motive, or some variation upon it, to depict the skeletal dance.

Example 7.5. "Neapolitan Tarantella," *Traditional*

The *A Passion Play* overture also brings to mind the tarantella, a traditional folk dance associated with death that originated in the southern Italian town of Taranto. Actually, the tarantella was used to prevent death, since, according to historical superstition, the vigorous dance could sweat out the venom of a certain wolf spider (the tarantula) whose bite was believed to cause death. There is a mention of spiders in Vocal 8 of *APP*, but it doesn't seem to have any connection to the dance. Like the Romantic-era manifestations of the dance of death, the tarantella has as its musical calling card the quarter-note/eighth-note motive, which dominates the *APP* overture. Example 7.5 shows the rhythm of the best-known tarantella, the traditional "Neapolitan Tarantella." In addition, both the tarantella and the *APP* overture are characterized by "repeated notes, the alternation of a note with its upper or lower auxiliary, scalic motion, leaps and arpeggios."[4]

Whether or not Anderson and the band intended the music in the overture to conjure up associations with the *Danse Macabre* or the tarantella, the connections are there for the discerning listener, and the experience of the music is all the richer for it. It is the subtext of the music.

THE FORM OF *A PASSION PLAY*

If the vocal sections of *Thick as a Brick* cling tenuously to the popular and rock music forms of strophic, AABA, and verse-chorus, the vocal sections of *A Passion Play* are barely hanging by a thread. Table 7.2 shows the song forms that the vocal sections of *APP* most closely resemble. Like *TAAB*, almost all of the vocal sections in *APP* are different, giving the album a broad and ambitious scope. There are only four places in *APP* where music and lyrics together are repeated verbatim, and they

Table 7.2. Song forms in *A Passion Play*

SECTION	SONG FORM	LYRICS
Vocal 1 Part 1	Strophic	"Do you still see me ..."
Vocal 1 Part 2	Strophic / through-composed	"Such a sense of glowing ..."
Vocal 1 Part 3	Strophic	"And who comes here ..."
Vocal 2	Strophic	"All along the icy wastes ..."
Vocal 3	Through-composed	"Take the prize ..."
Vocal 4	Strophic	"All of your best friends' ..."
Vocal 5 Part 1	Strophic / through-composed	"Lover of the black and white ..."
Vocal 5 Part 2	Reprise of the music of Vocal 2	"All of this and some of that's ..."
Vocal 5 Part 3	Strophic / through-composed	"Man of passion rise again ..."
Vocal 6	Reprise of lines 7–8 from Vocal 1 Part 1	"There was a rush ..."
Vocal 7	Through-composed	"This is the story ..."
Vocal 8	Strophic	"We sleep by the ..."
Vocal 9 Part 1	Strophic / through-composed	"Jack rabbit mister ..."
Vocal 9 Part 2	Strophic / through-composed	"Well, I'm all for leaving ..."
Vocal 10 Part 1	AABA	"Colours I've none ..."
Vocal 10 Part 2	Additional "A" of AABA	"Passionate play ..."
Vocal 11 Part 1	Verse-chorus	"Flee the icy Lucifer ..."
Vocal 11 Part 2	Verse-chorus	"Pick me up at ..."
Vocal 12 Part 1	"AAB" of AABA	"Hail! Son of Kings ..."
Vocal 12 Part 2	Final "A" of AABA	"Man, son of man ..."
Vocal 13	Reprise of lines 8–9 from Vocal 1 Part 2	"There was a rush ..."

are all short sections: first, the refrain of Vocal 1 ("There was a rush ...") is reprised in the middle of the piece in Vocal 6 and at the end in Vocal 13. Second, the refrain "Well, I'll go to the foot of our stairs" concludes each of the three stanzas in Vocal 8. Third, one line in Vocal 2 ("We've got you taped – you're in the play") returns in Vocal 5 Part 2. Fourth, one line in Vocal 10 Part 1 ("Summoned by name – I am the overseer over you") returns in Vocal 10 Part 2. This scanty amount of exact repetition is remarkable, since rock music is fundamentally governed by the repetition of music and lyrics at regular intervals.

The vocal sections labeled as "strophic" in table 7.2 have stanzas of equal length and roughly the same music for each stanza. While strophic form necessarily employs a high degree of repetition, this is not necessarily the case with *A Passion Play*. Those sections labeled "strophic/

through-composed" have stanzas of variable length or music that is altered in some significant way for each stanza.[5] They do not fall into a regular and repeated pattern or "groove." Thus, the first two-thirds of the piece (Vocals 1–9) have many irregular strophic and through-composed forms and give little familiar material for the listener's ear to grasp. The final one-third (Vocals 10–13) of the piece uses verse-chorus or AABA forms, which have repetition "built in." Yet even in these sections with repetition built in, it is only the music that is repeated, not the lyrics. The first two-thirds of the album (Vocals 1–9) stretch the attention span of the listener by continually presenting new material, while the final one-third (Vocals 10–13) eases the listener into the ending by retreading familiar territory. This trajectory was also employed on *Thick as a Brick* (where the last two sections reprise earlier music), showing Anderson and the band's innate ability to create challenging, yet accessible, large-scale rock songs.

The form of each of the vocal sections and the piece as a whole is obscured by the way the lyrics are presented on the inside gatefold of the album cover (see figure 6.3), much like the lyrics of *Thick as a Brick* in the accompanying newspaper, the *St. Cleve Chronicle*, obscure the form of that work. Regularizing the scansion of the text and showing the sequence of the vocal and instrumental sections allows one to get a better conception of *A Passion Play*'s form (see appendix 2). Although the form of *APP* works as a structure to sustain forty-five minutes of continuous music, it doesn't hold together as tightly as *TAAB*. The only vocal sections in *APP* that resemble popular song forms are Vocals 1, 2, 4, and 8, which are strophic, and Vocal 10, which is AABA. Vocal 10 ("Colours I've none . . . ") was excerpted from the album and made into a single, most likely because it is one of the few vocal sections with an easily identifiable form. The only other sections that have any connection with popular song forms are Vocal 11 (verse-chorus) and Vocal 12 (AABA) at the end, but they are loose connections at that. Thus the form of *APP* has less exact repetition than *TAAB*, itself an album with little exact repetition. Rob Mackie, a rock journalist for *Sounds* had a similar impression when he heard *APP* live for the first time in June 1973: "At first hearing, it seemed much more fragmented than Anderson's previous works on a theme, with less recurrence of easily identifiable riffs or phrases."[6] Table 7.3 shows the large-scale form of *APP*.[7]

Table 7.3. Large-scale form of *A Passion Play*

SIDE 1

SECTION	TIMING	METER	PITCH CENTER	LYRICS
Instr. 1	0:00–1:13	free	E Phrygian	
	1:13–1:46	8/8	B♭ Mixolydian	
	1:46–3:28	8/8	G Dorian	
Vocal 1 Part 1	3:28–4:36	mixed	G Phrygian	"Do you still see me…"
Vocal 1 Part 2	4:36–5:52	mixed		"Such a sense of glowing…"
Instr. 2	5:52–6:50	11/8	C Aeolian, D Aeolian	
Vocal 1 Part 3	6:50–7:55	mixed	G Phrygian	"And who comes here…"
Instr. 3	7:55–9:06	mixed	C Aeolian, C major	
Vocal 2	9:06–10:30	mixed	C major	"All along the icy wastes…"
Instr. 4	10:30–13:00	11/8	G Aeolian, D Dorian	
Vocal 3	13:00–13:26	4/4	D Dorian	"Take the prize…"
Vocal 4	13:26–14:51	4/4	B♭ major	"All of you best friends'…"
Instr. 5	14:51–15:41	mixed	D Dorian	
Vocal 5 Part 1	15:41–17:09	4/4	G Dorian	"Lover of the black and white"
Instr. 6	17:09–17:58	mixed	G Dorian, C major	
Vocal 5 Part 2	17:58–18:47	mixed		"All of this and some of that's"
Vocal 5 Part 3	18:47–19:33	4/4	G Dorian	"Man of passion rise again…"
Instr. 7	19:33–20:01	4/4, 8/8		
Vocal 6	20:01–20:22	mixed	G Phrygian	"There was a rush…"
Instr. 8	20:22–21:36	12/8	C major	

SIDE 2

SECTION	TIMING	METER	PITCH CENTER	LYRICS
Vocal 7	0:00–4:19	4/4	F Lydian	"This is the story…"
Instr. 9	4:19–5:30	12/8	C major	
Vocal 8	5:30–7:02	mixed	G Aeolian	"We sleep by the…"
Vocal 9 Part 1	7:02–7:22	4/4		"Jack Rabbit mister…"
Instr. 10	7:22–9:28	4/4	D Aeolian	
Vocal 9 Part 2	9:28–10:24	4/4	G Aeolian	"Well, I'm all for leaving…"
Vocal 10 Part 1	10:24–12:18	mixed		"Colours I've none…"
Instr. 11	12:18–12:57	mixed		
Vocal 10 Part 2	12:57–13:19	mixed		"Passionate play…"

Table 7.3. (cont.) **Large-scale form of *A Passion Play***

SECTION	TIMING	METER	PITCH CENTER	LYRICS
Instr. 12	13:19–14:21	mixed	E♭ Dorian	
Vocal 11 Part 1	14:21–16:01	mixed	G Aeolian	"Flee the icy Lucifer…"
Instr. 13	16:01–16:53	4/4		
Vocal 11 Part 2	16:53–17:47	mixed		"Pick me up at…"
Instr. 14	17:47–18:51	3/4	A minor	
	18:51–19:27	4/4	E Dorian	
Vocal 12 Part 1	19:27–21:04	4/4		"Hail! Son of Kings…"
Instr. 15	21:04–21:29	7/8	D Dorian	
	21:29–21:51	4/4	E Dorian	
Vocal 12 Part 2	21:51–22:45	4/4		"Man, son of man…"
Vocal 13	22:45–23:06	mixed	G Phrygian	"There was a rush…"
Instr. 16	23:06–23:26	free		

Like *Thick as a Brick*, *A Passion Play* builds to multiple climaxes. Table 7.4 shows how the song can be heard in six cycles. Although the overture (Instr. 1, 0:00–3:28 side 1) contains some stirring music, it functions as an introductory passage and therefore cannot be considered a climax. Like *TAAB*, the first two climaxes in *APP* are created by soft, acoustic vocal sections building to electric sections with intense instrumental soloing. Anderson solos on soprano saxophone in the first climax (Instr. 2, 6:18–6:50 side 1) and on double-tracked flute in the second (Instr. 4, 11:42–12:34 side 1). The $\frac{11}{8}$ meter of both solos gives the music a whirlwind effect. The long third cycle has a raw, visceral edge all the way through, making it feel "climactic" for its duration. The tension peaks in Instr. 7 (19:36–20:01 side 1) with the band playing again in a whirlwind fashion (this time in $\frac{6}{8}$ meter) and winding its way to Vocal 6, which is a return of the refrain of Vocal 1 ("There was a rush…").

The soft piano and vocal of Vocal 6 signal the beginning of the fourth cycle, which includes the spoof fable "The Story of the Hare Who Lost His Spectacles," bookended by the dreamy soundscapes of Instrs. 8 and 9. These two short instrumentals – and "The Story of the Hare" itself – build to mini-climaxes, but a greater climax occurs in Instr. 10, after the acoustic Vocal 8 and Vocal 9 Part 1. Instr. 10 (7:22–9:28 side 2) contains some of the most beautiful ensemble playing in *A Passion Play*, creating a brilliant, shimmering climax in contrast to the raw, intense ones that ended the first three cycles.

Table 7.4. Multiple climaxes in *A Passion Play*

CYCLE	BUILDUP	CLIMAX	TIMING
1	Vocal 1 Part 1 to Instr. 2	Soprano saxophone solo	3:28–6:50 side 1
2	Vocal 1 Part 3 to Instr. 4	Double-tracked flute solo	6:50–12:34 side 1
3	Instr. 4 to Instr. 7	Band accelerates to a whirlwind §	12:34–20:01 side 1
4	Vocal 6 to Instr. 10	Brilliant ensemble playing and soloing	20:01 side 1–9:28 side 2
5	Vocal 9 Part 2 to Vocal 11 Part 2	No definitive climax	9:28–17:47 side 2
6	Instr. 14 to Vocal 12 Part 2	Chaotic playing just before final refrain	17:47–22:45 side 2

The fifth cycle builds quickly from the acoustic guitar and vocal of Vocal 9 Part 2 to Vocal 10, which, in sharp contrast, is dominated by heavy electric guitar and synthesizer. This cycle fluctuates between hard rock and short acoustic passages and doesn't build to a definitive climax like the others do. The hypnotic acoustic guitar and soprano saxophone in Instr. 14 (17:47–18:51 side 2) mark a new cycle, the final one. The brash and angular guitar riff that Barre introduces at 18:51 side 2 brings an intensity that is sustained until the final reprise of the refrain of Vocal 1 in Vocal 13 (22:45 side 2). This refrain and the return of the heartbeat at the end provide the denouement to *A Passion Play*.

While there is an affinity between the large-scale forms of *Thick as a Brick* and *A Passion Play*, in that they alternate between vocal and instrumental sections, there are clear distinctions between them. First, APP begins with a grand instrumental overture, which intimates to the listener that it is a serious and even ostentatious work. TAAB begins quietly and unassumingly and gives no indication in its opening section that it is a grand work. Second, APP has more shifts in meter and more modulations to different keys/modes than TAAB. This, combined with its scanty use of repetition and avoidance of the common popular song forms, makes APP a more challenging and difficult listening experience. Third, APP has a darker harmonic palette than TAAB, since most of its sections are in modes that have the lowered third degree of the scale: Aeolian, Dorian, and Phrygian. One feature that APP does share with TAAB is its use of recurring motives.

MOTIVE 1

A Passion Play employs thematic development of musical motives, although it is not as sophisticated and subtle as that which is found in *Thick as a Brick*. APP has six motives that return periodically, one fewer than the seven motives that bind TAAB together. In comparing the motives between the two albums, one major difference becomes readily apparent. The primary themes in APP are a bit longer and more melodic than those in TAAB, many of which consist of motivic cells lasting only one or two measures. As a consequence there is less thematic development in APP, since these longer themes are less adaptable and malleable. Motive 1, the heartbeat, is the only motive that is put through any significant transformation (see example 7.6 and its appearances in table 7.5).

Example 7.6. *A Passion Play*, Motive 1: Heartbeat

While the heartbeat at the onset of *A Passion Play* may be forgotten by the listener once the band kicks in at the 1:13 mark, it is nevertheless a vital motive that binds the work together. As mentioned before, the heartbeat begins and ends not only the overture (Instr. 1, 0:00–3:28 side 1) but the work as a whole, much like an overture in a Romantic-era opera encapsulates an entire work. Between the heartbeat's two appearances in the overture is a lively gigue in $\frac{9}{8}$ meter (see examples 7.1 and 7.2). The primary motivic cell in the gigue is a quarter-note/eighth-note grouping that essentially turns the heartbeat rhythm into a dance.[8] The heartbeat also provides the rhythmic foundation for the $\frac{12}{8}$ meter in Instr. 8 and Instr. 9. These two occurrences, at the end of side 1 and the beginning of side 2, frame "The Story of the Hare Who Lost His Spectacles." In the heartbeat's appearance in Instr. 9, Motive 5 is appended to it (5:21–5:27 side 2), and then the band as a whole pound out the rhythm (5:27–5:30 side 2). This foreshadows the use of the heartbeat throughout Vocal 10 Parts 1–2 and Instrs. 11–12, Pilgrim's journey

Table 7.5. Appearances of *A Passion Play* Motive 1

SECTION	METER	TIMING	INSTRUMENTATION	FEATURES
Instr. 1	none	0:00–1:15 side 1	Studio effect	Slow ascent in pitch and volume
Instr. 1	$\frac{9}{8}$	1:15–3:06 side 1	Whole band	Heartbeat rhythm transformed into a gigue
Instr. 1	none	3:17–3:26 side 1	Studio effect	Fast decrease in pitch and tempo
Instr. 8	$\frac{12}{8}$	20:22–21:32 side 1	Studio effect or synthesizer	Moderate tempo
Instr. 9	$\frac{12}{8}$	4:20–5:30 side 2	Studio effect or synthesizer, then band as a whole	Swifter tempo
Vocal 10 Parts 1–2, Instr. 11–12	mixed	10:24–13:50 side 2	Synthesizer	Foundational rhythmic element symbolizing heart palpitations
Instr. 16	none	23:06–23:26 side 2	Synthesizer	Slow decrease in volume into silence

through hell, where it takes on a menacing tone with its unrelenting rhythm, loud dynamics, and distorted timbre. The sound can easily be interpreted as Ronnie Pilgrim's heart palpitating loudly in his chest as he meets Lucifer. While Jethro Tull were not the first to use a heartbeat as the pulse of a piece of music (Gustav Mahler based the opening of the first movement of his Ninth Symphony on his heart murmur), this rhythmic use of it to bind together *A Passion Play* is a stroke of genius. Charles Amenta writes: "The heartbeat holds a privileged position regarding music. Just think of the common terms in both music and the medicine of the heart: rhythm, beat, pulse. Indeed, it might well be that our universal attraction to musical rhythm is an epiphenomenon of our sense of our own heartbeat."[9] Besides the instances of the heartbeat listed in table 7.5, there are other quarter-note/eighth-note rhythms throughout *A Passion Play*, although the band does not explicitly associate them with the heartbeat motive. The quarter-note/eighth-note motive in examples 7.1 and 7.2 (Overture Themes 1 and 2) are the most obvious, since they occur shortly after the first appearance of the heartbeat that opens the work.

Example 7.7. *A Passion Play*, Motive 2

Table 7.6. Appearances of *A Passion Play* Motive 2

SECTION	TIMING	METER	PITCH CENTER	INSTRUMENTATION
Instr. 1	0:14 side 1	none	E Phrygian	Soprano saxophone (left channel)
Instr. 1	0:32 side 1	none	E Phrygian	Soprano saxophone (right channel)
Vocal 1 Part 1	3:42 side 1	mixed	G Phrygian	Voice and acoustic guitar
Vocal 1 Part 1	4:11 side 1	mixed	G Phrygian	Voice and piano
Vocal 1 Part 2	5:01 side 1	mixed	G Phrygian	Voice, electric guitar, and piano
Vocal 1 Part 2	5:29 side 1	mixed	G Phrygian	Voice, electric guitar, and piano
Vocal 1 Part 3	7:08 side 1	mixed	G Phrygian	Voice, electric guitar, and piano
Vocal 1 Part 3	7:38 side 1	mixed	G Phrygian	Voice, electric guitar, and piano
Vocal 6	20:01 side 1	mixed	G Phrygian	Voice and piano
Vocal 13	22:46 side 2	mixed	G Phrygian	Voice and piano

MOTIVE 2

This theme, the most identifiable in the piece, appears a total of ten times. Although it is not developed thematically, it is given different instrumental settings (see example 7.7 and table 7.6). The motive is faintly heard twice at the beginning of the piece on the soprano saxophone along with the heartbeat and other studio effects. It then appears six times in the three parts of Vocal 1 and acts as a refrain concluding each stanza. The most common words associated with the refrain ("There was a rush along the Fulham Road / There was a hush in the Passion Play") occur

Example 7.8. *A Passion Play*, Motive 3

Table 7.7. Appearances of *A Passion Play* Motive 3

SECTION	TIMING	METER	PITCH CENTER	INSTRUMENTATION
Vocal 2	9:27 side 1	mixed	C major	Piano, organ and electric guitar
Instr. 4	10:30 side 1	$\frac{11}{8}$	C major	Organ
Instr. 6	17:46 side 1	mixed	C major	Organ and electric guitar
Vocal 5 Part 2	18:05 side 1	mixed	C major	Organ and electric guitar
Instr. 10	9:16 side 2	mixed	C major	Organ and electric guitar

twice: first in Vocal 1 Part 1 and second in Vocal 6 in the middle of the piece. A closely related refrain ("There was a rush along the Fulham Road / Into the Ever-passion Play") also occurs twice: first, in Vocal 1 Part 2 and, second, at the end in Vocal 13. The other occurrences of the motive alter the melody in some fashion or have different words altogether (although the motive is easily recognizable). The refrain speaks of motion and action ("rush"), but this motive is the musical anchor of the work, its sense of "home." After its two initial appearances in E Phrygian, it is in G Phrygian in all subsequent appearances, establishing G as one of the major tonal centers of the piece.

MOTIVE 3

Motive 3 (shown in example 7.8 and table 7.7) is a primary melody in Vocal 2 ("All along the icy wastes . . ."), where it appears four times. Immediately after this, at the beginning of Instr. 4, the opening fragment of the motive is played on the organ in $\frac{11}{8}$ and combined contrapuntally with countermelodies played by the electric guitar and synthesizer. In Instr. 6 it returns twice, nicely dovetailed with Motive 4, the primary theme from Vocal 5 (see examples 7.9 and 7.10 below). It also appears twice in Vocal 5 Part 2 ("All of this and some of that's . . ."), since this section is a reprise of the music of Vocal 2. The motive's last appearance is at the end

Example 7.9. *A Passion Play*, Motive 4

Example 7.10. *A Passion Play*, Motives 4 and 3 combined, 17:41–17:58, side 1

Table 7.8. Appearances of *A Passion Play* Motive 4

SECTION	TIMING	METER	PITCH CENTER	INSTRUMENTATION
Instr. 5	15:24 side 1	mixed	D	Entire band
Vocal 5 Part 1	15:41 side 1	4/4	G Dorian	Entire band
Instr. 6	17:09 side 1	mixed	G Dorian	Entire band
Vocal 5 Part 2	18:33 side 1	mixed	G Dorian	Entire band
Vocal 5 Part 2	18:44 side 1	4/4	G Dorian	Entire band
Instr. 7	19:36 side 1	6/8	G Dorian	Entire band
Vocal 10 Part 1	10:28 and 11:46 side 2	12/8	G Aeolian	Entire band

of Instr. 10, where it punctuates an extended solo section and leads into Vocal 9 Part 2 ("Well, I'm all for leaving … ").

MOTIVE 4

Motive 4 (shown in example 7.9 and table 7.8) is the primary theme in Vocal 5 ("Lover of the black and white … "), and even engulfs Anderson's vocal melody in its raw power. It is simply a hard-rock guitar riff and is always played by the entire band in unison. Yet it is the B section that is heard first at the end of Instr. 5 just before Vocal 5. It begins slowly, and the band increases the tempo until it commences Vocal 5 Part 1, where the motive is played in its entirety. The motive continues into Instr. 6, where the B section is sequenced upward and lengthened. Near the end of Instr. 6, most of the A section is dovetailed with Motive 3, shown in example 7.10.

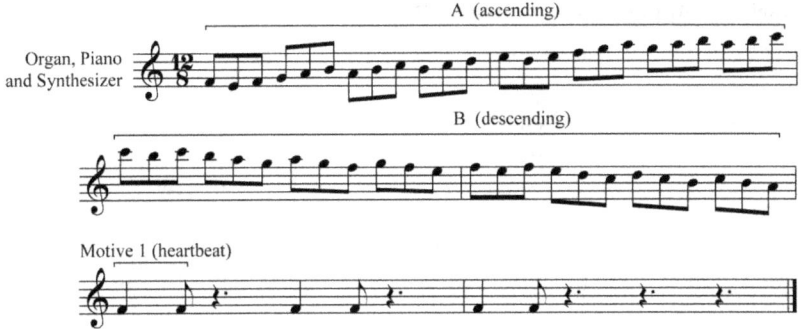

Example 7.11. *A Passion Play*, Motive 5

In Vocal 5 Part 2, a slightly modified version of section B of the motive is used to build tension on the repeated line "How does it feel to be in the play . . . " Section B alone is used again in Instr. 7, where it is turned into a swirling, churning theme (as it was in Instr. 5). Lastly, the introductory theme in Vocal 10 Part 1 ("Colours I've none . . . ") can be considered a close cousin to Motive 4. The Vocal 10 theme has a half-step descent followed by a rising and falling gesture, similar to sections A and B of Motive 4.

MOTIVE 5

This motive (shown in example 7.11 and table 7.9) appears for the first time in Instr. 9, with Evans playing organ and piano on the ascending section A and synthesizer on the descending section B. This appearance foreshadows its use in Vocal 10 Parts 1–2, where section A (at a much

Table 7.9. Appearances of *A Passion Play* Motive 5

SECTION	TIMING	METER	PITCH CENTER	INSTRUMENTATION
Instr. 9	5:21 side 2	12/8	C major	Organ, piano, and synthesizer
Vocal 10 Part 1	10:58, 11:21, 12:15 side 2	12/8	C major	Synthesizer and organ
Instr. 11	12:53 side 2	12/8	C major	Synthesizer and organ
Vocal 10 Part 2	13:16 side 2	12/8	C major	Synthesizer and organ
Instr. 12	13:39 side 2	12/8	C major	Synthesizer and organ

Table 7.10. Appearances of the phrase "Passion Play"

SECTION	TIMING	PHRASE
Vocal 1 Part 1	4:22 side 1	"Passion Play"
Vocal 1 Part 2	5:04 side 1	"Passion Play"
Vocal 1 Part 2	5:39 side 1	"Ever-passion Play"
Vocal 2	9:52 side 1	"you're in the play"
Vocal 2	10:28 side 1	"Passion Play"
Vocal 5 Part 1	16:03 side 1	"Passion Play"
Vocal 5 Part 2	18:31–18:45 side 1	"you're in the play," "be in the play," "play the play," "be the play"
Vocal 5 Part 3	18:51 side 1	"Man of passion"
Vocal 6	20:16 side 1	"Passion Play"
Vocal 10 Part 2	12:57 side 2	"Passionate play"
Vocal 13	22:58 side 2	"Ever-passion Play"

slower tempo) appears several times and functions as a structural element. Its final appearance in Instr. 12 includes both the ascending and descending sections. In its first and last appearances it has Motive 1 (the heartbeat) appended to it.

MOTIVE 6

This final motive is simply the phrase "Passion Play." It is heard many times along with the melody of Motive 2 (" . . . there was a hush in the Passion Play"), but the short phrase crops up numerous other times in the lyrics, with slight variations. In essence the phrase functions as both a melodic motive and a textual motive, reminding the listener of the theme of the album, since the music and lyrics continually veer into obscure territory. Since *A Passion Play* eschews the popular music forms that have repetition "built in" (such as strophic, AABA, and verse-chorus), this unorthodox method of repetition works well to help bind it together. Table 7.10 shows that the phrase appears quite often on side 1, and less so on side 2.

Tables 7.11 and 7.12 show where in the music the six motives occur throughout *A Passion Play*. The numbers above the lines indicate the motives, while the numbers below the lines indicate the timings for sides 1 and 2. These two tables show that the motives in *APP* appear more often than those in *TAAB*. This is an important factor in unifying *APP*, since it

Table 7.11. Appearances of all *A Passion Play* motives throughout side 1

1 2	1	1 2	2 6 2 6 2 6	2 2	3 6
0:00	2:30	5:00		7:30	10:00
6 3		4 4 6	4 4343 646	4 2 6 1	
10:01	12:30	15:00	17:30	21:36	

Table 7.12. Appearances of all *A Passion Play* motives throughout side 2

	1	5		3
0:00	2:30	5:00	7:30	10:00
1 4 5 4	5 5 6 5 5			2 6 1
10:01	12:30	15:00	17:30	23:26

doesn't cling as tightly to the popular song forms as *TAAB*. Unlike *TAAB*, the motives are not densely packed and combined at the conclusion of the piece.

INSTRUMENTAL PASSAGES

The instrumental passages in *Thick as a Brick* and *A Passion Play* are unique in progressive rock. While Pink Floyd, Yes, Genesis, and Emerson, Lake & Palmer were brilliant at creating substantial instrumental material between vocal sections in their extended works, Jethro Tull achieved more in this area on these two albums in terms of sheer quantity and quality. The instrumental passages are as noteworthy as the vocal sections and display a compositional density that is rare even by progressive rock standards. Some of the passages in *A Passion Play* have a chamber music quality to them, such as Instr. 3. Some, like Instr. 4, are dizzying in their play with odd meters and imitative counterpoint. Some have a floating, trance-like quality to them, evoking the non-corporal state of Ronnie Pilgrim, such as Instrs. 8, 9, and 14. Some simply have a wealth of beautiful melody, like Instr. 10.

Like their counterparts in *Thick as a Brick*, these passages serve different functions musically and can be placed into four categories: some function as transitions, some feature virtuosic soloing by individual band members or the band collectively, some provide stark contrasts and take the music in new directions, and some repeat and reinforce the musical material found in the previous vocal section. Almost all of the instrumental passages fall into more than one of these categories. (For a detailed analysis of the passages, see appendix 3.)

INSTRUMENTATION

The music of *A Passion Play*, like that of *Thick as a Brick* and much of Jethro Tull's music, can be described as a dialogue between acoustic instruments and electric instruments. While the acoustic sections of *TAAB* are clearly in a "folk" vein, being dominated by Anderson's acoustic guitar, the acoustic sections of *AAP* cannot be so narrowly defined. Although the acoustic guitar appears occasionally, Anderson plays as much in a pseudo-flamenco style than in an English folk style

Listening to *A Passion Play* may make one wonder if Anderson became disenchanted with his flute, since the album has the least amount of flute of all Jethro Tull albums. But when one hears the mastery that Anderson displays on the soprano and sopranino saxophones, this flagrant flute flub is quickly forgiven. In fact, Anderson's brilliant saxophone playing is one of the highlights of *APP*, and one may wonder why it is absent from the rest of Jethro Tull's albums after *War Child*. Surprisingly, Anderson's own assessment of his abilities on the saxophone is quite negative: "It is one of those deeply regrettable moments when I stuffed one of those things in my mouth, and I promised never to do it again. The saxophone, in all its shapes and forms and sizes, and I were not suited to be bedfellows, and so saxophones have remained in their cases for many a long year."[10] Anderson's virtuosity on the saxophone on *APP* seems to come from nowhere, since he uses it only sporadically on *TAAB*, the first album on which he plays it. Table 7.13 shows the presence of the saxophones in over half of the vocal and instrumental sections, while the presence of the flute is much more intermittent (compare the "SS" and "F" columns). On *APP* it is the first and last instrument to be heard, and there are numerous passages throughout where it dominates the soundscape, especially the solos in Instrs. 2, 10, and 15. Yet the flute does get its due with solos in Instrs. 4 and 13.

Another aspect that differentiates the soundscape of *A Passion Play* from *Thick as a Brick* is John Evans's heavy reliance on the synthesizer. Like Anderson with the saxophone, Evans's skill at incorporating the synthesizer into the band, and balancing it with the piano and organ, seems to come from nowhere. Table 7.13 and the accompanying legend in table 7.14 show the instrumentation of *APP*.

THE MUSIC OF "THE STORY OF THE HARE WHO LOST HIS SPECTACLES"

In my survey of the reception of *A Passion Play*, I have found that those who like the album also like "The Story of the Hare," while those who dislike the album think "The Story of the Hare" is, in Scott Allen Nollen's words, "the most obnoxious creation in the entire Tull canon."[11] Some listeners find that it distracts them from the narrative of Pilgrim's afterlife adventure. Since the concept of the album itself is a bit hare-brained, so to speak, I find that "The Story of the Hare" fits right into the album's weird and wonderful world. Although it is credited to Jeffrey Hammond, John Evans, and Ian Anderson, Anderson says that Hammond came up with the idea and words himself, and John Evans composed the music.[12] It shares some common ground with Serge Prokofiev's *Peter and the Wolf*, which is used as a point of comparison on Jethro Tull's official website.[13] Prokofiev's work is for a much larger ensemble and is longer due to the extended musical interludes between narrative sections. Hammond speaks over the music and shapes his narration to fit the contours of the orchestration – and even sings near the end – whereas Prokofiev's narrator is, for the most part, separated from the orchestra.

Although the primary melodies for the fable were composed by John Evans on piano, the arrangement and orchestration were done by David Palmer. The music is constructed from two closely related themes, shown in examples 7.12 and 7.13 as Story Theme 1 and Story Theme 2. These themes, while aptly portraying the whimsy of the story, do not seem to represent any of the animal characters in the way that Prokofiev portrayed each of his animals with a theme in *Peter and the Wolf*.

Story Theme 1 appears most often and is usually extended by sequencing upward the final sixteenth-note cell. Story Theme 2 appears

Table 7.13. Instrumentation of *A Passion Play*

SIDE 1

SECTION	AG	B	CO	D	EG	F	G	M	OR	P	SS	SW	SY	TI	VO
Instr. 1	*	*		*	*	*			*		*				
Vocal 1 Part 1	*								*						*
Vocal 1 Part 2	*	*			*				*						*
Instr. 2		*		*	*		*	*		*					
Vocal 1 Part 3		*			*				*						*
Instr. 3	*	*		*	*				*	*					
Vocal 2	*	*		*	*				*	*		*			*
Instr. 4		*		*	*	*			*	*			*		
Vocal 3		*		*	*				*	*			*		*
Vocal 4		*		*	*				*	*					*
Instr. 5		*		*	*				*		*		*		
Vocal 5 Part 1		*		*	*				*	*	*	*	*		*
Instr. 6		*		*	*				*	*	*		*		
Vocal 5 Part 2	*	*		*	*				*						*
Vocal 5 Part 3		*		*	*				*	*					*
Instr. 7		*		*	*				*	*	*		*		
Vocal 6									*						*
Instr. 8	*	*		*	*	*			*	*			*		

SIDE 2

SECTION	AG	B	CO	D	EG	F	G	M	OR	P	SS	SW	SY	TI	VO
Vocal 7		*	*	*	*		*	*	*	*	*	*	*		*
Instr. 9	*	*		*	*	*			*	*	*		*		
Vocal 8	*	*		*	*				*						*
Vocal 9 Part 1	*														*
Instr. 10		*		*	*				*	*	*		*		
Vocal 9 Part 2	*														*
Vocal 10 Part 1		*		*	*				*	*	*		*		*
Instr. 11		*		*	*				*	*	*		*		
Vocal 10 Part 2		*		*	*				*	*	*		*		*
Instr. 12									*				*		
Vocal 11 Part 1		*		*	*	*			*	*	*		*	*	*
Instr. 13		*		*	*	*			*	*	*		*	*	
Vocal 11 Part 2		*		*	*	*			*	*	*		*	*	*
Instr. 14	*	*		*	*	*				*			*		
Vocal 12 Part 1	*	*		*	*	*			*				*		*
Instr. 15		*		*	*				*	*			*		
Vocal 12 Part 2		*		*	*	*			*				*		*
Vocal 13		*		*	*				*	*	*		*		*
Instr. 16		*		*	*				*			*	*		

Table 7.14. Instrumentation legend of *A Passion Play*

ABBR.	INSTRUMENT	MUSICIAN
AG	Acoustic guitar	Ian Anderson
B	Bass guitar	Jeffrey Hammond
CO	Chamber orchestra	Arranged and conducted by David Palmer
D	Drums	Barrie Barlow
EG	Electric guitar	Martin Barre
F	Flute	Ian Anderson
G	Glockenspiel	Barrie Barlow
M	Marimba	Barrie Barlow
OR	Organ	John Evans
P	Piano	John Evans
SS	Soprano and sopranino saxophones	Ian Anderson
SW	Spoken word	Jeffrey Hammond, John Evans
SY	Synthesizer/Studio effects	John Evans
TI	Timpani	Barrie Barlow
VO	Vocals	Ian Anderson

in two places and, along with numerous passages of text painting, provides some melodic variety. The strings and woodwind instruments add progressively more countermelodies to the two themes, so as the plot of the story thickens, so do the texture and orchestration. Table 7.15 shows the appearances of the two themes and other features that characterize the story.

Example 7.12. *A Passion Play*, Story Theme 1

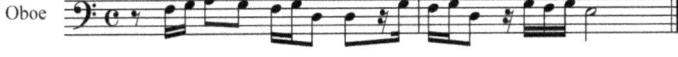

Example 7.13. *A Passion Play*, Story Theme 2

Table 7.15. Appearances of the two themes in "The Story of the Hare Who Lost His Spectacles"

TIMING	FEATURES
0:00–0:47	Theme 1 introduced and is sequenced upward
0:47–1:30	Switch to § meter, text painting
1:30–1:58	Theme 1 returns and is sequenced upward; strings provide countermelodies
1:58–2:13	Theme 2 introduced
2:13–2:37	Theme 1 returns and is sequenced upward; strings provide countermelodies
2:37–2:57	Theme 1 is varied and sequenced upward; strings provide countermelodies
2:57–3:18	Theme 2 returns
3:18–3:35	Theme 1 is varied and sequenced upward
3:35–4:19	Switch to § meter; band enters, punctuating Hammond's last words

Evans's piano and organ are the primary instruments, with the strings providing countermelodies and the woodwind instruments providing most of the text painting. The instrumentation in "The Story of the Hare Who Lost His Spectacles" consists of:

Narrators:	John Evans (introduction), Jeffrey Hammond (story)
Piano:	John Evans
Organ:	John Evans
Synthesizer:	John Evans
Glockenspiel:	Barrie Barlow
Marimba:	Barrie Barlow
Soprano saxophone:	Ian Anderson

Chamber orchestra consisting of clarinet, oboe, flute, horn, trumpet, trombone, strings

METER AND HARMONY

Assigning meters to the sections of *A Passion Play* is a difficult task, even more difficult than it is for *Thick as a Brick*. Transcribing some of the melodies is also problematic, since they can be interpreted metrically in a number of ways. The three sections of Vocal 1 in *APP* can be heard more or less in $\frac{4}{4}$ meter, but the constant stream of missing or misplaced accents, downbeats, and cadences contradicts such a simple interpretation.

Meters like $\frac{3}{4}$, $\frac{6}{4}$, and $\frac{5}{4}$ can be added to match the "misplaced" accents, downbeats, and cadences, but then the transcriptions appear overly complicated. Either way is imperfect, trying to imprison orally composed music into fixed musical notation. All of the band members – even Hammond, who was still a fledgling bassist in 1973 – reveled in playing in odd meters, switching meters, and implying odd meters within common ones (and vice versa). As a result, the word "mixed" appears several times in the "Meter" column in table 7.3.

The polyrhythmic passage in Instr. 4 is just one of many examples of this sophisticated treatment of meter. At 10:49 side 1, the band plays a two-measure twisting and turning phrase, interpreting the $\frac{11}{8}$ meter as $3 + 3 + 3 + 2$ (as if it were a more conventional $\frac{12}{8}$ with an eighth note dropped at the end). Then at 11:29 Anderson's soprano saxophone and Evans's synthesizer overlay a phrase that implies $2 + 2 + 2 + 2 + 3$, creating what, in the hands of lesser musicians, could be a hemiolic nightmare. The significance of the passage is not the fact that the band can play such complicated metrical games with a theme, but that it still sounds clear, beautiful, captivating, and quite tuneful.

Like *Thick as a Brick*, the harmony of *A Passion Play* is governed more by modes rather than keys. The primary key/mode area of *APP* is G. The overture is in G Dorian, the easily identifiable refrain ("There was a rush . . . ") is in G Phrygian in almost all of its appearances, and the most often played excerpt of the piece, which was released as a single (Vocal 10 – "Colours I've none . . . "), is in G Aeolian. The prominence of these minor tonalities along with the subject matter of the lyrics give the album a dark tone.

The harmonic areas in *A Passion Play* are murkier and more indistinct than those of *Thick as a Brick*. It is hard to pin down definite modes or keys in certain sections, since the fine distinctions between, for example, G Aeolian and G Dorian are not easily discerned by the ear. The difference between these two modes is the raised or lowered pitch of the sixth degree of the scale, a degree that has less importance than the tonic, the third, the fifth, or the seventh. Many of the modulations are by whole step or half step, building more tension than conventional modulations to closely related keys. For example, the primary key of most of the overture is G Dorian, yet it begins (1:15 side 1) in B♭ with a I-♭VII-vi-♭VII progression (B♭, A♭, G, A♭), modulates rapidly through A, B♭, C, C♯, and finally arrives at D, the V of G Dorian (1:46 side 1). This type of modulation by step and half step continues through the rest of the overture, as discussed in the section on the overture. The music's chromaticism makes it difficult to pin down the keys and modes of sections, and there are always scalar outliers that blur the lines between harmonic areas. Vocal 1 seems to be in G Phrygian, since A♭ appears several times in the melody. Yet there is an A♮ also (such as the one on the word "here" in the first line of Vocal 1 Part 1), giving it an inflection of G Aeolian.

The first eight minutes are saturated with minor key areas, with most of the overture in G Dorian, the three sections of Vocal 1 in G Phrygian, and Instrs. 2 and 3 mostly in C Aeolian. Thus, the first impression one receives from the music is that of a dour foreboding, which most likely prompted critics, fans, and Anderson himself to regard the album as too serious and humorless. The music begins to move away from these dark harmonic areas at the end of Instr. 3. The C Aeolian of this section turns to C major at the beginning of Vocal 2 (9:06 side 1, "All along the icy wastes..."), bringing the first sustained major key area in the piece. The other areas in bright keys are Instrs. 8 and 9 in C major, which bookend "The Story of the Hare Who Lost His Spectacles," in F Lydian. The remainder of side 2 is again in dark-sounding modes that have the lowered third degree of the scale: Dorian, Aeolian, and Phrygian.

Now that the inner workings of *A Passion Play* have been explored, does it deserve to stand alongside *Thick as a Brick* as one of the great Tull albums? Undoubtedly it does, although with certain caveats. It possesses most of the elements that make *Thick as a Brick* an enjoyable and intriguing record: an adventurous large-scale structure; dazzling instrumental virtuosity and ensemble playing; pleasant, memorable melodies; diverse instrumentation; and Anderson's sardonic vocal delivery, which makes the confusing lyrics captivating in spite of themselves. The album also has many novel features that distinguish it from its predecessor, such as the prominence of the soprano saxophone, the symbolic and musical use of the heartbeat motive, and the whimsical nature of "The Story of the Hare Who Lost His Spectacles." On the downside, the thematic development in *A Passion Play* is not as sophisticated as it is in *Thick as a Brick*, the live ambience and spontaneity is missing, and the album packaging is lackluster. Ultimately any attempt the band made to write and record an album-length work that was similar to *Thick as a Brick* was bound to fall short. Judged by itself, *A Passion Play* is one of the most creative progressive rock albums. Judged alongside *Thick as a Brick*, however, which it is inevitably bound to be, it is a lesser creation.

EIGHT

Monty Python, Reception, and Live Versions

THIS FINAL CHAPTER DISCUSSES THREE ASPECTS OF *THICK AS A Brick* and *A Passion Play* that are important but have not yet been considered. The first section shows how the two albums were influenced by British humor of the 1960s and 1970s, especially the television show *Monty Python's Flying Circus* (1969–1974). The second section describes how the albums were received by fans, critics, and the musicians themselves, and the third explores the live versions of the two pieces, which Jethro Tull performed in their entirety during their 1972 and 1973 tours.

A new brand of satire became a cultural force in 1960s Britain with the BBC radio show *The Goon Show* (1951–1960), the West End and Broadway comedy revue *Beyond the Fringe* (1960–1964), and television shows such as *That Was the Week That Was* (1962–1963) and *The Frost Report* (1966–1967). This "satire boom" brought a surreal, absurdist edge to the music hall tradition that dominated British humor in the first half of the twentieth century. The comedy team Monty Python (Graham Chapman, John Cleese, Terry Gilliam, Eric Idle, Terry Jones, and Michael Palin) took elements of the "satire boom," piled on even more surrealism and absurdity, and created *Monty Python's Flying Circus* in 1969. Jethro Tull was directly influenced by the surreal and absurd elements in these shows. When asked by an interviewer, "What makes you laugh?" Anderson replied: "The absurd. I suppose what makes me laugh is something that seems on the surreal and absurd side and in that way I'm probably right in the mainstream of what makes most British people laugh. With the landmark eras of The Goons and The Pythons and the current brigade, like Eddie Izzard . . . it may seem like it is all improvisation but there's a lot of structure and form underlying that illusion of randomness. But that's the stuff that makes me laugh – the surreal and the absurd."[1]

Humor and satire in rock music can be traced back to the 1950s and has taken many forms. Iain Ellis writes: "Though other art forms show their adaptability to various types of comedy, rock music's sensory range allows for a particular diversity of humorous styles. Satire, (self-)parody, irony, whimsy, cartoon, grotesque, and absurdism are just some of the humor techniques that have emerged from the lyrics, performances, sounds, artworks, and images of rock expression."[2] In the late 1960s, bands like the Beatles, the Who, the Small Faces, and the Kinks brought the madcap humor of the British music hall and the "satire boom" into rock music. The overt Britishness in these recordings was perhaps a reaction to the heavy influence of American rock, soul, blues, folk, and country music on British performers in the late 1950s and early 1960s. The Beatles' film *Magical Mystery Tour* (1967) and John Lennon's song "I Am the Walrus" (from the same film and album) are full of surreal and absurd elements. On *The Who Sell Out* (1967), a parody and homage to England's pirate radio stations like Radio London, the Who's "normal" songs are interspersed with jingles that advertise products such as Heinz's baked beans. The Small Faces devote the latter portion of *Ogdens' Nut Gone Flake* (1968) to a surreal fairy tale about Happiness Stan, a lad in search of the missing half of a half moon. Interspersed between the Small Faces' psychedelic songs, British comedian Stanley Unwin narrates the tale in his whimsical gobbledygook language "Unwinese." On the concept album *The Kinks Are the Village Green Preservation Society* (1968), the Kinks celebrate the quaint and quirky denizens of England's hamlets. While this album is principally a loving and nostalgic ode to the countryside, it also has a satirical edge, as Andy Miller and Barry Faulk point out.[3] These recordings show how sophisticated humor in British rock became in the 1960s. Although they may not have been a direct influence on Jethro Tull, they did create a fun house – or holiday camp – in British rock for other bands and musicians to enter into.

What about humor in British progressive rock bands? These bands tended to take themselves and their art seriously, since they strove to imbue their music with influences from "serious" or art music. It was this seriousness that was a catalyst for Jethro Tull to make *Thick as a*

Brick into a spoof of the style. Yet even progressive rock is not devoid of humor, satire, and irreverence. Genesis' Peter Gabriel created preposterous scenarios in songs like "The Return of the Giant Hogweed" from *Nursery Cryme* (1971), a tale of deadly plants gone amok. Emerson, Lake & Palmer recorded several humorous songs, the best of which is "Bennie the Bouncer" on *Brain Salad Surgery* (1973), a ditty with lyrics by Peter Sinfield about a drunken brawl in a music hall. Some of Sinfield's lyrics on King Crimson's albums employ dark humor, such as "Cat Food" from *In the Wake of Poseidon* (1970) and "Happy Family" from *Lizard* (1971). *Thick as a Brick* has some satirical elements in its lyrics and music, but its packaging (see chapter 3) and live presentation (see below) have cemented its reputation as satire, a spoof of concept albums. Thus *Thick as a Brick* is both a product and a parody of the monumentality of progressive rock. *A Passion Play* has satirical elements in its music, lyrics, packaging, and live presentation. "The Story of the Hare Who Lost His Spectacles" is full of the same whimsy and lightness of the latter half of the Small Faces' *Ogdens' Nut Gone Flake*. Yet ironically, *A Passion Play* is considered to be one of Jethro Tull's darker albums by critics, fans, members of the band, and Anderson himself.

The members of Jethro Tull have used humor all through their career in a variety of ways. Their penchant for self-parody can be seen on numerous album covers with band members – especially Anderson – appearing in a number of guises. The band's videos almost always have a satirical edge with heavy doses of self-parody. In the video for "Too Old to Rock 'n' Roll, Too Young to Die" on the *Slipstream* (1981) video, Anderson and the band dress up as monocle-wearing, brandy-sipping gentlemen; seasick sailors; and grizzled lechers. Especially in the 1970s, their live shows were rife with outrageous costumes, bizarre stage antics, and bawdy stage banter. Lyrical humor and satire can be found in songs such as "Fat Man" (1969), "Down at the End of Your Road" (1981), and "The Dog-Ear Years" (1999). Musical humor can be found in "Bourrée" (in which a Bach piece for lute is turned into cocktail lounge jazz), in the clever text painting in "The Story of the Hare Who Lost His Spectacles" on *A Passion Play*, and in Anderson's entertaining flute solos, where he sings, snorts, and coughs through the flute and comically quotes snippets from well-known pieces of classical music and Christmas carols. Rock journalist Lester Bangs describes the following bit of musical tomfoolery from the *Thick as a Brick* tour:

> Jethro Tull are such solid entertainers that even if you can't stand the music, they're usually providing something for you to gawk at. A lot of it is real vaudeville: [drummer] Barlow walks up to the mike during a pause, holds up a toy cymbal, raises a drumstick and hits it with an extravagant flourish. He gets cheers and an echoing cymbal shot which seems to come from nowhere. He looks around, scratches his head and hits the cymbal again. Again the echo. Getting really worked up, he hits the cymbal again and again, faster and faster, the echoes coming at the same pace, and suddenly the rest of the band converges on him, each of them holding identical cymbal and stick and wildly bashing away. The audience eats it up.[4]

MONTY PYTHON'S FLYING CIRCUS AND JETHRO TULL

Ian Anderson has said in numerous interviews that *Thick as a Brick* was influenced by the surreal, Monty Python–esque style of English humor that was prominent in the early 1970s. In fact, Jethro Tull helped to finance the 1975 movie *Monty Python and the Holy Grail*, and John Cleese was hired to be the "humor consultant" for the *War Child* movie project in 1974, which, unfortunately, never materialized. What, if any, connection is there between *Thick as a Brick* and *A Passion Play* and *Monty Python's Flying Circus*? While it would be a stretch to claim that the structure and flow of the *Flying Circus* episodes were a direct influence on the structure and flow of these two albums, there are uncanny resemblances between them.

First, unlike the British music hall tradition, the 1960s satire boom, and American shows like *Saturday Night Live* (which feature individual sketches), each *Flying Circus* episode was conceived as a continuous narrative with thematic connections binding the sketches together. Some episodes, such as "The Cycling Tour" and "Mr. Neutron," were governed by an overriding theme while others were simply a hodgepodge of incongruous elements thrust together. Terry Jones recounts how the Pythons formulated their stream-of-consciousness approach: "Terry Gilliam had done an animation for one of the *Do Not Adjust Your Sets* called *Beware of Elephants* and I suddenly thought: that's what we could do: break up the sketch format and just do a whole thing that's stream-of-consciousness, and Terry's animations can go in and out and link things, and the whole show would just flow like that."[5] In the same fashion, Jethro Tull was able to reject the idea that an album had to be a collection of separate songs and instead composed two albums that were continuous pieces of music with linking material connecting the songs and song fragments.

Second, both the show and the two Jethro Tull albums place a great deal of emphasis on the linking material. The Pythons used Terry Gilliam's animation, stock footage, deliberate interruptions, free association, and other visual and audio devices to link unrelated sketches together. This gave each episode a unique form, each with its own surreal flow and logic. Reiterating a quote from above about the Pythons, Anderson said, "It may seem like it is all improvisation but there's a lot of structure and form underlying that illusion of randomness." This "illusion of randomness" in *Flying Circus* is emphasized in one of the catchphrases of the show – "and now for something completely different." Likewise, both of the Jethro Tull albums give great weight and importance to the linking material, since they have as many, or even more, instrumental passages as they do vocal sections. The instrumental passages bind together the "completely different" vocal sections, which have varying keys, tempos, instrumentation, and musical styles. Although many of the passages have instrumental solos, and therefore are improvisatory, they do provide structure and form to the albums.

Third, elements in a *Flying Circus* episode are repeated or developed. Some elements, such as the "Knight with the Raw Chicken" and the "Women's Institute Applause," appear in many different episodes. Part of the enjoyment of watching a *Flying Circus* episode, or listening to *Thick as a Brick* or *A Passion Play*, is not knowing what, or when, bits will be repeated or developed. This adds a great degree of surprise and unpredictability, which may put off some viewers or listeners but is refreshing to others. As Michael Palin explains: "The shows in the first series certainly, and some in the second, could encompass a traditional sketch which had a beginning, middle and an end . . . or you could just have a fragment and repeat it at various times during the show. Even a little fragment, a gesture, a line, a bit of costume or whatever, could be in, even if it didn't relate to anything else around it and that was both exciting and exhilarating, and fresh and also funny."[6] Thus, both the show and the albums use repetition at irregular intervals, varied repetition, and thematic development to unify a work that eschews conventional structures.

Fourth, although each show consists of one continuous piece, individual sketches in the *Flying Circus* episodes can be viewed out of the context of the show in which they originally appeared. The DVD box set of the complete series gives the viewer the option to just watch the individual sketches in each episode. Yet the sketches are an integral part of the unbroken narrative of the episodes. In the same way, the first three-minute section of *Thick as a Brick* has become one of the band's most popular "singles" and is played to this day on classic rock radio stations, even though it was never released as a single. Just as *Monty Python's Flying Circus* can be enjoyed as either complete episode or individual sketch, *Thick as a Brick* can be enjoyed as either album or single.

A closer look at the individual elements in a *Flying Circus* episode, such as "How to Recognize Different Types of Trees from Quite a Long Way Away" from season one, reveals a structure that is similar to that of *Thick as a Brick* and *A Passion Play* (see table 8.1). This *Flying Circus* episode, like all of them, uses such a wide range of satire, humor, visual styles, and modes of expression that it could easily appear completely incoherent. Yet the show also employs the linking and unifying elements explained in the second and third points above. As table 8.1 shows, there are five elements (or motives, in musical terms) in this episode that are repeated or developed: the It's Man (appearing twice), Terry Gilliam's animation (appearing four times), The Larch (appearing four times), the Knight with the Raw Chicken (appearing three times), and the Beach Scene (appearing twice).

This unorthodox method of employing repetition is similar to what is found in *Thick as a Brick* and *A Passion Play*, as explored in the sections on thematic development in chapters 4 and 7. Even more specific similarities can be found between this episode and the two albums. The It's Man appears at the beginning and end of this episode, as he does in most of them. Likewise, *Thick as a Brick* begins and ends with the same refrain ("So you ride yourselves . . . "), and *A Passion Play* begins and ends with a heartbeat. More by way of coincidence than design, both

Table 8.1. Form of *Flying Circus* episode: "How to Recognize Different Types of Trees from Quite a Long Way Away"

TIMING	SECTION	REPEATED ELEMENTS
0:00–0:20	It's Man	It's Man #1
0:20–0:54	Main Titles – Terry Gilliam animation	Animation #1
0:54–1:15	The Larch	The Larch #1
1:15–9:22	Court Scene	Knight with the Raw Chicken #1
9:22–9:47	The Larch	The Larch #2
9:47–12:54	Bicycle Repair Man	
12:54–13:25	Tirade against Communists	Knight with the Raw Chicken #2
13:25–14:56	Children's Stories	Animation #2
14:56–15:21	Terry Gilliam animation	Animation #3
15:21–15:36	Beach Scene	Beach Scene #1
15:36–20:30	Restaurant Sketch	
20:30–20:49	Beach Scene	Beach Scene #2 Knight with the Raw Chicken #3
20:49–22:34	Terry Gilliam animation	Animation #4
22:34–23:32	Seduced Milkmen	
23:32–26:04	Stolen Newsreader	
26:04–26:38	The Larch	The Larch #3
26:38–27:38	Children's Interview	
27:38–29:51	Nudge Nudge Wink Wink	
29:51–30:41	It's Man and End Credits	It's Man #2 The Larch #4

the *Flying Circus* episode and *A Passion Play* have children's fairy tales in the middle of them. At the 13:31 mark of the thirty-minute show, Terry Gilliam provides animation of bouncing bunnies as Eric Idle begins to read naughty fairy tales such as this: "Rumpletweezer ran the Dinky Tinky shop in the foot of the magic oak tree by the wobbly dum dum bush in the shade of the magic glade down in Dingly Dell. Here he sold contraceptives and . . ."[7] Likewise, a fairy tale is placed in the middle of *A Passion Play* with, as some Jethro Tull fans have speculated, a title that sounds quite like "The Story of the Hare Who Lost His Testicles." In addition, anyone who is familiar with the visual style of a *Flying Circus* episode will think of the show when they see the short film that Jethro Tull made for "The Story of the Hare Who Lost His Spectacles,"[8] as they are cut from the same cloth.

RECEPTION OF THE TWO ALBUMS

So how did *Thick as a Brick* and *A Passion Play*, two of the "most uncompromising and uncommercial albums" in the history of popular music, both reach number one on the U.S. *Billboard* 200 Album Chart?[9] Jethro Tull's constant touring in America and the success of *Aqualung* were important factors in making *Thick as a Brick* a hit album, but it still remains a mystery. The deeper mystery is how *A Passion Play* reached number one. A forty-five-minute song with impenetrable lyrics, a dark subject matter, and a dead ballet dancer on the album cover aren't the usual ingredients that endear a work to the general populace. The period from late 1972 to late 1973 was a difficult time for Jethro Tull. The recording problems at the Château, negative reviews of *A Passion Play*, the announcement from manager Terry Ellis that the band was retiring from touring (which outraged the band, who never intended it), and the disappointing reviews of the *A Passion Play* tour were the first major setbacks for the group.[10] This begs the question: how did *A Passion Play* hit number one while selling half the number of records as *Thick as a Brick*, plus everything else that was going wrong for Jethro Tull in 1973?[11] Were the other albums released at the time lackluster? Was the popular music audience interested in listening to forty-five-minute songs? The simple answer is that *A Passion Play* piggybacked onto the success of *Thick as a Brick* and *Living in the Past* (which reached number three on the *Billboard* chart). Greg Russo opines that it was "one of the most deceiving #1 *Billboard* album placements in US chart history."[12] Here's Anderson's perspective from a 1979 interview:

> It was only number one in the States for one week, which meant that a lot of people went out and bought it on the assumption that Jethro Tull's last album had been at number one for several weeks [actually two weeks] and was a good album and they'd all loved it, and this next album must also be a great album and they would love it and they all rushed out and bought it. But it didn't generate throughout its initial sales period enough confidence in the album to sustain those kinds of sales. So in the long run it didn't sell as many, in America, as other albums. In fact it only sold half as many. It was a gold album, but it didn't sell a million units or anything.[13]

What do the three Jethro Tull historians think of *A Passion Play*? Rees raves ("perhaps their finest work to date"), Russo reproaches ("a bit too serious and highbrow for its own good"), and Nollen nixes ("it suffers from an overwrought theatricality").[14] Anderson himself has mixed feeling about the album:

> *Thick as a Brick* was very successful, and when it came to the next album I guess we all fell into the trap of thinking we should do the same kind of thing again, but instead of being silly about it maybe we should take it seriously. I think the problem with it was that the humor that was there on *Thick as a Brick* was not there on *A Passion Play*. And I think that's because a lot of the humor had been knocked out of it by the circumstances leading up to the making of the album. A year of being on tour, living in Switzerland, rehearsing, recording it in France then finally coming back to England to start it all over again, rehearsing and recording virtually all new material. That really took the humor out of it! The result is that *A Passion Play* is too deadpan, it doesn't have those slightly irreverent and humorous little interludes or moments of light relief that would have made it more listenable.[15]

It is puzzling to read this comment when it is obvious that both *The Château d'Isaster Tapes* and *A Passion Play* are filled to the brim with humor that elicits at least a snigger or a smirk: the numerous puns and twists of phrase, the scatological humor of "Look at the Animals," the razor-sharp portrayal of a businessman as a tiger in "Law of the Bungle," and of course, the absurd and amusing "The Story of the Hare Who Lost His Spectacles." Some of the music of *A Passion Play* is indeed serious and somber (such as Vocals 1, 8, and 9 and the two reprises of the couplet "There was a rush . . . "), but the rest of the album balances these sections out. As I noted previously, these two daunting works don't sound so daunting because they are so tuneful, with a profusion of melody that enthralls the ear but doesn't overwhelm it.

LIVE VERSION OF *THICK AS A BRICK*

Jethro Tull, like many other progressive bands, thought of their songs as composed pieces of music and faithfully reproduced them live. Even though the band members had opportunities for solo improvisation, and even impromptu comedy bits, they performed *Thick as a Brick* and *A Passion Play* on their respective tours much like they were on the albums. This practice contrasts with other rock bands like Led Zeppelin, the Allman Brothers Band, and the Grateful Dead, who saw some of their songs as having open or elastic forms and used them as vehicles for lengthy solos or group improvisation. The Grateful Dead's twenty-three-minute version of "Dark Star" from *Live/Dead* (1969) and Led Zeppelin's twenty-six-minute version of "Dazed and Confused" (recorded in 1973 and released on 1976's *The Song Remains the Same*) come to mind.

By the time of Jethro Tull's 1972 tour for *Thick as a Brick*, the band's concerts had become quite theatrical. Anderson explains that this theatricality stems from the progression the band made from playing pubs and clubs in the mid to late 1960s to playing theaters by 1969:

> As soon as I discovered theatres, and theatre stages, and [the] proscenium arch, and dressing rooms, and flushing toilets that you didn't have to share with the punters at the Marquee Club, then theatres to me... that was it! I never liked playing the clubs, the booze,... the smoke, the cigarettes. I never liked the clubs, hated pubs. I think that's when I started to discover the idea of "concerts," as opposed to just doing "gigs." I like to create that neutrality of the concert environment where you can shape it the way you want. Places that have too much atmosphere, like the Marquee Club,... you can't do anything to change it. The theatre is neutral. You make of it what you can with lighting and atmosphere and the way you address an audience. That's the blank canvas I've always liked to work with.[16]

Imagine seeing Jethro Tull for the first time during their tour for *Thick as a Brick* in 1972–1973. While the crowd is still mulling about and chatting, a group of roadies dressed in long white jackets check and adjust the instruments onstage. They tear off their jackets, reveal themselves to be the five members of the band, and begin playing. The madcap lead singer, brandishing a flute and wearing a tattered Victorian waistcoat, bounds across the stage looking like he's trying to find his way back to the Dickens novel from which he escaped. Suddenly a telephone on stage rings, and the singer stops the music on a dime to answer it. After listening for a moment, he announces, "Would the gentleman who has left the thoroughbred racehorse parked outside the theatre please remove it, because it's now got in and is fouling the foyer." In the front row a roadie dressed in a jockey outfit jumps up, grabs the saddle in the seat next to him, and frantically runs out of the theater. The band tears back into the music. The electric guitarist and drummer disappear into a tent onstage and emerge a few minutes later wearing each other's clothes. The music rages on but stops again when the keyboard player walks to the center of the stage and reads the current news and weather report. The music rages on again. A giant white rabbit hops across the stage. A gorilla appears, gesticulating madly. The music ends, the band exits the stage, and the lights go out. Again the telephone (which soon became known among fans as the "Tullephone") begins to ring. The singer comes out, picks up the receiver, listens for a moment, holds the receiver out to the audience and mutters laconically, "It's for you." One might expect to see this sort of thing in a music hall performance or on *Monty Python's Flying Circus*, but not at a rock concert.

Jethro Tull's tour for *Thick as a Brick* was truly original, with the band playing the entire song and extending it to over an hour with the integration of surreal comedy bits. Yet they were not the only band putting a theatrical spin on a rock concert in 1972, which, because of this theatricality, has to be counted as one of the strangest years in rock history. Peter Gabriel was donning a fox's head and a red dress for the song "The Musical Box" during Genesis concerts. David Bowie was becoming Ziggy Stardust, a freaky rock star from outer space with orange hair. Alice Cooper was dying many a gruesome onstage death either by the electric chair, the guillotine, or the gallows. While there is ample footage of these artists performing their outlandish antics, alas, there are no recordings or video of a complete live version of *Thick as a Brick* commercially available. There are bootleg recordings and video, and short clips on YouTube, but the sound and picture quality are, for the most part, poor. Andrew Jackson's website Jethro Tull Press includes numerous articles on the concerts written by rock journalists, plus his own detailed description with photographs of a typical performance.[17] Scott Allen Nollen, Greg Russo, and David Rees also have descriptions of the tour in their books. Another way to get a glimpse of these live shows is through personal remembrances. Steve Valdez shared with me his experience hearing *Thick as a Brick* live, and Gilbert Head shared his recollections of *A Passion Play* (see below). Dr. Valdez, a music professor at the University of Georgia, told me in an email:

> The very first rock concert I ever saw was for Jethro Tull promoting *Thick as Brick*. It was on June 22, 1972, at the University of New Mexico basketball arena, better known as "The Pit." This was the summer before my first year at college, and I had barely known Jethro Tull's music. The concert began with a warm-up

band, a British blues band called Head Hands and Feet featuring blues guitarist Albert Lee. They were decent, but the crowd was itching for Tull to get started. HH&F wound it up to an appreciative response and the lights went up. The crowd began to mess around, throwing Frisbees, while the roadies began to readjust the stage. These roadies looked a little different from the roadies earlier. I just figured they were associated with Tull while the others were part of HH&F. At 9:00 the roadies threw off their coats and grabbed their instruments. The lights went off and a spotlight shined on Ian Anderson as he began to pick the acoustic guitar introduction of *Thick as a Brick*. The roadies were actually the band! The crowd went completely wild. As I was at the time unfamiliar with *Thick as a Brick*, I was totally entranced by the long performance. Tull ended up playing this one, continuous musical piece for approximately one hour and fifteen minutes. As I later compared the performance to the album, I realized that for the most part the band had played the song almost exactly as it appeared on the album. The performance was stretched out an extra half hour by the comedic presentation and by the expansions of improvisations within the musical connectors between the songs. I remember especially how entranced the audience was with the final acoustic reprise. The audience remained standing and clapping for around ten minutes, hoping that the band would return for an encore. It was a marvelous, and unexpectedly long, encore. The band played through nearly every song on *Aqualung* and also played a few numbers from both *Benefit* and *Stand Up*. We finally left The Pit sometime after 12:30 a.m. or so, one of the longest concerts I've ever attended. It was hands down the best concert I've ever seen in my life.[18]

Jethro Tull has not performed *Thick as a Brick* in its entirety since the 1973 tour for *A Passion Play* – that is, until the 2012–2013 tour. In April 2012 Anderson embarked on an eighteen-month world tour in which he and his bandmates performed both the original *Thick as a Brick* and the sequel album *Thick as a Brick 2: Whatever Happened to Gerald Bostock?* in their entirety. (This tour is discussed in the epilogue.) From 1973 to 2011 an eight-to-twelve-minute edited version of the song was a staple of their concert repertoire. Examining how the piece has been presented in live concerts reveals the malleable nature of its form, which portions are the most popular, and which transfer the best to live performance. The following section briefly describes five versions of *Thick as a Brick* (four are live recordings and one is a studio recording) from 1978, 1986, 1992, 2001, and 2008, and show how the form of the piece has been altered in various ways. This song has gained a chameleon-like reputation over the years among concert-going fans, sparking a debate about how it will be reshaped each time the band revisits it.

Table 8.2. Form of *Thick as a Brick*, Live at Madison Square Garden 1978 version

SECTION	TIMING	LYRIC
Vocal 1	0:00–3:11	"Really don't mind if you sit this one out..."
Vocal 2	3:11–3:52	"See there! A son is born..."
Instr. 1	3:52–5:02	
Vocal 3 Part 1	5:02–6:09	"The Poet and the painter..."
Instr. 2	6:09–8:22	
Instr. 4	8:22–9:03	
Vocal 5 Part 1	9:03–9:31	"I've come down from the upper class..."
Instr. 5	9:31–10:29	
Instr. 19	10:29–10:54	
Vocal 14	10:54–11:35	"So you ride yourselves..."

MADISON SQUARE GARDEN, NEW YORK, OCTOBER 9, 1978

This is the best live version of *Thick as a Brick* commercially available, performed by most of the band members who originally recorded the song.[19] This version, which lasts eleven and a half minutes, is on the *Jethro Tull: Live at Madison Square Garden 1978* DVD, released in 2009. It is also included as a bonus track on the remastered CD of *Thick as a Brick*, released in 1997 (see table 8.2). Vocal 1 is slightly condensed by leaving off the final A section ("Spin me back down the years..."). Vocal 2 is similar to the album version, but Instr. 1 does not have the organ and electric guitar solos, leaving only the section that introduces Vocal 3. Vocal 3 Part 1 is consistent with the album version, and Instr. 2 contains some amazing interplay between Anderson on flute and Barre on electric guitar. The band skips over Vocal 3 Part 2 and Instr. 3 and jumps right into Instr. 4, which serves as an introduction to Vocal 5. Anderson sings the first two lines of Vocal 5, then plays the flute solo that characterizes Instr. 5. After this, the band leaps over twenty-five minutes of music on the album version and begins playing the $^6_8$ ostinato rhythm in Instr. 19. They leave out the string orchestra interludes, reach a climax on the final three chords of Instr. 19, and end on Vocal 14, with Anderson encouraging the crowd to sing the final word of the song: "brick." The form of *Thick as a Brick* on Jethro Tull's live album *Bursting Out* from 1978 is similar to this version from Madison Square Garden.

Table 8.3. Form of *Thick as a Brick*, live "Out in the Green" Festival version (1986)

SECTION	TIMING	LYRIC
Vocal 1	0:00–2:41	"Really don't mind if you sit this one out..."
Vocal 2	2:41–3:28	"See there! A son is born..."
Vocal 12 Part 3	3:28–4:05	"Let me help you to pick up your dead..."
Instr. 16	4:05–4:31	
Instr. 4	4:31–5:12	
Vocal 5 Part 1	5:12–5:39	"I've come down from the upper class..."
Instr. 5	5:39–6:46	
New music	6:46–8:43	

"OUT IN THE GREEN" FESTIVAL, DINKELSBUHL, GERMANY, JULY 5, 1986

This version is probably the most unusual version the band has ever done. It lasts a little less than nine minutes and is found on the *Jack in the Green* DVD, released in 2008. It was recorded in 1986 in Germany with Anderson, Barre, Dave Pegg on bass, Peter-John Vettese on keyboards, and Doane Perry on drums. Its unusual form is shown in table 8.3. Vocals 1 and 2 are played just as they are from the 1978 Madison Square Garden concert. Then the band starts playing music from near the end of side 2: Vocal 12 Part 3 and Instr. 16. Then they jump back to side 1 and play Instr. 4 and the familiar Vocal 5. Yet, instead of going into Instr. 19 and ending with the expected reprise of Vocal 14, they start playing new music that sounds like an Irish jig, featuring Dave Pegg on bass and Peter-John Vettese on keyboards.

STUDIO VERSION FROM 25TH ANNIVERSARY BOX SET, CD 3: BEACONS BOTTOM TAPES, 1993

This studio version, which lasts nine minutes, was recorded in late 1992 for the four-CD box set celebrating the band's twenty-fifth anniversary in 1993 (see table 8.4). Vocals 1 and 2 and Instr. 1 are very similar to the original version, yet the band ends Instr. 1 early and goes into the jig-like introduction to Vocal 5 at the end of Instr. 4. Anderson sings the first two lines of Vocal 5, then plays the flute solo in Instr. 5. The rumbling ostinato of Instr. 19 and the conclusion in Vocal 14 round out the record-

Table 8.4. Form of *Thick as a Brick*, 25th Anniversary Box Set studio version (1992)

SECTION	TIMING	LYRIC
Vocal 1	0:00–3:15	"Really don't mind if you sit this one out..."
Vocal 2	3:15–3:56	"See there! A son is born..."
Instr. 1	3:56–5:17	
Instr. 4	5:17–6:04	
Vocal 5 Part 1	6:04–6:34	"I've come down from the upper class..."
Instr. 5	6:34–7:48	
Instr. 19	7:48–8:21	
Vocal 14	8:21–9:01	"So you ride yourselves..."

ing. The form of this version is similar to the Madison Square Garden performance, except that Vocal 3 Part 1 ("The Poet and the painter...") and Instr. 2 are left out. This version includes Anderson, Barre, Dave Pegg on bass, Andy Giddings on keyboards, and Doane Perry on drums.

HAMMERSMITH APOLLO THEATRE, LONDON, NOVEMBER 25, 2001, AND AVO SESSION BASEL, SWITZERLAND, NOVEMBER 15, 2008

These final two performances are included on the *Living with the Past* DVD, released in 2002, and the *Live at AVO Session Basel* DVD released in 2009. The form of these renditions of *Thick as a Brick* are the same as the studio version from 1992 (table 8.4), implying that the form remained the same from the 1990s through the 2000s. With his penchant for mock melodrama and stage banter, Anderson introduces the song on the *Living with the Past* DVD by saying:

> We've been everything to everybody. We started off as being a little old blues band, and then became a blues-rock band, a classic rock band, a folk rock band, art rock band, even a progressive rock band. Back in '72, '73 we were just for a little while a progressive rock band who made [waving his arms and raising his voice] concept albums! Don't worry, we're not going to do that to you tonight... well, maybe just for eight minutes and fifty-four seconds... which is going to seem like a bloody hour and three quarters.[20]

When Jethro Tull has played *Thick as a Brick* live, Vocals 1, 2, 5, and the reprise of Vocal 14 are almost always present. Vocal 1 is one of the best-known Jethro Tull "singles," even though it was never released as one, so it is instantly recognized by audiences once Anderson starts to play the acoustic introduction. Vocal 2 is heavy, fast, and intense and comes off well in a live setting. Vocal 5 was included on Jethro Tull's second greatest hits album, *Repeat*, so it is also a well-known passage. Of the instrumental passages, Instrs. 1, 4, and 5 are usually included, since they give opportunities for electric guitar, organ, and flute solos. So, in summary, the edited versions of *Thick as a Brick* present its most identifiable sections, allow ample time for soloing, and give an impression of its large-scale form with the reprise of Vocal 14 at the end. These live versions are still substantial musical creations, even though they present less than one-fourth of the music from the original version.

LIVE VERSION OF *A PASSION PLAY*

During the *Thick as a Brick* tour, the band found that they were able – for the most part – to keep the audience's attention throughout forty-three minutes of new music, a telephone ringing, a gorilla rambling across the stage, and a weather report. For the *A Passion Play* tour, they were keen on stretching the boundaries of a rock concert even further, creating a stage performance that was the most complex and challenging the band had yet attempted. Not only did they perform the *A Passion Play* album (over forty minutes of new and extremely difficult music), but they also produced an elaborate film to accompany "The Story of the Hare Who Lost His Spectacles" and showed short films at the beginning and end of the music. While such multimedia spectacles are common today, they were still novel in the early 1970s. On the creation of the film for "The Story of the Hare Who Lost His Spectacles" Anderson says:

> On the record there was a piece of totally programmed synthesizer music and when it came to doing that live on stage it was a bit soft, just having a two-minute gap of totally electronic music.[21] If we mime to it that's cheating, and if we try to play it live it'll be a disaster because it's impossible to play live. And yet we couldn't just leave it out because then we wouldn't be playing the "whole thing" on stage, which we very much wanted to do. So what we did was make a film: we wrote a little thing around "The Story of the Hare Who Lost His Spectacles" and the synthesizer music which was front and back ... and filmed that at enormous expense. Even back then it was a lot of money: a day's shooting with three camera crew, 35 mm, the real thing; catering trucks, unions, 6 o'clock calls, mobile dressing rooms ... it was about £12,000 for a one-day shoot.[22]

The film that the band made for "The Story of the Hare Who Lost His Spectacles" is superb and silly, a perfect respite from the difficult music. It is clever and engaging and makes connections between the album concept, ballet, and the lyrics to "The Story of the Hare." The film can be found on the DVD *A New Day Yesterday: The 25th Anniversary Collection* (2003), the remastered CD of *A Passion Play* (2003), and on YouTube.[23] More recently, Ian Anderson narrated the story at his concerts in the fall of 2010 with John O'Hara accompanying on keyboard. A video of this was made by an audience member at a concert in Peekskill, New York, on October 19, 2010, and can be seen on YouTube.[24]

As if presenting an extremely long and difficult piece of new music with an accompanying film were not enough, Jethro Tull then played *Thick as a Brick* in its entirety. After *A Passion Play* was over, almost an hour into the show, Anderson would slyly announce "and now for our second number . . . " Gilbert Head attended his first Jethro Tull concert at the Mid-South Coliseum in Memphis, Tennessee, on May 27, 1973.[25] He vividly recalls hearing both pieces played back-to-back:

> With regard to that show, it was begun with a darkened hall into which the sound of a heartbeat was pumped; gradually, synched up with the pulse was an increasingly larger spot of light thrown onto an onstage screen. This pulse gradually began to boom in the SRO hall, then gave way to a short film of a ballerina coming to life, and then immediately to the whole band on a fully lit stage launching headlong into *A Passion Play*. As I did not own the record prior to the concert, I cannot report as to the fidelity with which the performance matched the vinyl, but I can report that there were varying pieces of stagecraft, including a parade involving a fellow in a yellow slicker (not a "jet black mac," sadly . . .). At the close of *A Passion Play*, I recall a pretty seamless segue into *Thick as a Brick*. Now this, which I did already own, was a pretty faithful recreation of the music on the disc, including the fade down/fade up transition that marked the side one/side two switch on the disc. I greatly enjoyed singing along, as did a sizeable portion of the crowd, who much more enthusiastically embraced this (and the subsequent *Aqualung* and *Benefit* songs which followed) than they did *A Passion Play*. Mostly, the reception for *A Passion Play* was polite confusion, giving way to the sort of restless impatience you can sense more than actually note in its specifics, all of which was obliterated in the cacophony which greeted the opening bars of *Thick as a Brick*. Then, too, the deeper we got into the Memphis show, the harder it was to see the stage clearly, as the cannabis sativa fog rolled forth like a San Francisco tide or an evening on the moors.[26]

Despite all the time and effort put into the show, most of the reviews of the *A Passion Play* concerts by rock journalists were disappointing. This would not be surprising for the U.S. shows before July 23, the day the album was released, since the audiences would have been unfamiliar with the album. Yet even after the album was released – and went to number one – the bad concert reviews still rolled in. Anderson speculated that the critics were already predisposed to dislike the show because most of them disliked the album. Whether it was because the critics and the audience were not willing to have their rock concert expectations meddled with, or because the band executed their ideas poorly, the show did not dazzle as it could have. A major criticism by the musical press was the confusion the band caused as to when the concert actually began. Anderson explains, with unrestrained glee, how the band used both film and sound to toy with the audience as they entered the venue:

> We opened the *Passion Play* with a little bit of movie which I shot with a high-speed camera: the ballet dancer being dead, in the position of the album cover, and slowly getting up in slow motion. It was rather elaborate and rather difficult to do because the movie screen had to be lowered from above the stage. It was *not* part of the show, it was part of what was happening when the audience walked into the hall, took their seats, talked to their mates, when what appeared to be still on the screen came up, and a subsonic pulse began [i.e., the heartbeat]. And it gradually went up in pitch, so it became noticeable at a low level and gradually built up as the [ballet dancer] started to move. I used to watch that every night... to see if I could spot the first person in the audience who said: "She's moving!" And nobody knew when the show began, and I thought it was great. So there was an opening piece of film, the piece of film in the middle, and then a little bit at the end, so the whole thing (I thought) made quite a nice stage presentation. And that irritated some people because they don't like to be ...confused.[27]

Unfortunately like the *Thick as a Brick* tour, there is no high-quality footage of any of the concerts from the *A Passion Play* tour. According to Jethro Tull collector "TullTapes," the best quality audio that has been found to date is from the July 23, 1973, concert at the Oakland Coliseum, while the best video is from the August 28–29, 1973, concerts at Madison Square Garden. TullTapes has synched the audio from Oakland with the video from both Oakland and Madison Square Garden, giving the best possible impression of the concert experience.[28]

Conclusions

IN THE LINER NOTES FROM THE 1988 COMPILATION *20 YEARS OF Jethro Tull,* David Rees and Martin Webb encapsulate the band's career in a way that is difficult to improve upon:

> If ever there was a band beset by paradox, Jethro Tull is it. In a medium where gimmicks are the norm, the group's success has always come from the music itself – and yet, in the wild-eyed, one-legged flute player, Ian Anderson has created one of the strongest images in the rock world.
>
> The content of the music is intelligent, analytical, even cerebral – and yet there is a constant thread of self-depreciating and often vulgar humor running through every album and stage presentation.
>
> Over the years, Jethro Tull has become ever more eclectic, drawing on all kinds of musical sources, from jazz and blues to folk and classical – and yet, their music has an instantly recognizable identity.
>
> They are often written off by a fickle music press as "Too Old to Rock 'n' Roll" – yet each new album and tour produces a new generation of fans.
>
> They maintain a very low media profile – yet all over the world their concerts sell out.
>
> Whatever the paradoxes, the ultimate reason for their success over the last 20 [now 45] years is their music. It's evolved and progressed, it's never stood still, and it's always been superb.[1]

Thick as a Brick and *A Passion Play* are among the most original, and bizarre, rock albums from the late 1960s and early 1970s, an era that had its fair share of musical curiosities by the likes of Frank Zappa, Miles Davis, Pink Floyd, the Doors, King Crimson, and the Beatles. How are these two albums unique and inventive among the multiplicity of approaches to the medium that came out in this period? To begin with, they were the first rock albums that consisted of one continuous song. Second, their forms are unique, blending vocal music and instrumental music in equal measures, and even resembling older classical forms such as the medieval *lai* and late Romantic-era symphonic poem. Third, their packaging was as expansive and entertaining as the music. Fourth, they achieved mainstream success while being esoteric and uncompromisingly complex.

Because they are both highbrow and lowbrow at the same time, these two albums raise interesting questions about experimental and mainstream music. How can albums that consist of forty-minute-plus songs, with no successful singles to help promote them, reach number one on the pop chart? Were listeners truly interested in such long songs, or was it just the novelty that attracted people to the albums? What does it take to get a mainstream popular music audience interested in listening to a large-scale piece of music? The two albums succeed as long songs because they present a large amount of continually new musical material yet also contain just enough repetition and thematic development to prevent them from sounding incoherent, or as if they were wandering aimlessly. This balance of new musical material, repetition, and thematic development in both lyrics and music was a hallmark of the progressive rock style and created an audience, even a mainstream popular audience, that appreciated large-scale pieces of music.

Progressive rock scholars such as Edward Macan, Kevin Holm-Hudson, John Covach, and Allan Moore have brought new attention in the musicological community to progressive rock in the last two decades. One can find scholarly, book-length studies and numerous journal articles on Yes, Genesis, King Crimson, and Emerson, Lake & Palmer. Yet Jethro Tull, who was just as innovative and significant as these bands, has received less attention. There has been a fair share of biographies of the band written by fans and rock journalists, but few scholars besides Allan Moore have delved deeply into Jethro Tull's music in order to delineate their characteristic style. I hope this book will spur more musicological interest in this band and their fascinating music.

What does the future hold for Ian Anderson and Jethro Tull? Is Ian Anderson, who will be sixty-six in 2013, past his prime? One of the themes of *Thick as a Brick*, and indeed the primary theme of *Thick as a Brick 2: Whatever Happened to Gerald Bostock?* is the harsh reality of encroaching old age. This is a subject that Anderson has addressed often in his career. For the cover of Jethro Tull's first album, *This Was,* the band members – then in their early twenties – dressed up as old men. The concept album *Too Old to Rock 'n' Roll, Too Young to Die!* tells the story of an aging rocker who has passed his prime yet becomes popular again with the next generation of fans. In the 1990 song "I Don't Want to Be Me," the protagonist decides to give up his career as a traveling musician and take on "the simple life." But he stops and ponders "maybe I'm not done yet." In "The Dog-Ear Years" from *J-Tull Dot Com* (1999), Anderson refers to himself as "vintage and classic, or just plain Jurassic." In several interviews he has questioned when he should retire and has admitted that rock musicians often extend their careers far past their primes. On the one hand, Anderson's voice has deteriorated and he is less dynamic onstage as he was in the 1970s. On the other hand, his songwriting and his flute and guitar playing have continued to improve and expand. The continual lineup changes and the way certain band members have been "let go" are disappointing, yet each new player sustains the high musical standards of the band and brings new talents to the mix. Judging from *Thick as a Brick 2* and the live shows in 2012–2013, most of Anderson's talents remain undiminished, and he appears to have many fruitful years ahead of him.

Epilogue: Whatever Happened to Gerald Bostock?

ON FEBRUARY 1, 2012, ON THE OFFICIAL JETHRO TULL WEBSITE, Ian Anderson announced something as unexpected as *Thick as a Brick* and *A Passion Play* hitting number one on the *Billboard* chart: he had written and recorded a sequel to *Thick as a Brick*. The new album recounts the further possible adventures of Gerald "Little Milton" Bostock, the fictional boy genius and supposed author of the *Thick as a Brick* lyrics. Titled *Thick as a Brick 2: Whatever Happened to Gerald Bostock?* it was released on April 2, 2012, forty years and three weeks after the original album. Of the concept, Anderson writes:

> The theme of this anniversary 'part two' album is to examine the possible different paths that the precocious young schoolboy, Gerald Bostock, might have taken later in life. Not just for Gerald but to echo how our own lives develop, change direction and ultimately conclude through chance encounters and interventions, however tiny and insignificant they might seem at the time. The imagination-filled process of thinking how things might have turned out for the young and older Gerald kept me fascinated.[1]

In addition to the album, Anderson conceived a new "online edition" of the *St. Cleve Chronicle* (called www.StCleve.com), full of more stories about the quaint and quirky denizens of St. Cleve and neighboring Linwell and Little Cruddock. In yet another strange twist, he reported that the fictional Gerald Bostock (who appears on the front cover of *Thick as a Brick*) is alive and well and living in England. Anderson even provided links to Bostock's Facebook page and Twitter account on Jethro Tull's website.

How did this unlikely project come about? Anderson was approached by Mike Andrews and Royston Eldridge, who designed the newspaper for *Thick as a Brick,* about doing a follow-up to the album. Anderson was skeptical about the suggestion until Derek Shulman, a record producer and founding member of progressive rock band Gentle Giant, approached him with the same idea. Just as he did with the writing of *Thick as a Brick* and *A Passion Play,* Anderson churned out most of the lyrics and music of *Thick as a Brick 2* in an astonishingly short period of time, two or three weeks. The audacity of revisiting one of the oddest concept albums in rock music was not lost on Anderson, who wrote: "It was a little daunting to consider the impact – or perhaps lack of – which this release might have on old and new fans alike but I eventually decided that I would embark on this for my own benefit and enjoyment rather than trying to please anyone else."[2]

There are many musical links, both obvious and subtle, between *Thick as a Brick* and *Thick as a Brick 2.* First, several musical themes in TAAB reappear in altered forms in TAAB2, such as the three-chord riff in Instr. 10 (heard at the beginning of TAAB2) and the organ theme of Vocal 5 (refashioned in "Old School Song"). Another example is the main flute melody from Vocal 1 of TAAB (shown in example 4.1), which appears in TAAB2's "From a Pebble Thrown," played by Florian Opahle on electric guitar at 2:05 and 2:40. But there is more to this musical allusion. John O'Hara on accordion and organ surreptitiously plays the melody heard in the second verse of Vocal 1 (shown in example 4.2) underneath Ophale. Thus, the two predominant instrumental melodies in Vocal 1 of TAAB are played simultaneously in "From a Pebble Thrown." The most obvious link between the two albums is the Vocal 1 refrain ("So you ride yourselves . . . "), which brings both TAAB and TAAB2 to a conclusion. Another type of musical tie between the two albums is the instrumentation. The instrumentation of TAAB is closely replicated on TAAB2, with ample use of the Hammond organ, glockenspiel, and harpsichord. Overall, a discerning listener can spot dozens of lyrical, melodic, textural, and instrumental allusions to Jethro Tull songs from the past. For example, in "Swing It Far," John O'Hara plays the celesta, a keyboard instrument not heard in a Jethro Tull song since "Just Trying to Be" and "Wond'ring Again" from 1972's *Living in the Past.*

Like *Thick as a Brick,* the sequel album is one continuous piece of music. Yet there is less transitional material between the seventeen sections, making them feel more like "songs." *Thick as a Brick* 2 has a separate title and cue for each track; this is to accommodate contemporary listening habits, where downloading single tracks to a MP3 player is more popular than purchasing an entire album. Anderson says:

> I think it would be unreasonable of me to expect to have it a completely unbroken piece of music, available on iTunes or a CD in your car and not have any ID points to be able to listen to bits again. We need to accept that people have a different cultural way of absorbing entertainment and the arts. People snack on the arts these days; they don't banquet like they might have done 15 years ago. And I can understand that because I do the same. I feel a bit naughty about it, but nonetheless, there are some bits of Beethoven's "Ninth Symphony" I'm going to want to hear every time and some bits I can do without more than once every couple years.[3]

In April 2012 Anderson began an eighteen-month world tour, performing both the original *Thick as a Brick* and the sequel album in their entirety. The band consisted of Anderson, David Goodier (bass guitar, double bass), John O'Hara (piano, keyboards, accordion), Florian Opahle (electric and acoustic guitars), and Scott Hammond (drums and percussion). The tour also featured Ryan O'Donnell, who acted the part of Bostock, did a fair imitation of a younger Ian Anderson, and sang sections of both pieces to give Anderson's voice a break. The original *Thick as a Brick* studio recording had several vocal passages with flute overdubs, creating difficulties over the years in presenting the music in concert. Ryan's singing solved this problem, allowing Anderson to play all the flute parts on the album. When asked if the band was still called Jethro Tull, Anderson left the matter vague, calling the affair "Jethro Tull's Ian Anderson." He did say in an interview: "I don't think it would be appropriate if I went out under the name Ian Anderson to expect Martin Barre to just be one of the musicians."[4] He also mentioned in several interviews that whenever the band tours as Jethro Tull, the audience expects them to play many of the favorite hits such as "Aqualung," "Locomotive Breath," and "Living in the Past." Billing the show as "Jethro Tull's Ian Anderson" gave him more freedom to devise something new and unexpected, such as a theatrical performance of two hour-long songs. The concerts briefly revived many of the absurd escapades and sight gags of the original 1972 performances while adding new video bits and O'Donnell's acting. The lighting, stage props, video, and spoken-word passages were all integrated with the music to create a captivating audio/video presentation. Although Anderson stressed at the beginning of the tour that the band would perform only *Thick as a Brick* and *Thick as a Brick 2* with no encore, he changed his mind later on and the band encored with "Locomotive Breath" and sometimes "Aqualung." The tour was a great success and showed Anderson's ability to take risks and push his talents in innovative directions yet provide just enough of the "oldies" to please the fans.

In November 2012 the celebration of the fortieth anniversary of *Thick as a Brick* continued with the release of a sonically improved collector's edition of the album. This two-disc set contained a CD with a new stereo mix and an audio DVD with more new mixes (5.1 DTS and Dolby Digital, 96 kHz/24-bit stereo, and a flat transfer of the 1972 stereo mix). These remixes were done by Steven Wilson, English musician/producer/sound engineer and leader of Porcupine Tree, who did the same for the *Aqualung* fortieth anniversary collector's edition (2011). Wilson worked with the original master tapes, something that was not done with the 1997 remastered edition. Anderson explains the difference between a remix and a remaster this way: "A 'remix' is not the same as a 're-master.' Remixing involves going back to the original studio multi-track masters and balancing and perfecting the sound on all the individual instrumental and vocal tracks and creating from them a new stereo or 5.1 surround master. Re-mastering is just the cleaning up and making a new copy of the original stereo master."[5] The 2012 remix is a feast for the ears. Even though the original LP recording and 1997 remaster were already superb, the new remix greatly enhances both the overall sound and the individual timbres of the instruments: the crispness of Anderson's acoustic guitar, the multiple textures of Evans's Hammond organ, the variety of sounds Barlow gets from his ride and crash cymbals, the presence of Anderson's double-tracked voice. The two-disc set came packaged with a 104-page hardback book that also duplicated in miniature the newspaper of the original album.

Also released was a box set of vinyl LP versions of both *Thick as a Brick* and *Thick as a Brick 2*, remixed by Wilson at 96 kHz/24-bit stereo. It included a 72-page book with a replication of the original *TAAB* newspaper, a similar newspaper for *TAAB2*, the lyrics in several translations, and interviews with band members and others associated with the group.

This release gives the listener both the expansive packaging of the 1972 album and the crystal-clear sound of the 2012 remix.

So how does *Thick as a Brick 2* stand up to the original album? Is the sequel a worthy successor to the masterwork? Indeed, it is. The lyrics to *Thick as a Brick 2* have all the quaint quirkiness of the original and are easier to follow, since they contain a coherent narrative: five possible life paths for Gerald Bostock (banker, homeless person, military man, corrupt pastor, and ordinary man). The lyrics to the original album have a certain mystery and fascination, but they come across mostly as perplexing and keep the listener at a bit of a distance. What about the packaging? On the original album, the small village English culture of the *St. Cleve Chronicle* (explored in chapter 3) gives the album its peculiar charm. Yet this is conveyed primarily in the newspaper articles and ads rather than in the lyrics. With the sequel album, one gets a strong sense of hamlet culture in both the packaging (the online newspaper) and lyrics, and the connection between them is stronger. What about the music? *Thick as a Brick 2* has compositional depth, expansive instrumentation, virtuoso musicianship, and skillful integration of introspective folk passages and boisterous rock passages, but it can't match the audacity and originality of the 1972 album.

APPENDIX ONE

The Complete Lyrics to *Thick as a Brick*

The lyrics are shown with regularized scansion, rhyme schemes, timings, and approximate song forms.

"Thick as a Brick"
Words and Music by Ian Anderson.
Copyright ©1976 Chrysalis Music Ltd.
Copyright Renewed.
All Rights for the U.S. and Canada Administered by Chrysalis Music.
All Rights Reserved. Used by Permission.
Reprinted by Permission of Hal Leonard Corporation.

SIDE 1

Vocal 1 : AABA (last "A" section is altered) (0:00–3:01)

Really don't mind if you sit this one out.	a
My words but a whisper – your deafness a SHOUT.	a
I may make you feel but I can't make you think.	b
Your sperm's in the gutter – your love's in the sink.	b
So you ride yourselves over the fields	c
And you make all your animal deals	c
And your wise men don't know how it feels	c
To be thick as a brick.	d
And the sand-castle virtues are all swept away	e
In the tidal destruction the moral melee.	e
The elastic retreat rings the close of play	e
As the last wave uncovers the newfangled way.	e

But your new shoes are worn at the heels	c
And your suntan does rapidly peel	c
And your wise men don't know how it feels	c
To be thick as a brick.	d

And the love that I feel is so far away:	e
I'm a bad dream that I just had today –	e
And you shake your head and say it's a shame.	f

Spin me back down the years and the days of my youth.	g
Draw the lace and black curtains and shut out the whole truth.	g
Spin me down the long ages: let them sing the song.	h

Vocal 2 : through-composed (3:01–3:36)

See there! A son is born –	a
And we pronounce him fit to fight.	b
There are black-heads on his shoulders,	c
And he pees himself in the night.	b

We'll make a man of him	d
Put him to a trade	e
Teach him to play Monopoly	f
And how to sing in the rain.	e

Instrumental passage 1 (3:36–6:08)

Vocal 3 Part 1 : verse-chorus (6:08–7:15)

The Poet and the painter casting shadows on the water –	a
As the sun plays on the infantry returning from the sea.	b
The do-er and the thinker: no allowance for the other –	a
As the failing light illuminates the mercenary's creed.	b

The home fire burning: the kettle almost boiling –	c
But the master of the house is far away.	d
The horses stamping – their warm breath clouding	c
In the sharp and frosty morning of the day.	d

And the poet lifts his pen while the soldier sheaths his sword.	e

And the youngest of the family	f

Is moving with authority.	f
Building castles by the sea,	f
He dares the tardy tide	g
To wash them all aside.	g

Instrumental passage 2 (7:15–9:20)

Vocal 3 Part 2 : verse-chorus (9:20–10:30)

The cattle quietly grazing at the grass down by the river	a
Where the swelling mountain water moves onward to the sea:	b
The builder of the castles renews the age-old purpose	c
And contemplates the milking girl whose offer is his need.	b
The young men of the household have all gone into service	c
And are not to be expected for a year.	d
The innocent young master – thoughts moving ever faster –	e
Has formed the plan to change the man he seems.	f
And the poet sheaths his pen while the soldier lifts his sword.	g
And the oldest of the family	h
Is moving with authority.	h
Coming from across the sea,	h
He challenges the son	i
Who puts him to the run.	i

Instrumental passage 3 (10:30–11:19)

Vocal 4 : through-composed (11:19–11:52)

What do you do when the old man's gone –	a
Do you want to be him?	b
And your real self sings the song.	a
Do you want to free him?	b
No one to help you get up steam –	c
and the whirlpool turns you 'way off-beam.	c

Instrumental passage 4 (11:52–13:16)

Vocal 5 Part 1 : strophic (13:16–14:13)

LATER.

I've come down from the upper class to mend your rotten ways.	a
My father was a man-of-power whom everyone obeyed.	a
So come on all you criminals! I've got to put you straight	b
Just like I did with my old man – twenty years too late.	b

Instrumental passage 5 (14:13–15:26)

Vocal 5 Part 2 : strophic (15:26–15:54)

Your bread and water's going cold. Your hair is short and neat.	c
I'll judge you all and make damn sure that no-one judges me.	c

Instrumental passage 6 (15:54–16:35)

Vocal 6 : through-composed (16:35–17:06)

You curl your toes in fun	a
As you smile at everyone –	a
You meet the stares.	b
You're unaware	b
That your doings aren't done.	a
And you laugh most ruthlessly	c
As you tell us what not to be.	c
But how are we	d
Supposed to see	d
Where we should run?	a

Instrumental passage 7 (17:06–17:41)

Vocal 7 Part 1 : 1st "A" of AABA (17:41–18:08)

I see you shuffle in the courtroom	a
With your rings upon your fingers	b
And your downy little sidies	c
And your silver-buckle shoes	d
Playing at the hard-case,	e
You follow the example	f

Of the comic-paper idol	g
Who lets you bend the rules.	d

Instrumental passage 8 (18:08–18:39)

Vocal 7 Part 2 : 2nd "A" of AABA (18:39–19:06)
So!	
Come on ye childhood heroes!	a
Won't you rise up from the pages	b
Of your comic-books? your super-crooks	c
And show us all the way.	b
Well! Make your will and testament.	d
Won't you? Join your local government.	d
We'll have superman for president	d
Let Robin save the day.	b

Vocal 7 Part 3 : "B" of AABA (19:06–19:29)
You put your bet on number one and it comes up every time.	a
The other kids have all backed down and they put you first in line.	a
And so you finally ask yourself just how big you are –	b
And you take your place in a wiser world of bigger motor cars.	b
And you wonder who to call on.	c

Instrumental passage 9 (19:29–20:00)

Vocal 7 Part 4 : last "A" of AABA (20:00–20:25)
So! Where the hell was Biggles	a
When you needed Him last Saturday?	b
And where are all the Sportsmen	c
Who always pulled you through?	d
They're all resting down in Cornwall –	e
Writing up their memoirs	f
For a paper-back edition	g
Of the Boy Scout Manual.	h

Instrumental passage 10 (20:25–22:43) side 1, (0:00–0:48) side 2

SIDE 2

Vocal 8 : through-composed (0:48–1:24)
LATER.
See there! A man is born –   a
And we pronounce him fit for peace.   b
There's a load lifted from his shoulders   c
With the discovery of his disease.   b

We'll take the child from him   d
Put it to the test   e
Teach it to be a wise man   f
How to fool the rest.   e

Instrumental passage 11 (with spoken-word passages) (1:24–4:04)

QUOTE
We will be geared toward the average rather than the exceptional
God is an overwhelming responsibility
We walked through the maternity ward and saw 218 babies wearing nylons
Cats are on the upgrade
Upgrade?
Hipgrave.
Oh, Mac.[1]

Vocal 9 : strophic (4:04–5:12)
LATER
In the clear white circles of morning wonder,   a
I take my place with the lord of the hills.   b
And the blue-eyed soldiers stand slightly discoloured   c
(In neat little rows) sporting canvas frills.   b

With their jock-straps pinching, they slouch to attention,   d
While queueing for sarnies at the office canteen.   e
Saying – how's your grannie and good old Ernie: f
He coughed up a tenner on a premium bond win.   e

Instrumental passage 12 (5:12–5:59)

Vocal 10 : through-composed (5:59–6:29)

The legends (worded in	a
The ancient tribal hymn)	a
Lie cradled in the seagull's call.	b
And all the promises they made are ground beneath the sadist's fall.	b

Vocal 11 : strophic (6:29–10:57)

The poet and the wise man stand behind the gun,	a
And signal for the crack of dawn.	a
Light the sun.	a
Do you believe in the day?	b
Do you? Believe in the day!	b
The Dawn Creation of the Kings has begun.	a
Soft Venus (lonely maiden) brings	c
The ageless one.	a
Do you believe in the day?	b
The fading hero has returned to the night –	d
And fully pregnant with the day,	b
Wise men endorse the poet's sight.	d
Do you believe in the day?	b
Do you? Believe in the day!	b

Instrumental passage 13 (10:57–13:11)

Vocal 12 Part 1 : 1st verse of verse-chorus (13:11–13:47)

Let me tell you the tales of your life	a
Of the cut and the thrust of the knife[2]	a
The tireless oppression	b
The wisdom instilled	c
The desire to kill or be killed.	c
Let me sing of the losers who lie	a
In the street as the last bus goes by.	a
The pavements are empty:	d
The gutters run red –	e
While the fool toasts his god in the sky.	a

Instrumental passage 14 (13:47–14:49)

Vocal 12 Part 2 : 1st chorus of verse-chorus (14:49–15:03)

So come all ye young men who are building castles!	a
Kindly state the time of the year	b
And join your voices in a hellish chorus.	c
Mark the precise nature of your fear.	b

Instrumental passage 15 (15:03–16:07)

Vocal 12 Part 3 : 2nd verse of verse-chorus (16:07–16:43)

Let me help you pick up your dead	a
As the sins of the father are fed	a
With the blood of the fools	b
And the thoughts of the wise	c
And from the pan under your bed.	a
Let me make you a present of song	d
As the wise man breaks wind and is gone	d
While the fool with the hour-glass	e
Is cooking his goose	f
And the nursery rhyme winds along.	d

Instrumental passage 16 (16:43–17:13)

Vocal 12 Part 4 : 2nd chorus of verse-chorus (17:13–17:44)

So! Come all ye young men who are building castles!	a
Kindly state the time of the year	b
And join your voices in a hellish chorus.	c
Mark the precise nature of your fear.	b
See! The summer lightning casts its bolts upon you	d
And the hour of judgement draweth near.	b
Would you be the fool stood in his suit of armour	e
Or the wiser man who rushes clear.	b

Instrumental passage 17 (17:44–18:08)

Vocal 13 Part 1 : (same music and lyrics as Vocal 7 Part 2) (18:08–18:31)

So! Come on ye childhood heroes!	a
Won't you rise up from the pages	b
Of your comic-books? your super-crooks	c
And show us all the way.	b
Well! Make your will and testament.	d
Won't you? Join your local government.	d
We'll have superman for president	d
Let Robin save the day.	b

Instrumental passage 18 (18:31–18:52)

Vocal 13 Part 2 : (same music and lyrics as Vocal 7 Part 4) (18:52–19:21)

So! Where the hell was Biggles	a
When you needed Him last Saturday?	b
And where are all the Sportsmen	c
Who always pulled you through?	d
They're all resting down in Cornwall –	e
Writing up their memoirs	f
For a paper-back edition	g
Of the Boy Scout Manual.	h

Instrumental passage 19 (19:21–20:26)

Vocal 14 : (same music and lyrics as lines 5–8 of Vocal 1) (20:26–20:54)

OF COURSE

So you ride yourselves over the fields	a
And you make all your animal deals	a
And your wise men don't know how it feels	a
To be thick as a brick.	b

APPENDIX TWO

The Complete Lyrics to *A Passion Play*

The lyrics are shown with regularized scansion, timings, and approximate song forms.

"Passion Play"
Words and Music by Ian Anderson.
Copyright ©1973 Chrysalis Music Ltd.
Copyright Renewed.
All Rights for the U.S. and Canada Administered by Chrysalis Music.
All Rights Reserved. Used by Permission.
Reprinted by Permission of Hal Leonard Corporation.

SIDE 1

Instrumental passage 1 (0:00–3:28)

Vocal 1 Part 1 : strophic (3:28–4:36)
"Do you still see me even here?"
(The silver cord lies on the ground.)
"And so I'm dead," the young man said –
Over the hill (not a wish away).

My friends (as one) all stand aligned,
Although their taxis came too late.
There was a rush along the Fulham Road.
There was a hush in the Passion Play.

Vocal 1 Part 2 : strophic/through-composed (4:36–5:52)
Such a sense of glowing in the aftermath
Ripe with rich attainments all imagined
Sad misdeeds in disarray
The sore thumb screams aloud,
Echoing out of the Passion Play.

All the old familiar choruses come crowding in a different key:
Melodies decaying in sweet dissonance.
There was a rush along the Fulham Road
Into the Ever-passion Play.

Instrumental passage 2 (5:52–6:50)

Vocal 1 Part 3 : strophic (6:50–7:55)
And who comes here to wish me well?
A sweetly-scented angel fell.
She laid her head upon my disbelief
And bathed me with her ever-smile.

And with a howl across the sand
I go escorted by a band
Of gentlemen in leather bound –
NO-ONE (but someone to be found).

Instrumental passage 3 (7:55–9:06)

Vocal 2 : strophic (9:06–10:30)
All along the icy wastes there are faces smiling in the gloom.
Roll up roll down, feeling unwound?
Step into the viewing room.
The cameras were all around.
We've got you taped – you're in the play.

Here's your I.D. (Ideal for identifying one and all.)
Invest your life in the memory bank –
Ours the interest and we thank you.

The ice-cream lady wet her drawers,
To see you in the Passion Play:

Instrumental passage 4 (10:30–13:00)

Vocal 3 : through-composed (13:00–13:26)
Take the prize for instant pleasure
Captain of the cricket team
Public speaking in all weathers
A knighthood from a queen.

Vocal 4 : strophic (13:26–14:51)
All of your best friends' telephones never cooled
    from the heat of your hand.
There's a line in a front-page story, 13 horses that also-ran.
Climb in your old umbrella. Does it have a nasty tear in the dome?
But the rain only gets in sometimes and the sun never leaves you alone.

Instrumental passage 5 (14:51–15:41)

Vocal 5 Part 1 : strophic/through-composed (15:41–17:09)
Lover of the black and white – it's your first night.
The Passion Play goes all the way, spoils your insight.
Tell me, how the baby's made, how the lady's laid,
Why the old dog howls in sadness.

And your little sister's immaculate virginity wings away
On the bony shoulder of a young horse named George
Who stole surreptitiously into her geography revision.
(The examining body examined her body.)

Actor of the low-high Q, let's hear your view.
Peek at the lines upon your sleeve since your memory won't do.
Tell me, how the baby's graded, why the lady's faded,
Why the old dog howls with madness.

Instrumental passage 6 (17:09–17:58)

Vocal 5 Part 2 : reprise of the music of Vocal 2 (17:58–18:47)
All of this and some of that's the only way to skin the cat.
And now you've lost a skin or two –
Where you're for us and we for you.
The dressing room is right behind.
We've got you taped – you're in the play.
How does it feel to be in the play?
How does it feel to play the play?
How does it feel to be the play?[1]

Vocal 5 Part 3 : strophic/through-composed (18:47–19:33)
Man of passion rise again, we won't cross you out –
For we do love you like a son – of that there's no doubt.
Tell us, is it you who is here for our good cheer?
Or are we here for the glory, for the story, for the gory satisfaction
Of telling you how absolutely awful you really are.

Instrumental passage 7 (19:33–20:01)

Vocal 6 : reprise of lines 7–8 from Vocal 1 Part 1 (20:01–20:22)
There was a rush along the Fulham Road.
There was a hush in the Passion Play.

Instrumental passage 8 (20:22–21:36)

SIDE 2[2]

Vocal 7 : through-composed (0:00–4:19)
THE STORY OF THE HARE WHO LOST HIS SPECTACLES
This is the story of the hare who lost his spectacles.

Owl loved to rest quietly whilst no one was watching.
Sitting on a fence one day, he was surprised when
    suddenly a kangaroo ran close by.
Now this may not seem strange, but when Owl overheard Kangaroo
Whisper to no one in particular,

"The hare has lost his spectacles," well, he began to wonder.
Presently, the moon appeared from behind a cloud
    and there, lying on the grass, was Hare.
In the stream that flowed by the grass – a newt
And sitting astride a twig of a bush – a bee.

Ostensibly motionless, the hare was trembling with excitement,
For without his spectacles he appeared completely helpless.
Where were his spectacles? Could someone have stolen them?
Had he mislaid them? What was he to do?

Bee wanted to help, and thinking he had the answer began:
"You probably ate them thinking they were a carrot."
"No!" interrupted Owl, who was wise.
"I have good eye-sight, insight, and foresight.
How could an intelligent hare make such a silly mistake?"
But all the time Owl had been sitting on the fence, scowling!

Kangaroo were hopping mad at this sort of talk.
She thought herself far superior in intelligence to the others.
She was their leader; their guru. She had the answer:
"Hare, you must go in search of the optician."
But then she realized that Hare were completely
    helpless without his spectacles.
And so, Kangaroo aloudly proclaimed, "I can't
    send Hare in search of anything!"
"You can guru, you can!" shouted Newt.
"You can send him with Owl."
But Owl had gone to sleep.
Newt knew too much to be stopped by so small a problem –
"You can take him in your pouch."
But alas, Hare was much too big to fit into Kangaroo's pouch.

All this time, it had been quite plain to Hare that the
    others knew nothing about spectacles.
As for all their tempting ideas well, Hare didn't care.
The lost spectacles were his own affair.

And after all, Hare *did* have a spare a-pair.
A-pair.
THE END

Instrumental passage 9 (4:19–5:30)

Vocal 8 : strophic (5:30–7:02)
We sleep by the ever-bright hole in the door,
Eat in the corner, talk to the floor –
Cheating the spiders who come to say "Please,"
(Politely). They bend at the knees.
Well, I'll go to the foot of our stairs.

Old gentlemen talk of when they were young
Of ladies lost, of erring sons.
Lace-covered dandies revel (with friends)
Pure as the truth – tied at both ends.
Well I'll go to the foot of our stairs.

Scented cathedral – spire pointed down.
We pray for souls in Kentish Town.
A delicate hush – the gods floating by
Wishing us well – pie in the sky.
God of ages, Lord of Time – mine is the right to be wrong.
Well I'll go to the foot of our stairs.

Vocal 9 Part 1 : strophic/through-composed (7:02–7:22)
Jack rabbit mister – spawn a new breed
Of love hungry pilgrims (no bodies to feed).
Show me a good man and I'll show you the door.
The last hymn is sung and the devil cries "More."

Instrumental passage 10 (7:22–9:28)

Vocal 9 Part 2 : strophic/through-composed (9:28–10:24)
Well, I'm all for leaving and that being done,
I've put in a request to take up my turn

In that forsaken paradise that calls itself "Hell" –
Where no-one has nothing and nothing is
Well meaning fool,
Pick up thy bed and rise up from your gloom *smiling*.
Give me your hate and do as the loving heathen do.

Vocal 10 Part 1 : AABA (10:24–12:18)
Colours I've none – dark or light, red, white or blue.
Cold is my touch (freezing).
Summoned by name – I am the overseer over you.

Given this command to watch o'er our miserable sphere.
Fallen from grace, called on to bring sun or rain.
Occasional corn from my oversight grew.

Fell with mine angels from a far better place,
Offering services for the saving of face.
Now you're here, you may as well admire
All whom living has retired from the benign reconciliation.

Legends were born surrounding mysterious lights
Seen in the sky (flashing).
I just lit a fag then took my leave in the blink of an eye.

Instrumental passage 11 (12:18–12:57)

Vocal 10 Part 2 : Additional "A" of AABA (12:57–13:19)
Passionate play – join round the maypole in dance
(Primitive rite) (wrongly).
Summoned by name, I am the overseer over you.

Instrumental passage 12 (13:19–14:21)

Vocal 11 Part 1 : verse-chorus (14:21–16:01)
Flee the icy Lucifer. Oh, he's an awful fellow!
What a mistake! I didn't take a feather from his pillow.

Here's the everlasting rub: neither am I good nor bad.
I'd give up my halo for a horn and the horn for the hat I once had.

I'm only breathing. There's life on my ceiling.
The flies there are sleeping quietly.

Twist my right arm in the dark. I would give two or three for
One of those days that never made impressions on the old score.

I would gladly be a dog barking up the wrong tree.
Everyone's saved – we're in the grave. See you there for afternoon tea.

Time for awaking – the tea-lady's making
A brew up and baking new bread.

Instrumental passage 13 (16:01–16:53)

Vocal 11 Part 2 : verse-chorus (16:53–17:47)
Pick me up at half past none – there's not a moment to lose.
There is the train on which I came. On the platform are my old shoes.

Station master rings his bell. Whistles blow and flags wave.
A little of what you fancy does you good. (Or so it should)

I thank everybody for making me welcome.
I'd stay but my wings have just dropped off.

Instrumental passage 14 (17:47–19:27)

Vocal 12 Part 1 : "AAB" of AABA (19:27–21:04)
Hail! Son of Kings make the ever-dying sign
Cross your fingers in the sky for those about to BE.
There am I waiting along the sand.
Cast your sweet spell upon the land and sea.

Magus Perdé, take your hand from off the chain.
Loose a wish to still the rain, the storm about to BE.
Here am I (voyager into life).
Tough are the soles that tread the knife's edge.

Break the circle, stretch the line, call upon the devil.
Bring the gods, the gods' own fire.
In the conflict revel.
The passengers upon the ferry crossing, waiting to be born,
Renew the pledge of life's long song, rise to the reveille horn.
Animals queueing at the gate that stands upon the shore
Breathe the ever-burning fire that guards the ever-door.

Instrumental passage 15 (21:04–21:51)

Vocal 12 Part 2 : Final "A" of AABA (21:51–22:45)
Man, son of man, buy the flame of ever-life
(Yours to breathe and breath the pain of living): living BE!
Here am I! Roll the stone away
From the dark into ever-day.

Vocal 13 : Reprise of lines 8–9 from Vocal 1 Part 2 (22:45–23:06)
There was a rush along the Fulham Road
Into the Ever-passion Play.

Instrumental passage 16 (23:06–23:26)

APPENDIX THREE

Analysis of the Instrumental Passages

The following is a detailed description of all the primary musical events in the nineteen instrumental passages of *Thick as a Brick*.

INSTR. 1 (3:36–6:08 SIDE 1) SOLOING, TRANSITION, AND CONTRAST

3:36–4:05 Organ solo in C Dorian over $\frac{3}{4}$ ostinato (Motive 2) on bass and electric guitar

4:05–4:20 Electric guitar solo over bass, which leaves the ostinato behind in favor of more melodic, sequential lines

4:20–4:30 Shift to $\frac{4}{4}$ meter and a short acoustic guitar interlude

4:30–5:01 Staccato rhythms by entire band in $\frac{3}{4}$, ending on a diminished chord

5:01–5:12 Shift to $\frac{4}{4}$ meter and G Aeolian

5:12–6:08 Introduction to the harmonic and melodic material of Vocal 3

INSTR. 2 (7:15–9:20 SIDE 1) SOLOING

7:15–7:26 Electric guitar and flute play Motive 3

7:26–9:04 Electric guitar solo in the left channel and another in the right channel (starting at 7:45) playing related material

9:04–9:20 Electric guitar and flute play Motive 3

INSTR. 3 (10:30–11:19 SIDE 1) TRANSITION

10:30–10:46 Codetta of Vocal 3: descending, sequential passages

10:46–10:58 Organ trades motives with electric guitar, soprano saxophone, and flute

10:58–11:19 Descending, sequential passages in $\frac{6}{8}$ leading to D Mixolydian

INSTR. 4 (11:52–13:16 SIDE 1) CONTRAST AND TRANSITION

11:52–12:00 Organ and flute play syncopated, staccato figure

12:00–12:32 Shift to B Aeolian. Organ plays syncopated melody and fragments of the accompanimental melody of Vocal 5

12:32–13:16 Introduction to Vocal 5: shift from $\frac{4}{4}$ to $\frac{12}{8}$ meter and modulation to D pitch center. Organ, electric guitar, and bass play accompanimental melody of Vocal 5 with flute punctuations

INSTR. 5 (14:13–15:26 SIDE 1) SOLOING

14:13–14:56   Flute solo
14:56–15:26   Electric guitar and organ play a theme derivative of accompanimental melody of Vocal 5

INSTR. 6 (15:54–16:35 SIDE 1) CONTRAST AND TRANSITION

15:54–16:24   Organ, then electric guitar, play variation of accompanimental melody of Vocal 5, augmented by acoustic guitar
16:24–16:35   Introduction to Vocal 6: shift to F pitch center, reappearance of Motive 1

INSTR. 7 (17:06–17:41 SIDE 1) TRANSITION

17:06–17:15   Descending sequences in piano and bass
17:15–17:30   Acoustic guitar strumming and change of meter from $\frac{6}{8}$ to $\frac{4}{4}$
17:30–17:41   Introduction to Vocal 7 and reappearance of Motive 3 on organ

INSTR. 8 (18:08–18:39 SIDE 1) REPETITION

18:08–18:39   Repetition of the same melodic and harmonic material of Vocal 7 Part 1, with different instrumentation

INSTR. 9 (19:29–20:00 SIDE 1) REPETITION AND SOLOING

19:29–20:00   Repetition of the same melodic and harmonic material in Vocal 7 Part 1. Flute solo in the left channel and another in the right channel (starting at 19:39) playing related material

INSTR. 10 (20:25 SIDE 1–0:48 SIDE 2) REPETITION, SOLOING, CONTRAST, AND TRANSITION

20:25–21:11   Repetition of the same melodic and harmonic material in Vocal 7 Part 1, with double flute solo. Brief shifts in meter between $\frac{4}{4}$ and $\frac{6}{8}$
21:11–22:07   Shift to C Dorian. Three chord staccato riffs from electric guitar, piano, bass, and drums interspersed with two organ flourishes (Motive 6), then treated with echo and reverb effects. The riffs grow softer while the echo and reverb grow louder.
22:07–22:43   Swirling wind sounds with *pianissimo* organ murmurs.
0:00–0:48   Swirling wind sounds. Flute and soprano saxophone play Motive 6. Three-chord riff returns played at half speed.

INSTR. 11 (1:24–4:04 SIDE 2) CONTRAST AND SOLOING

1:24–1:32   Motive 6 played on electric guitar and organ in G
1:32–3:00   Barlow drum solo in $\frac{6}{8}$ interspersed with Motive 5 on flute and tubular bells and interrupted twice by Motive 6 on organ, electric guitar, and bass
3:00–4:04   Free-form playing, spoken-word dialogue, and silence

INSTR. 12 (5:12–5:59 SIDE 2) REPETITION AND TRANSITION

5:12–5:38   Codetta of Vocal 9: Acoustic guitar, then entire band repeat riff in ascending intervals

5:38–5:59   Introduction to Vocal 10: acoustic guitar plays
            Motive 1, modulation to G Aeolian

INSTR. 13 (10:57–13:11 SIDE 2) REPETITION AND TRANSITION
10:57–12:33   Gradually intensified repetition of riff
              from Vocal 11 by entire band
12:33–12:47   Riff lengthened by scalar passages and Motive 7A
12:47–13:11   Introduction to the harmonic and melodic material
              of Vocal 12: flute, electric guitar, and organ
              play Motive 7. Modulation to C Dorian

INSTR. 14 (13:47–14:49 SIDE 2) REPETITION AND TRANSITION
13:47–14:04   Repeat of Motive 7 on flute, electric guitar, and organ
14:04–14:33   Busy theme played by flute and harpsichord
14:33–14:49   Dotted theme on flute, organ, and electric
              guitar punctuated by timpani

INSTR. 15 (15:03–16:07 SIDE 2) TRANSITION
15:03–15:18   Descending flute line repeated twice
15:18–15:32   Trills and scalar passages on flute, harpsichord, and organ
15:32–16:07   March theme alternating between $\frac{3}{4}$ and $\frac{5}{4}$ meter with Motive 7A

INSTR. 16 (16:43–17:13 SIDE 2) REPETITION AND TRANSITION
16:43–16:58   Repeat of Motive 7 on flute, electric guitar, and organ
16:58–17:13   Dotted theme on flute, organ, and electric
              guitar punctuated by timpani

INSTR. 17 (17:44–18:08 SIDE 2) TRANSITION AND CONTRAST
17:44–17:58   Descending flute line repeated twice
17:58–18:08   Abrupt modulation to F. Introduction to Vocal 13 Part 1

INSTR. 18 (18:31–18:52 SIDE 2) TRANSITION AND REPETITION
18:31–18:42   Varied and augmented version of Motive
              7B on organ and electric guitar
18:42–18:52   Faster tempo *fortspinnung* version of Motive 2 on
              electric guitar, organ, and bass in odd meters

INSTR. 19 (19:21–20:26 SIDE 2) CONTRAST AND TRANSITION
19:21–19:31   Flute, organ, and electric guitar play Motive 3
19:31–19:41   Flute and organ play ascending sequence
19:41–20:01   Organ, electric guitar, and bass play $\frac{6}{8}$ version of Motive 2
              interspersed with string orchestra interludes playing Motive 4
20:01–20:21   Band play $\frac{6}{8}$ version of Motive 2 while organ, flute,
              and soprano saxophone overlay Motive 6
20:21–20:26   Scalar passage leading to a climax on three repeated chords
     20:26   Introduction to Vocal 14: band cuts out
              while acoustic guitar plays Motive 1

The following is a detailed description of all the primary musical events in the sixteen instrumental passages of *A Passion Play*.

INSTR. 1 (0:00–3:28 SIDE 1) TRANSITION, SOLOING

0:00–1:13   Heartbeat (Motive 1) ascends in pitch. Soprano saxophone plays Motive 2 and flourishes of melody. Studio effects

1:13–1:46   Gigue in $\frac{9}{8}$ beginning in B-flat with electric guitar and soprano saxophone sharing melody. Modulation to G Dorian

1:46–2:08   Overture Theme 1 on flute, synthesizer, organ, bass, and drums. Anderson solos on flute at the repeat of the theme

2:08–2:47   Overture Theme 2. Synthesizer and soprano saxophone trading Motive 1

2:47–3:06   Overture Theme 1 returns with Anderson soloing on flute

3:06–3:17   Whistling and acoustic guitar

3:17–3:28   Heartbeat descends in pitch, slows in tempo, and ceases

INSTR. 2 (5:52–6:50 SIDE 1) TRANSITION, SOLOING

5:52–6:14   Marimba and organ play theme in $\frac{11}{8}$ evocative of a music box

6:14–6:50   Band plays similar theme in $\frac{11}{8}$ (interpreted metrically as 3 + 3 + 3 + 2) with Anderson soloing on soprano saxophone

INSTR. 3 (7:55–9:06 SIDE 1) REPETITION, SOLOING, TRANSITION

7:55–8:22   Acoustic guitar, then band play theme reminiscent of Vocal 1

8:22–9:06   Acoustic guitar plays flamenco-influenced solo passage, with organ, electric guitar, and bass accompaniment

INSTR. 4 (10:30–13:00 SIDE 1) TRANSITION, SOLOING

10:30–10:49   Organ plays opening fragment of Motive 3, which is combined contrapuntally with countermelodies played by the electric guitar and synthesizer in $\frac{11}{8}$ meter

10:49–11:29   Synthesizer, organ, and electric guitar play $\frac{11}{8}$ theme (interpreted metrically as 3 + 3 + 3 + 2) in unison, increasing in volume and intensity

11:29–11:39   Synthesizer and soprano saxophone add countermelody, interpreting $\frac{11}{8}$ meter as 2 + 2 + 2 + 2 + 3

11:39–12:36   Anderson double-tracks two similar, but distinct, flute solos in left and right channels

12:36–13:00   Electric guitar, synthesizer, organ, and soprano saxophone play rising figure, then trade motives contrapuntally

INSTR. 5 (14:51–15:41 SIDE 1) TRANSITION, CONTRAST

14:51–15:11   Electric guitar, synthesizer, organ, and soprano saxophone trade motives contrapuntally, as at the end of Instr. 4

15:11–15:41   Music disintegrates, band collectively improvises, then repeatedly plays section B of Motive 4 (which will dominate Vocal 5) while increasing the tempo

ANALYSIS OF THE INSTRUMENTAL PASSAGES   209

          INSTR. 6 (17:09–17:58 SIDE 1) REPETITION
17:09–17:58   Motive 4 from Vocal 5 repeated and developed, then
                interspersed with Motive 3 from Vocal 2

         INSTR. 7 (19:33–20:01 SIDE 1) REPETITION, TRANSITION
19:33–20:01   Section B of Motive 4 repeated, as at the end of
                Instr. 5, then band modulates to G Phrygian

         INSTR. 8 (20:22–21:36 SIDE 1) CONTRAST, TRANSITION
20:22–21:36   Motive 1 (heartbeat) returns, acoustic guitar strumming,
                and melodic fragments on flute and synthesizer

         INSTR. 9 (4:19–5:30 SIDE 2) CONTRAST, TRANSITION
4:19–5:21   Motive 1 (heartbeat) and acoustic guitar return at faster tempo.
              Melodic fragments on flute, soprano saxophone, and synthesizer
5:21–5:30   Motive 5 and Motive 1 on organ, piano, and synthesizer

         INSTR. 10 (7:22–9:28 SIDE 2) SOLOING, TRANSITION
7:22–9:17   Soprano saxophone, electric guitar, and synthesizer solos
9:17–9:28   Motive 3 and organ chords

         INSTR. 11 (12:18–12:57 SIDE 2) REPETITION, SOLOING
12:18–12:57   Soprano saxophone and synthesizer solos

         INSTR. 12 (13:19–14:21 SIDE 2) REPETITION,
         SOLOING, CONTRAST, TRANSITION
13:19–13:39   Soprano saxophone solo (on the melody of Vocal 10)
13:39–13:50   Motive 5 (ascending and descending) and Motive 1 (heartbeat)
13:50–14:21   Organ and synthesizer play mock melodramatic theme

         INSTR. 13 (16:01–16:53 SIDE 2) SOLOING
16:01–16:53   Short soprano saxophone, electric guitar, and flute solos

         INSTR. 14 (17:47–19:27 SIDE 2) CONTRAST, TRANSITION
17:47–18:51   Acoustic guitar and soprano saxophone solo
                over tranquil accompaniment in $\frac{3}{4}$ meter
18:51–19:27   Electric guitar disrupts preceding section with angular
                riff accompanied by synthesizer and flute flourishes

         INSTR. 15 (21:04–21:51 SIDE 2) SOLOING, TRANSITION
21:04–21:29   Oriental-sounding synthesizer melody in $\frac{7}{8}$ meter
                followed by soprano saxophone solo
21:29–21:51   Return of angular electric guitar riff from Instr. 14

         INSTR. 16 (23:06–23:26 SIDE 2) TRANSITION
23:06–23:26   Return of Motive 1 (heartbeat), flourishes
                of soprano saxophone melody

Notes

PREFACE

1. There were no singles released from *Thick as a Brick* in America or in the United Kingdom, but the first three minutes of the album have been included on practically all of Jethro Tull's greatest hits compilations. From these compilations, the edit garnered heavy radio airplay and thus became a well-known Jethro Tull "single."

2. Edward Macan, *Rocking the Classics: English Progressive Rock and the Counterculture* (New York: Oxford University Press, 1997). Two other thorough progressive rock histories are Bill Martin, *Listening to the Future: The Time of Progressive Rock, 1968–1978* (Chicago: Open Court, 1998), and Paul Stump, *The Music's All That Matters: A History of Progressive Rock* (London: Quartet Books, 1997).

3. Two excellent Jethro Tull resources besides Russo are Scott Allen Nollen, *Jethro Tull: A History of the Band, 1968–2001* (Jefferson, NC: McFarland, 2002), and David Rees, *Minstrels in the Gallery: A History of Jethro Tull* (Middlesex, Eng.: Firefly, 1998).

4. Allan F. Moore, *Rock: The Primary Text: Developing a Musicology of Rock*, 2nd ed. (Aldershot: Ashgate, 2001).

5. Allan F. Moore, *Aqualung* (New York: Continuum, 2004).

6. John Covach, "Jethro Tull and the Long Song," *Progression Magazine* (Summer 1996), http://www.ibiblio.org/john covach/jethrotull.htm.

1. LIFE IS A LONG SONG: PROVIDING A CONTEXT FOR *THICK AS A BRICK* AND *A PASSION PLAY*

1. Craig Rosen, *The Billboard Book of Number One Albums: The Inside Story behind Pop Music's Blockbuster Records* (New York: Billboard Books, 1996), 144. Also available online at http://number1albums .com/1972/06/03/thick-as-a-brick–jethro -tull-june-3-1972.aspx.

2. Neil Warwick, Jon Kutner, and Tony Brown, *The Complete Book of the British Charts: Singles and Albums,* 3rd ed. (London: Omnibus Press, 2004), 565.

3. Rosen, *Billboard Book of Number One Albums.*

4. Warwick, Kutner, and Brown, *Complete Book of the British Charts.*

5. Edward Macan, *Rocking the Classics: English Progressive Rock and the Counterculture* (New York: Oxford University Press, 1997), 72–73.

6. Ibid., 13.

7. Ian Anderson, interview by Steve Demorest, "Ian Anderson's Pearls of Wisdom," *Circus* (April 14, 1977), http://www .tullpress.com/c14apr77.htm.

8. Ian Anderson, quoted in David Rees's and Martin Webb's liner notes to *20 Years of Jethro Tull: The Definitive Collec-*

tion. Chrysalis Records V5X 41653, 1988, 5 LP box set, [12].

9. Ian Anderson, 1969 documentary "Swing In – Rock In mit Jethro Tull (A Film by Wim Van Der Linden)," in *Jethro Tull: Classic Artists: Their Fully Authorized Story*, produced and directed by Jon Brewer, DVD (Image Entertainment, 2008), 16:56–17:16.

10. Ian Anderson, interview by Michael Castner, "Jethro Tull E! Television Interview, 1991," http://www.youtube.com/watch?v=V91BzJ8mlIo.

11. Kevin Holm-Hudson, ed., *Progressive Rock Reconsidered* (New York: Routledge, 2002), 2.

12. Martin Barre, extended interview portion "Martin Barre: On Ian Going Solo" in *Jethro Tull: Classic Artists*, DVD, at 3:23.

13. Palmer was a full-time member of the band from 1976 to 1980.

14. An EP (which stands for "extended play") is a recording that contains more music than a single, but not as much as a full-length album (an LP).

15. Jethro Tull's song "Up the 'Pool" (1971) addresses this specifically in its first line, "I'm going up the 'pool from down the smoke below."

16. Pete Shelton, *Rock-n-Roll Fever: Blackpool in the 60's* (Houston: Martin Powers Publishing, 2011), 40.

17. Dee Palmer, from *Jethro Tull: Classic Artists*, DVD, 1:38:04.

18. Ian Anderson, "Roy Harper by Ian Anderson," *Classic Rock* magazine blog archive, December 15, 2006, http://www.classicrockmagazine.com/uncategorized/roy_harper_by_ian_anderson.

19. Greg Russo, *Flying Colours: The Jethro Tull Reference Manual*, 2nd rev. ed. (New York: Crossfire Publications, 2009),12.

20. Anderson, "Roy Harper by Ian Anderson."

21. Another Anderson song about Blackpool is "Big Dipper" from *Too Old to Rock 'n' Roll, Too Young to Die!*

22. Roy Shuker, *Popular Music: The Key Concepts*, 2nd ed. (New York: Routledge, 2005), 7–8.

23. John Lennon, in David Sheff, *All We Are Saying: The Last Major Interview with John Lennon and Yoko Ono* (New York: St. Martin's/Griffin Press, 2000), 197.

24. John Covach, "Jethro Tull and the Long Song," *Progression* (Summer 1996), http://www.ibiblio.org/john covach/jethrotull.htm.

25. Macan, *Rocking the Classics*, 41.

26. Some examples include "In Held 'Twas in I" by Procol Harum (1968), "Dark Star" by the Grateful Dead (from *Live/Dead*, 1969), "Atom Heart Mother" and "Echoes" by Pink Floyd (1970, 1971), "Tarkus" by Emerson, Lake & Palmer (1971), "A Plague of Lighthouse Keepers" by Van der Graaf Generator (1971), and "Mountain Jam" by the Allman Brothers Band (1972).

27. This recording is also included as a bonus track on the deluxe edition of *Stand Up* (2010).

28. Ian Anderson, in Russo, *Flying Colours*, 84.

29. Ian Anderson, interview by Christopher Scapelliti, "Jethro Tull: Tull Tales," *Guitar World* (September 1999), http://www.guitarworld.com/article/jethro_tull_tull_tales.

30. Ian Anderson, interview by Dick Williams in Australia. Broadcast on July 22, 1972, http://www.youtube.com/watch?v=EsMYOO_lZeo, at 6:35-6:47.

31. Eric Tamm, *Robert Fripp: From King Crimson to Guitar Craft* (Boston: Faber and Faber, 1990), xiii.

2. GALLIARDS AND LUTE SONGS

1. This lip-synched performance can be seen on the DVD *A New Day Yesterday: The 25th Anniversary Collection* (EMI Records Ltd., 2003) and on YouTube, http://www.youtube.com/watch?v=-0GAuexrVzo.

2. Anderson's clothes, mannerisms, and facial expressions bear an uncanny resemblance to Ron Moody's depiction of the tramp Fagin in the 1968 musical *Oliver!* (based on Charles Dickens's novel *Oliver Twist* [1838]), especially in the song "Be Back Soon," in which Fagin plays his umbrella as if it were a flute.

3. Martin, *Listening to the Future*, 133.

4. Britta Sweers describes the style of the "electric folk" bands, and how they were different from "folk-rock" bands such as the Byrds and Simon and Garfunkel, in her *Electric Folk: The Changing Face of English Traditional Music* (New York: Oxford University Press, 2005), 21–43.

5. Paul Hardwick, "If I Lay My Hands on the Grail: Arthurianism and Progressive Rock," in *Mass Market Medievalism: Essays on the Middle Ages in Popular Culture*, ed. David W. Marshall (Jefferson, NC: McFarland, 2007), 28.

6. Rob Young, *Electric Eden: Unearthing Britain's Visionary Music* (New York: Faber and Faber, 2010), 5.

7. I have created labels (such as Vocal 12 and Instr. 4) for the vocal and instrumental sections of the two albums as a convenient way of referring to them. The vocal and instrumental sections of *TAAB* (including the first lines of the lyrics in the vocal sections) are listed in table 4.2 in chapter 4. The sections of *APP* are in table 7.3 in chapter 7. I use these labels extensively throughout the book, so a familiarization with these two tables will greatly aid the reader.

8. Ian Anderson, "Jethro Tull: Sweet Dream and Band Interviews 1979," http://www.youtube.com/watch?v=yaF7cms3MJc, at 5:20.

9. Beatrice K. Otto, *Fools Are Everywhere: The Court Jester around the World* (Chicago: University of Chicago Press, 2001), 9–10.

10. This shift away from the blues is even evident in the lyrics to the song "Play in Time" from *Benefit* (1970): "Blues were my favorite colour, till I looked around and found another song that I felt like singing."

11. Russo, *Flying Colours*, 33–34.

12. Ian Anderson, interview by Tom Silvestri, "Ian Anderson: The Jethro Tull Autodiscography," *Trouser Press* (October 1982), http://www.tullpress.com/tpoct82.htm.

13. Jeremy Montagu, Howard Mayer Brown, Jaap Frank, and Ardal Powell, "Flute," in Grove Music Online. Oxford Music Online, http://www.oxfordmusiconline.com/subscriber/article/grove/music/40569?q=flute&search=quick&pos=2&_start=1#firsthit.

14. Macan, *Rocking the Classics*, 52.

15. Ian Anderson, Jethro Tull: Official Website, http://jtull.com/musicians/iananderson/equipment.html.

16. Thanks to Dr. Stephen Valdez for suggesting this to me.

17. Christopher Page, *Voices and Instruments of the Middle Ages: Instrumental Practice and Songs in France, 1100–1300* (Berkeley: University of California Press, 1987), 93.

18. Richard H. Hoppin, *Medieval Music* (New York: W. W. Norton, 1978), 404.

19. Isabelle Ragnard, liner notes from *Ay Mi!: Lais et Virelais: Guillame de Machaut*. Emmanuel Bonnardot. OPS 30–171. CD (Paris, France: Opus 111, 1997), 11.

20. Ian Anderson, interview in Russo, *Flying Colours*, 78–79, and phone interview by Tim Smolko, February 9, 2012.

21. Ian Anderson, interview by Eric "Air-Wreck" Genheimer, "Ian Anderson: Too Old to Rock 'n' Roll? Never!" *Creem* (June 1977), http://www.tullpress.com/crjun77.htm.

22. Ian Anderson, phone interview by Tim Smolko.

23. Ian Anderson, interview by Graham Fuller, *Rolling Stone* 668 (October 1993), http://www.tullpress.com/rsoct93.htm.

24. Interestingly, Anderson shows evidence of his knowledge of the *lai* when he uses the word in "Cup of Wonder" from the *Songs from the Wood* album: "And those who ancient lines did lay will heed the song that calls them back." Ernest Adams points out that with the word "lay," Anderson creates a homophone (or more precisely a heterograph) with three different spellings and meanings: lay, ley, and *lai*. Adams's lucid explanation of "lay" is on Jan Voorbij's website, Cup of Wonder: The Annotated Jethro Tull Lyrics Page, http://www.cupofwonder.com/songs3.html#ancient.

25. The video *Slipstream* is included as a bonus DVD with the remastered CD of the 1980 album *A* (2004).

3. GEARED TOWARD THE EXCEPTIONAL RATHER THAN THE AVERAGE

1. Roger Dean, "Rock and Roll Relics," in *45 rpm: A Visual History of the Seven-Inch Record*, ed. Spencer Drate (New York: Princeton Architectural Press, 2002), 97.

2. Steve Jones and Martin Sorger, "Covering Music: A Brief History and Analysis of Album Cover Design," *Journal of Popular Music Studies* 11–12, no. 1 (2006): 75.

3. Ian Inglis, "'Nothing You Can See That Isn't Shown': The Album Covers of the Beatles," *Popular Music* 20, no. 1 (2001): 83–84.

4. Jones and Sorger, "Covering Music," 77.

5. The Doors intended to include an extended musical performance of the poem on their *Waiting for the Sun* album, but only the last section, "Not to Touch the Earth," was included. A live recording of the entire work appears on *Absolutely Live* (1970).

6. Ian Anderson, interview by Bryan Matthew, "The Jethro Tull Story, Part 3: *Thick as a Brick* to *A Passion Play*," BBC Radio, World Service, March 1979, http://www.tullpress.com/bbc79c.htm.

7. *Thick as a Brick*, Special Collector's Edition 40th Anniversary Set, Chrysalis Records 5099970461923, 2012, CD and audio DVD, "The Colour Supplement," 13, 20.

8. Russo, *Flying Colours*, 78.

9. *Thick as a Brick*, Special Collector's Edition 40th Anniversary Set, Chrysalis Records 5099970461923, 2012, CD and audio DVD, "The Colour Supplement," 13, 21.

10. Ian Anderson, interview by Christopher Scapelliti, "Jethro Tull: Tull Tales," *Guitar World* (September 1999), http://www.guitarworld.com/article/jethro_tull_tull_tales; Ian Anderson, from interview on the remastered CD of *Thick as a Brick*, Chrysalis Records 7243 4 95400 2 6, 1997, at 6:20–6:45.

11. Ian Anderson, quoted in Scott Allen Nollen, *Jethro Tull: A History of the Band, 1968–2001*, 82.

12. Jeffrey Hammond, from interview on the remastered CD of *Thick as a Brick*, at 9:41–9:59.

13. Rees, *Minstrels in the Gallery*, 49.

14. Royston Eldridge, from interview in *Jethro Tull: Classic Artists* DVD, at 51:24–52:39.

15. The online review of TAAB2: *Whatever Happened to Gerald Bostock?* is credited to Julian's son, Adrian Stone-Mason, which also contains "Ian." http://www.jethrotull.com/discography/taab2/stonemasonreview.html. "Adrian" was kind enough to write the foreword for this book.

16. John Covach, "Jethro Tull and the Long Song," *Progression* (Summer 1996), http://www.ibiblio.org/johncovach/jethrotull.htm.

17. The name Derek Small can be found in many places in the *Thick as a Brick* newspaper as well as in the *A Passion Play* playbill (Martin Barre). Harry Shearer's mutton-chopped bass player, Derek Smalls, in the rock mockumentary *This Is Spinal Tap* was most likely inspired by this.

18. Jim Curtis, *Rock Eras: Interpretations of Music and Society, 1954–1984* (Bowling Green, OH: Bowling Green State University Popular Press, 1987), 130.

19. Lester Bangs, *Psychotic Reactions and Carburetor Dung*, ed. Greil Marcus (New York: Knopf, 1987), 129.

20. *Thick as a Brick* and *A Passion Play* can each be downloaded in two twenty-minute-plus "slices."

21. Covach, "Jethro Tull and the Long Song."

22. Greg Keogh, "Nancy Street Network," *Thick as a Brick*, http://www.orthogonal.com.au/collections/taab/index.htm.

23. Ian Anderson, interview by John Alan Simon, "The Codpiece Chronicles," *Down Beat* 43 (March 11, 1976), http://www.tullpress.com/db11mar76.htm.

24. Ian Anderson, interview on the remastered CD of *Thick as a Brick*, at 2:12–3:29.

25. Ian Anderson, interview by Bryan Matthew, "The Jethro Tull Story, Part 3."

26. Anderson misspeaks here. Bostock is said to be eight years old on the album cover.

27. Ian Anderson, interview by Scapelliti, "Jethro Tull: Tull Tales."

28. My labels (Instr. 11, etc.) for the instrumental sections in *TAAB* are listed in table 4.2 in chapter 4 in the section on form.

29. Voltaire, *Candide, or Optimism* (New Haven, CT: Yale University Press, 2005), 14.

30. Ian Anderson, interview by Scapelliti, "Jethro Tull: Tull Tales."

31. This song, recorded in 1981, appears on the compilation *20 Years of Jethro Tull* (1988) and on the remastered version of *The Broadsword and the Beast* (2005).

32. Ian Anderson, interview with Jeune Pritchard, broadcast in Australia on GTK on July 18, 1972, http://www.youtube.com/watch?v=pSeTTL2_swk&feature=channel, at 1:50–2:03.

33. Covach, "Jethro Tull and the Long Song."

34. From, respectively, Jethro Tull's *Too Old to Rock 'n' Roll, Too Young to Die!* (1976), the Who's *Tommy* (1969), Genesis' *The Lamb Lies Down on Broadway* (1974), and Pink Floyd's *The Wall* (1979).

35. Ian Anderson, phone interview by Tim Smolko, February 9, 2012.

36. Stephen Akey, *A Guide to My Record Collection* (Bloomington: XLibris, 2009), 58.

37. Kari Kallioniemi, "Peter Gabriel and the Question of Being Eccentric," in *Peter Gabriel, From Genesis to Growing Up*, ed. Michael Drewett, Sarah Hill, and Kimi Kärki (Surrey, Eng.: Ashgate, 2010), 34.

38. Chris Riley, from an interview by Martin Webb in David Rees and Martin Webb, *Jethro Tull: The A New Day Tapes Volume One* ([Newcastle upon Tyne]: A New Day, 2012), 134; Shelton, *Rock-n-Roll Fever: Blackpool in the 60's*, 47.

39. John Stuart Mill, *On Liberty*, 2nd ed. (London: John W. Parker & Son, 1859), 120–21.

4. THE MUSIC OF *THICK AS A BRICK*: FORM AND THEMATIC DEVELOPMENT

1. Julian Stone-Mason B.A. (Ian Anderson), "Music Review, New Tull L.P.," from newspaper section of Jethro Tull's *Thick as a Brick*, Reprise Records MS 2072, 1972, 7.

2. John J. Sheinbaum, "Progressive Rock and the Inversion of Musical Values," in *Progressive Rock Reconsidered*, ed. Kevin Holm-Hudson (New York: Routledge, 2002), 35.

3. Edward Macan finds the multi-movement suite to be the most common form adopted by progressive rock bands in their large-scale works. See Macan, *Rocking the Classics*, 42. Both Macan and Dirk von der Horst trace elements of

sonata form in Yes' "Close to the Edge." See Macan, *Rocking the Classics*, 99–103, and Dirk von der Horst, "Precarious Pleasures: Situating 'Close to the Edge' in Conflicting Male Desires," in Holm-Hudson, *Progressive Rock Reconsidered*, 173–77. Mark Spicer describes the Genesis piece "Supper's Ready" in terms of Arnold Schoenberg's *Grundgestalt* ("basic shape") theory, showing how the nearly twenty-three-minute piece grows out of the first four measures. See Mark S. Spicer, "Large-Scale Strategy and Compositional Design in the Early Music of Genesis," in *Expression in Pop-Rock Music: A Collection of Critical and Analytical Essays*, ed. Walter Everett (New York: Garland, 2000), 85, 101. Lastly, Nors Josephson devotes an entire article to finding antecedents of progressive rock forms in classical music from the Renaissance to the twentieth century. See Nors S. Josephson, "Bach Meets Liszt: Traditional Formal Structures and Performance Practices in Progressive Rock," *Musical Quarterly* 76, no. 1 (1992): 67–92.

4. David Nicholls, "Virtual Opera, or Opera between the Ears," *Journal of the Royal Musical Association* 129, no. 1 (2004): 103.

5. Ian Anderson, quoted in Martin Webb and David Rees, *Jethro Tull 25th Anniversary Programme* (England: Adrian Hopkins Promotions, Ltd., 1993), [9].

6. Ian Anderson, *Jethro Tull 25th Complete Lyrics*, ed. Karl Schramm and Gerard J. Burns, 2nd ed. (Heidelberg, Germany: Palmyra, 1996), 10–11, 14.

7. Richard Middleton, *Studying Popular Music* (Milton Keynes, Eng.: Open University Press, 1990), 34–63.

8. Theodor Adorno, "On Popular Music," in *Essays on Music*, selected, with introduction, commentary, and notes by Richard Leppert. New translations by Susan H. Gillespie (Berkeley: University of California Press, 2002), 438, 442–43. Also available online at http://www.icce.rug.nl/~soundscapes/DATABASES/SWA/On_popular_music_1.shtml.

9. Ian Anderson, interview in Russo, *Flying Colours*, 86.

10. For deeper analyses of popular songs forms, see John Covach, "Form in Rock Music: A Primer," in *Engaging Music: Essays in Music Analysis*, ed. Deborah Stein (New York: Oxford University Press, 2005), 65–75; Walter Everett, "Forms: Phrases and Sections," in *The Foundations of Rock: From "Blue Suede Shoes" to "Suite: Judy Blue Eyes"* (Oxford: Oxford University Press, 2009), 134–56; Ken Stephenson, "Form," in *What to Listen for in Rock: A Stylistic Analysis* (New Haven, CT: Yale University Press, 2002), 121–43; Richard Middleton, "Form," in *Key Terms in Popular Music and Culture*, ed. Bruce Horner and Thomas Swiss (Malden, MA: Blackwell, 1999), 141–55.

11. Covach, "Form in Rock Music," 70; Everett, *Foundations of Rock*, 144.

12. Ian Anderson, interview in Russo, *Flying Colours*, 78–79, and phone interview by Smolko on February 9, 2012.

13. Regarding the "Timing" column, I have divided *Thick as a Brick* into two large sections in order to follow the tracking of the original LP (Reprise Records MS 2072, 1972), the remastered CD (Chrysalis Records 7243 4 95400 2 6, 1997), the remixed CD (Chrysalis Records 5099970461923, 2012), and the downloadable MP3 version of the album on websites like iTunes. The timings in the text and the tables are based on the 2012 remix of the album by Steven Wilson. Anyone listening to the 1997 remastered version will notice the timings are off in various sections by a few seconds. The audio DVD included with the 2012 remixed CD is cued as one continuous forty-three-minute track.

14. Regarding the "Pitch Center" column, some sections cannot be placed in

a specific mode or key. For instance, Vocal 1 could be said to be in both F major and F Mixolydian, since the opening acoustic guitar pattern contains both an E♮ and an E♭. In cases such as this I chose pitch centricity ("F") for the sake of clarity and simplicity. This will be discussed further in the section on harmony at the end of chapter 5.

15. Ian Anderson, phone interview by Smolko.

16. See Michael Broyles, "Organic Form and the Binary Repeat," *Musical Quarterly* 66, no. 3 (1980): 339–60, and Hugh MacDonald, "Repeats," in *Beethoven's Century: Essays on Composers and Themes* (Rochester, NY: University of Rochester Press, 2008), 144–60.

17. In this section I use the phrase "thematic development" to encompass "cyclical variation," "developing variation," and "thematic transformation," since the fine distinctions between them are beyond the scope of this book.

18. Middleton, "Form," 146.

19. Macan, *Rocking the Classics*, 58; Kevin Holm-Hudson, *Genesis and The Lamb Lies Down on Broadway* (Aldershot, Eng.: Ashgate, 2008), 15; David Nicholls, "Virtual Opera," 103; Spicer, "Large-Scale Strategy," 78.

20. Detlef Altenberg, "Franz Liszt and the Legacy of the Classical Era," *19th-Century Music* 18, no. 1, Brahms – Liszt – Wagner (1994): 54.

21. Middleton, "Form," 146.

22. Ian Anderson, interview by Dick Williams, Australia, broadcast on July 22, 1972, http://www.youtube.com/watch?v =EsMYOO_lZeo, at 5:56–6:21.

23. Doane Perry, interview in Nollen, *Jethro Tull: A History*, 189–90.

24. This theme actually appears for the first time at 0:20 side 1, echoing the word "shout."

25. Ian Anderson, interview by Steve Ditlea, "Ian Anderson Shows You How to Lose Your Way through 'Thick as a Brick,'" *Circus* (April 1972), http://www.tullpress .com/capr72.htm.

26. Ian Anderson, phone interview by Smolko.

27. Ian Anderson, interview in Russo, *Flying Colours*, 86.

28. William Drabkin, "Fortspinnung," in Grove Music Online, Oxford Music Online, http://www.oxfordmusiconline .com/subscriber/article/grove/music /10024.

29. From Jethro Tull: Official Website: Discography: *Thick as a Brick,* http://www .jtull.com/discography/thickasabrick /index.html.

30. Ian Anderson, Martin Barre, and Jeffrey Hammond, interview on the remastered CD of *Thick as a Brick,* at 6:20–7:53.

31. Ian Anderson, interview by Steve Gaines, "Ian Anderson Fights Back with *War Child,*" *Circus Raves* (November 1974), http://www.tullpress.com/cnov74 .htm.

32. Ian Anderson, phone interview by Smolko.

33. Samuel Taylor Coleridge, *Coleridge's Criticism of Shakespeare,* ed. R. A. Foakes (Detroit: Wayne State University Press, 1989), 53.

34. Ian Anderson, YouTube video uploaded by TullTapes, "Part 2 Jethro Tull Thick as a Brick Making of 1972 8mm Film + Pics, Real Sound," http://www.youtube .com/watch?v=nnbeI2EZfPM&feature =related, at 0:00–1:12.

5. THE MUSIC OF *THICK AS A BRICK*: OTHER FEATURES

1. Ian Anderson, interview by John Pidgeon, July 3, 1989, in *Classic Albums: Interviews from the Radio One Series* (London: BBC Books, 1991), 65.

2. Ian Anderson, July 2003 interview, in T. Virgil Parker, Jessica Hopsicker, and

Carri Anne Yager, *Sausage Factory: The College Crier's Infamous Interviews of the Freaks and the Famous* (Portland, OR: Inkwater Press, 2009), 5.

3. Peter Gabriel, "Reissues interview 2007," *Trespass* DVD audio, *Genesis 1970–1975*. (Atlantic/Rhino R2 513942, 2008, 1970), at 14:40.

4. Ian Anderson, interviewed by Steve Boisson, "Passion Plays: Ian Anderson's Three Decades of Visual Songwriting with Jethro Tull," *Acoustic Guitar* (November 2000), http://www.tullpress.com/agnov00.htm.

5. Allan F. Moore, "Jethro Tull and the Case for Modernism in Mass Culture," in *Analyzing Popular Music,* ed. Allan F. Moore (Cambridge, UK: Cambridge University Press, 2003), 160.

6. Ian Anderson, interview by Bryan Matthew, "The Jethro Tull Story, Part 4: *War Child* to *Minstrel in the Gallery,*" BBC Radio, World Service, March 1979, http://www.tullpress.com/bbc79d.htm.

7. Ian Anderson, phone interview by Smolko.

8. In the 1970s John Evans subtracted the "s" from his last name, Jeffrey Hammond added an extra "Hammond" to his last name, and Barrie Barlow added "more" to his first name.

9. These winds sounds may have been a studio effect added by Anderson or the sound engineers in the recording studio.

10. Macan, *Rocking the Classics,* 135.

11. Martin Barre interview from "Mostly Rock "N Roll" show, November 2003, http://www.youtube.com/watch?v=z7P-DAGWG1Q, at 1:17–1:36.

12. Anderson, interview by Pidgeon, in *Classic Albums,* 52.

13. Ian Anderson, interview by Teri Saccone, "The Drummers of Jethro Tull," *Modern Drummer* (December 1990), http://www.tullpress.com/mddec90.htm.

14. Macan, *Rocking the Classics,* 51.

15. Allan F. Moore, "The So-Called 'Flattened Seventh' in Rock," *Popular Music* 14, no. 2 (May 1995): 190.

16. Macan, *Rocking the Classics,* 53.

6. THE CHÂTEAU D'ISASTER TAPES AND THE ALBUM COVER AND LYRICS OF A PASSION PLAY

1. Anderson, *Jethro Tull 25th Complete Lyrics,* 13–14.

2. Ian Anderson, interview in Rees, *Minstrels in the Gallery,* 51.

3. Ian Anderson, "Jethro's Disneyland," *New Musical Express* (March 24, 1973), http://www.tullpress.com/nme24mar73.htm.

4. Ian Anderson, "Songwriter Interviews: Ian Anderson of Jethro Tull," Songfacts, http://www.songfacts.com/blog/interviews/ian_anderson_of_jethro_tull.

5. Desmond Morris, *The Naked Ape: A Zoologist's Study of the Human Animal* (New York: MacGraw-Hill, 1967), 9.

6. "Bungle in the Jungle" was written during the "Château d'Isaster" sessions but was not released until the *War Child* album (1974), http://www.jethrotull.com/discography/warchild/index.cfm.

7. "Solitaire" was recorded during the "Château d'Isaster" sessions but was titled "Only Solitaire" when it was released on the *War Child* album, http://www.jethrotull.com/discography/warchild/index.cfm.

8. "Skating Away on the Thin Ice of the New Day" was written during the "Château d'Isaster" sessions but was not released until the *War Child* album, http://www.jethrotull.com/discography/warchild/index.cfm.

9. I have created labels (such as Vocal 2) for the vocal and instrumental sections of *A Passion Play* as a convenient way of referring to them. The sections of APP are in table 7.3.

10. Anderson, *Jethro Tull 25th Complete Lyrics,* 94.

11. Rees, *Minstrels in the Gallery*, 146–47.

12. Ian Anderson, liner notes to *20 Years of Jethro Tull: The Definitive Collection*, Chrysalis Records V5X 41653, 1988, 5 LP box set, [3].

13. Jon Tiven, "Jethro Tull," *Melody Maker* (November 25, 1972), http://www.tullpress.com/mm25nov72.htm.

14. Nollen, *Jethro Tull: A History*, 93.

15. Ian Anderson, phone interview by Smolko.

16. Jethro Tull: Official Website: Discography: *A Passion Play*, http://www.jtull.com/discography/passionplay/index.cfm.

17. Anderson has an interest in ballet, and one can find references to it in Jethro Tull songs such as "Black Satin Dancer" and "Baker Street Muse" from *Minstrel in the Gallery*. Ian's brother Robin was the administrator of the Royal Scottish Ballet and even commissioned Ian to compose music for the 1979 ballet *The Water's Edge* (although David Palmer wrote most of it).

18. It is unclear from the lyrics when act IV begins. I have followed the lead of Neil Thomason on his Ministry of Information website, where he indicates that act IV begins at the lyrics "Flee the icy Lucifer . . . ," http://www.ministry-of-information.co.uk/app/a4.htm.

19. Lester Bangs, "Dear Creem Readers . . . " *Creem* (October 1973) http://www.tullpress.com/croct73.htm.

20. Ian Anderson, phone interview by Smolko.

21. Neil Thomason, Ministry of Information website, *A Passion Play*, Introduction, http://www.ministry-of-information.co.uk/app/index.htm.

22. Jan Voorbij, Cup of Wonder website. "Annotations for *A Passion Play*," www.cupofwonder.com/apassion.html; Neil Thomason, Ministry of Information website, "*A Passion Play*."

23. Ian Anderson, interview by Bryan Matthew, "Jethro Tull Story, Part 3."

24. The severing of the silver cord is also invoked in the song "Two Fingers" from *War Child*: "And when the Old Man with the telescope cuts the final strand . . . "

25. Ecclesiastes 12:6–7, New International Version UK, Bible Gateway website, http://www.biblegateway.com/passage/?search=Ecclesiastes%2012:6-7&version=NIVUK.

26. Dave Morice, *The Dictionary of Wordplay* (New York: Teachers & Writers Collaborative, 2001), 41.

27. Dmitri A. Borgmann, *Language on Vacation: An Olio of Orthographical Oddities* (New York: Charles Scribner's Sons, 1965), 111–12.

28. I Peter 5:8, New International Version UK. Bible Gateway website. http://www.biblegateway.com/passage/?search=I%20Peter%205:8&version=NIVUK.

29. Jethro Tull: Official Website: Discography: *A Passion Play*.

7. THE MUSIC OF *A PASSION PLAY*

1. It is difficult to hear a distinction between the two instruments through speakers, but the separation becomes more apparent when listening on headphones.

2. Malcolm Boyd, "Dance of Death," in Grove Music Online. Oxford Music Online, http://www.oxfordmusiconline.com/subscriber/article/grove/music/07153.

3. The grace notes in this example have been taken out to reveal more clearly the quarter-note/eighth-note rhythm.

4. Erich Schwandt, "Tarantella," in Grove Music Online, Oxford Music Online, http://www.oxfordmusiconline.com/subscriber/article/grove/music/27507.

5. For example, Vocal 1 as a whole is in strophic form, but each of its three parts is

treated slightly differently. The melodies of Vocal 1 Parts 1 and 3 are similar and contain two stanzas of four lines each, but Part 3 concludes with different words from the characteristic refrain "There was a rush..." Vocal 1 Part 2 does include this refrain, but has nine lines instead of eight, different melodic contours, and is more through-composed.

6. Rob Mackie, "Road Report: Rob Mackie Reports from Wembley on Jethro's 'Passion Play,'" *Sounds* (June 30, 1973), http://www.tullpress.com/s30jun73.htm.

7. Regarding the "Timing" column, I have divided *A Passion Play* into two large sections in order to follow the tracking of the remastered CD (Chrysalis Records 7243 5 81569 0 4, 2003) and the downloadable MP3 version of the album on websites like iTunes. On the original LP, side 2 begins in the middle of "The Story of the Hare Who Lost His Spectacles" at the line "Ostensibly motionless..." On the remastered CD, side 2 begins at the first line of "The Story of the Hare."

8. Although the heartbeat as it sounds at the beginning of the album has no definite meter, I have notated it as a quarter-note/eighth-note grouping in $\frac{9}{8}$ meter to closely associate it with the gigue in the overture.

9. Charles Amenta, "The Opening of the Mahler Ninth Symphony and the Bernstein 'Heart-Beat' Hypothesis," The Mahler Archives, http://www.mahlerarchives.net/archives/amentaM9.pdf.

10. Ian Anderson, phone interview by Smolko.

11. Nollen, *Jethro Tull: A History*, 94.

12. Ian Anderson, phone interview by Smolko.

13. From Jethro Tull: Official Website: Discography: *A Passion Play*, http://www.jtull.com/discography/passionplay/index.cfm.

8. MONTY PYTHON, RECEPTION, AND LIVE VERSIONS

1. Ian Anderson, "Ian Anderson Interview," Retrosellers, http://www.retrosellers.com/features198.htm.

2. Iain Ellis, *Rebels Wit Attitude: Subversive Rock Humorists* (Berkeley, CA: Soft Skull Press, 2008), 13.

3. Andy Miller, *The Kinks Are the Village Green Preservation Society* (New York: Continuum, 2003), 48; Barry J. Faulk, *British Rock Modernism, 1967–1977: The Story of Music Hall in Rock* (Burlington, VT: Ashgate, 2011), 107, 110.

4. Lester Bangs, *Psychotic Reactions and Carburetor Dung*, ed. Greil Marcus (New York: Knopf, 1987), 131.

5. Terry Jones, in David Morgan, *Monty Python Speaks!* (New York: Spike/Avon, 1999), 30–31.

6. The Pythons (John Cleese, Terry Gilliam, Michael Palin, Eric Idle, Terry Jones, and the Estate of Graham Chapman), *The Pythons: Autobiography by the Pythons* (New York: Thomas Dunne Books, 2003), 141–42.

7. Eric Idle, in *The Complete Monty Python's Flying Circus: All the Words*, written and Conceived by Graham Chapman, John Cleese, Terry Gilliam, Eric Idle, Terry Jones, Michael Palin (New York: Pantheon Books, 1989), 1:35.

8. Jethro Tull, film for "The Story of the Hare Who Lost His Spectacles," YouTube, http://www.youtube.com/watch?v=oQCTe_50Sy8.

9. Rosen, *Billboard Book of Number One Albums*, 144. Also available online at http://number1albums.com/1972/06/03/thick-as-a-brick–jethro-tull-june-3-1972.aspx.

10. These incidents are well covered in the Rees, Russo, and Nollen histories of the band.

11. Russo, *Flying Colours*, 86.

12. Ibid.

13. Ian Anderson, interview by Bryan Matthew, "Jethro Tull Story, Part 3."

14. Rees, *Minstrels in the Gallery*, 52; Russo, *Flying Colours*, 86; Nollen, *Jethro Tull: A History*, 96.

15. Ian Anderson, in Rees, *Minstrels in the Gallery*, 53.

16. Ian Anderson, extended interview portion "Ian Anderson: On Venues," *Jethro Tull: Classic Artists*, DVD, at 16:10–17:45.

17. Andrew Jackson, "Thick as a Brick live," Jethro Tull Press, http://www.tullpress.com/brick.htm.

18. Stephen Valdez, interview by Tim Smolko, March 16, 2012.

19. On this recording, bassist Tony Williams replaced John Glascock, who was recovering from heart surgery. Glascock joined Jethro Tull late in 1975, replacing Jeffrey Hammond, who played bass on the studio recording of *Thick as a Brick*.

20. *Jethro Tull: Living with the Past*, DVD, produced by Ian Anderson and Classic Rock Productions, 302 061 201 9 (Fuel 2000 Records, 2002), at 23:33–24:12.

21. The synthesizer music Anderson is referring to here is the sections labeled Instr. 8 (20:22–21:36 side 1) and Instr. 9 (4:19–5:30 side 2) in table 7.3. These sections frame "The Story of the Hare Who Lost His Spectacles" and are called "Forest Dance #1" and "Forest Dance #2" on the Mobile Fidelity Sound Labs remastered edition.

22. Ian Anderson, interview by Bryan Matthew, "Jethro Tull Story, Part 3."

23. Jethro Tull, film for "The Story of the Hare," YouTube.

24. "Ian Anderson – The Story of the Hare Who Lost His Spectacles," YouTube, http://www.youtube.com/watch?v=aZrFRPQgkDc&feature=related.

25. This concert is listed as occurring on May 15, 1973, in Greg Russo's exhaustive tour date listing in his *Flying Colours: The Jethro Tull Reference Manual*. But Mr. Head still has the actual ticket from the show, so the May 27 date must be correct.

26. Gilbert Head, interview by Tim Smolko, January 30, 2012.

27. Ian Anderson, interview by Bryan Matthew, "Jethro Tull Story, Part 3."

28. "Part 1 of 4 Jethro Tull *A Passion Play* Concert Film 8mm Oakland CA, New York NY, 1973 Tulltapes," http://www.youtube.com/watch?v=445HDZlQ5p0.

CONCLUSIONS

1. David Rees and Martin Webb, liner notes to *20 Years of Jethro Tull: The Definitive Collection*, Chrysalis Records V5X 41653, 1988, 5 LP box set, [4].

EPILOGUE

1. Ian Anderson, "TAAB2: Whatever Happened to Gerald Bostock?" Jethro Tull: Official Website, http://www.jtull.com/discography/taab2/iancomments.html.

2. Ibid.

3. Ian Anderson, interviewed by Joe Reinartz, "The Ian Anderson Interview," Pollstar, http://www.pollstar.com/blogs/news/archive/2012/03/09/798862.aspx.

4. Ian Anderson, interview with Nancy Dunham, "Ian Anderson 'Would Never Say That It Is the End of Jethro Tull,'" Ultimate Classic Rock, http://ultimateclassicrock.com/jethro-tull-ian-anderson-interview.

5. Ian Anderson, "Ian's Comments," Jethro Tull: Official Website, http://www.jtull.com/discography/aqualungcollectors/index.html.

APPENDIX 1. THE COMPLETE LYRICS TO *THICK AS A BRICK*

1. These last two lines of the spoken-word section do not appear in the lyrics on the original LP, but were added in *Jethro Tull 25th Complete Lyrics*, ed. Karl Schramm

and Gerald J. Burns, 2nd ed. (Heidelberg, Germany: Palmyra, 1996), 65.

2. What is actually sung here is "Of your luck and the cut of the knife."

APPENDIX 2. THE COMPLETE LYRICS TO *A PASSION PLAY*

1. These last three lines are not included in the lyrics on the original album, the remastered CD, nor *Jethro Tull 25th Complete Lyrics*.

2. On the original LP, side 2 begins in the middle of "The Story of the Hare Who Lost His Spectacles" at the line "Ostensibly motionless..." On the remastered CD, side 2 begins at the first line of "The Story of the Hare."

Bibliography

Adorno, Theodor W. "On Popular Music." In *Essays on Music*, 437–69. Selected, with introduction, commentary, and notes by Richard Leppert. New translations by Susan H. Gillespie. Berkeley: University of California Press, 2002.

Akey, Stephen. *A Guide to My Record Collection*. Bloomington, IN: XLibris, 2009.

Altenberg, Detlef. "Franz Liszt and the Legacy of the Classical Era." *19th-Century Music* 18, no. 1, Brahms – Liszt – Wagner (Summer 1994): 46–63.

Amenta, Charles. "The Opening of the Mahler Ninth Symphony and the Bernstein "Heart-Beat" Hypothesis." Mahler Archives. http://www.mahlerarchives.net/archives/amentaM9.pdf.

Anderson, Ian. *Jethro Tull 25th Complete Lyrics*. Edited by Karl Schramm and Gerald J. Burns. 2nd ed. Heidelberg, Germany: Palmyra, 1996.

———. Phone interview by Tim Smolko. February 9, 2012.

———. "Roy Harper by Ian Anderson." *Classic Rock* Magazine Blog Archive. December 15, 2006. http://www.classicrockmagazine.com/uncategorized/roy_harper_by_ian_anderson.

Bach, Johann Sebastian. *Französische Suiten: BWV 812–817*. Herausgegeben von Rudolf Steglich. 1071. München: G. Henle, 2008.

Bangs, Lester. "Dear *Creem* Readers . . . " *Creem* (October 1973). http://www.tullpress.com/croct73.htm.

———. *Psychotic Reactions and Carburetor Dung*. Edited by Greil Marcus. New York: Knopf, 1987.

Berlioz, Hector. *Fantastic Symphony: An Authoritative Score, Historical Background, Analysis, Views and Comments*. Edited by Edward T. Cone. New York: W. W. Norton, 1971.

Bible Gateway. New International Version UK. http://www.biblegateway.com.

Boisson, Steve. "Passion Plays: Ian Anderson's Three Decades of Visual Songwriting with Jethro Tull." *Acoustic Guitar* (November 2000). http://www.tullpress.com/agnov00.htm.

Borgmann, Dmitri A. *Language on Vacation: An Olio of Orthographical Oddities*. New York: Charles Scribner's Sons, 1965.

Boyd, Malcolm. "Dance of Death." In Grove Music Online. Oxford Music Online. http://www.oxfordmusiconline.com/subscriber/article/grove/music/07153.

Broyles, Michael. "Organic Form and the Binary Repeat." *Musical Quarterly* 66, no. 3 (July 1980): 339–60.

Castner, Michael. "Jethro Tull E! Television interview, 1991." http://www.youtube.com/watch?v=V91BzJ8mlIo.

Coleridge, Samuel Taylor. *Coleridge's Criticism of Shakespeare*. Edited by R.A. Foakes. Detroit: Wayne State University Press, 1989.

The Complete Monty Python's Flying Circus: All the Words. Written and conceived by Graham Chapman, John Cleese, Terry Gilliam, Eric Idle, Terry Jones, Michael Palin. 2 vol. New York: Pantheon Books, 1989.

Covach, John. "Form in Rock Music: A Primer." In *Engaging Music: Essays in Music Analysis*, edited by Deborah Stein, 65–75. New York: Oxford University Press, 2005.

———. "Jethro Tull and the Long Song," *Progression* (Summer 1996). http://www.ibiblio.org/johncovach/jethrotull.htm.

Curtis, Jim. *Rock Eras: Interpretations of Music and Society, 1954–1984*. Bowling Green, OH: Bowling Green State University Popular Press, 1987.

Dean, Roger. "Rock and Roll Relics." In *45 rpm: A Visual History of the Seven-Inch Record*, edited by Spencer Drate, 96–139. New York: Princeton Architectural Press, 2002.

Demorest, Steve. "Ian Anderson's Pearls of Wisdom." *Circus* (April 14, 1977). http://www.tullpress.com/c14apr77.htm.

Ditlea, Steve. "Ian Anderson Shows You How to Lose Your Way through 'Thick as a Brick.'" *Circus* (April 1972). http://www.tullpress.com/capr72.htm.

Drabkin, William. "Fortspinnung." In Grove Music Online. Oxford Music Online. http://www.oxfordmusiconline.com/subscriber/article/grove/music/10024.

Dunham, Nancy. "Ian Anderson 'Would Never Say That It Is the End of Jethro Tull.'" Ultimate Classic Rock. http://ultimateclassicrock.com/jethro-tull-ian-anderson-interview.

Ellis, Iain. *Rebels Wit Attitude: Subversive Rock Humorists*. Berkeley, CA: Soft Skull Press, 2008.

Everett, Walter. *The Foundations of Rock: From "Blue Suede Shoes" to "Suite: Judy Blue Eyes."* Oxford: Oxford University Press, 2009.

Fuller, Graham. "Ian Anderson." *Rolling Stone*, 668 (October 1993). http://www.tullpress.com/rsoct93.htm.

Gaines, Steve. "Ian Anderson Fights Back with *War Child*." *Circus Raves* (November 1974). http://www.tullpress.com/cnov74.htm.

Genesis 1970–1975. R2 513942. CD/DVD box set. Atlantic/Rhino, 2008, 1970.

Genheimer, Eric "Air-Wreck." "Ian Anderson: Too Old to Rock 'n' Roll? Never!" *Creem* (June 1977). http://www.tullpress.com/crjun77.htm.

Hardwick, Paul. "If I Lay My Hands on the Grail: Arthurianism and Progressive Rock." In *Mass Market Medievalism: Essays on the Middle Ages in Popular Culture*, edited by David W. Marshall, 28–41. Jefferson, NC: McFarland, 2007.

Head, Gilbert. Interview by Tim Smolko, January 30, 2012.

Holm-Hudson, Kevin. *Genesis and The Lamb Lies Down on Broadway*. Aldershot, Eng.: Ashgate, 2008.

———, ed. *Progressive Rock Reconsidered*. New York: Routledge, 2002.

Hoppin, Richard H. *Medieval Music*. New York: W. W. Norton, 1978.

"Ian Anderson Interview." Retrosellers. http://www.retrosellers.com/features198.htm.

"Ian Anderson–The Story of the Hare Who Lost His Spectacles." http://www.youtube.com/watch?v=aZrFRPQgkDc&feature=related.

Inglis, Ian. "'Nothing You Can See That Isn't Shown': The Album Covers of the Beatles." *Popular Music* 20, no. 1 (2001): 83–97.

Jackson, Andrew. Jethro Tull Press. http://www.tullpress.com.

Jethro Tull. Official Website. http://www.j-tull.com.

"Jethro's Disneyland," *New Musical Express* (March 24, 1973). http://www.tullpress.com/nme24mar73.htm.

Jones, Steve, and Martin Sorger. "Covering Music: A Brief History and Analysis of Album Cover Design" *Journal of Popular Music Studies* 11–12, no. 1 (2006): 68–102.

Josephson, Nors S. "Bach Meets Liszt: Traditional Formal Structures and Performance Practices in Progressive Rock." *Musical Quarterly* 76, no. 1 (1992): 67–92.

Kallioniemi, Kari. "Peter Gabriel and the Question of Being Eccentric." In *Peter Gabriel, From Genesis to Growing Up*, edited by Michael Drewett, Sarah Hill, and Kimi Kärki, 31–42. Surrey, Eng.: Ashgate, 2010.

Koegh, Greg. "Nancy Street Network." *Thick as a Brick*. http://www.orthogonal.com.au/collections/taab/index.htm.

Letts, Marianne Tatom. *Radiohead and the Resistant Concept Album: How to Disappear Completely*. Bloomington: Indiana University Press, 2010.

Macan, Edward. *Rocking the Classics: English Progressive Rock and the Counterculture*. New York: Oxford University Press, 1997.

MacDonald, Hugh. "Repeats." In *Beethoven's Century: Essays on Composers and Themes*, 144–60. Rochester, NY: University of Rochester Press, 2008.

Mackie, Rob. "Road Report: Rob Mackie Reports from Wembley on Jethro's 'Passion Play.'" *Sounds* (June 30, 1973). http://www.tullpress.com/s30jun73.htm.

———. *Listening to the Future: The Time of Progressive Rock, 1968–1978*. Chicago: Open Court, 1998.

Matthew, Bryan. "The Jethro Tull Story, Part 3: *Thick as a Brick* to *A Passion Play*." BBC Radio, World Service, March 1979. http://www.tullpress.com/bbc79c.htm.

———. "The Jethro Tull Story, Part 4: *War Child* to *Minstrel in the Gallery*." BBC Radio, World Service, March 1979. http://www.tullpress.com/bbc79d.htm.

Middleton, Richard. "Form." In *Key Terms in Popular Music and Culture*, edited by Bruce Horner and Thomas Swiss, 141–55. Malden, MA: Blackwell, 1999.

———. *Studying Popular Music*. Milton Keynes, Eng.: Open University Press, 1990.

Mill, John Stuart. *On Liberty*. 2nd ed. London: John W. Parker & Son, 1859.

Miller, Andy. *The Kinks Are the Village Green Preservation Society*. New York: Continuum, 2003.

Montagu, Jeremy, Howard Mayer Brown, Jaap Frank, and Ardal Powell. "Flute." In Grove Music Online. Oxford Music Online. http://www.oxfordmusiconline.com/subscriber/article/grove/music/40569?q=flute&search=quick&pos=2&_start=1#firsthit.

Moore, Allan F. *Aqualung*. New York: Continuum, 2004.

———. "Jethro Tull and the Case for Modernism in Mass Culture." In *Analyzing Popular Music*, edited by Allan F. Moore, 158–72. Cambridge, UK: Cambridge University Press, 2003.

———. *Rock: The Primary Text: Developing a Musicology of Rock*. 2nd ed. Aldershot, Eng.: Ashgate, 2001.

———. "The So-Called 'Flattened Seventh' in Rock." *Popular Music* 14, no. 2 (May 1995): 185–201.

Morgan, David. *Monty Python Speaks!* New York: Spike/Avon, 1999.

Morice, Dave. *The Dictionary of Wordplay*. New York: Teachers & Writers Collaborative, 2001.

Morris, Desmond. *The Naked Ape: A Zoologist's Study of the Human Animal*. New York: MacGraw-Hill, 1967.

"Mostly Rock' N Roll" show. November 2003. Martin Barre interview. http://www.youtube.com/watch?v=z7P-DAGWG1Q.

Nicholls, David. "Virtual Opera, or Opera between the Ears." *Journal of the Royal Musical Association* 129, no. 1 (2004): 100–42.

Nollen, Scott Allen. *Jethro Tull: A History of the Band, 1968–2001*. Jefferson, NC: McFarland, 2002.

Otto, Beatrice K. *Fools Are Everywhere: The Court Jester around the World*. Chicago: University of Chicago Press, 2001.

Page, Christopher. *Voices and Instruments of the Middle Ages: Instrumental Practice and Songs in France, 1100–1300*. Berkeley: University of California Press, 1987.

Parker, T. Virgil, Jessica Hopsicker, and Carri Anne Yager. *Sausage Factory: The College Crier's Infamous Interviews of the Freaks and the Famous*. Portland, OR: Inkwater Press, 2009.

Pidgeon, John, comp. *Classic Albums: Interviews from the Radio One Series*. London: BBC Books, 1991.

Pritchard, Jeune. "GTK: Jethro Tull 1972." Ian Anderson interview on GTK. Broadcast in Australia. July 18, 1972. http://www.youtube.com/watch?v=pSeTTL2_swk&feature=channel.

The Pythons. *The Pythons: Autobiography by the Pythons*. New York: Thomas Dunne Books, 2003.

Ragnard, Isabelle. Liner notes from *Ay Mi!: Lais et Virelais: Guillaume de Machaut*. Emmanuel Bonnardot. OPS 30–171. CD. Paris: Opus 111, 1997.

Rees, David. *Minstrels in the Gallery: A History of Jethro Tull*. Middlesex, Eng.: Firefly, 1998.

Rees, David, and Martin Webb. *Jethro Tull: The A New Day Tapes Volume One*. [Newcastle upon Tyne]: A New Day, 2012.

———. Liner notes to *20 Years of Jethro Tull: The Definitive Collection*. 5 LP box set. V5X 41653. Chrysalis Records, 1988.

Reinartz, Joe."The Ian Anderson Interview." Pollstar website. http://www.pollstar.com/blogs/news/archive/2012/03/09/798862.aspx

Rosen, Craig. *The Billboard Book of Number One Albums: The Inside Story behind Pop Music's Blockbuster Records*. New York: Billboard Books, 1996.

Russo, Greg. *Flying Colours: The Jethro Tull Reference Manual*. 2nd rev. ed. New York: Crossfire Publications, 2009.

Saccone, Teri. "The Drummers of Jethro Tull." *Modern Drummer* (December 1990). http://www.tullpress.com/mddec90.htm.

Scapelliti, Christopher. "Jethro Tull: Tull Tales." *Guitar World* (September 1999). http://www.guitarworld.com/article/jethro_tull_tull_tales.

Schwandt, Erich. "Tarantella." In Grove Music Online. Oxford Music Online. http://www.oxfordmusiconline.com/subscriber/article/grove/music/27507.

Sheff, David. *All We Are Saying: The Last Major Interview with John Lennon and Yoko Ono*. New York: St. Martin's/Griffin Press, 2000.

Sheinbaum, John J. "Progressive Rock and the Inversion of Musical Values." In *Progressive Rock Reconsidered*, edited by Kevin Holm-Hudson, 21–42. New York: Routledge, 2002.

Shelton, Pete. *Rock-n-Roll Fever: Blackpool in the 60's*. Houston: Martin Powers Publishing, 2011.

Shuker, Roy. *Popular Music: The Key Concepts*. 2nd ed. New York: Routledge, 2005.

Silvestri, Tom. "Ian Anderson: The Jethro Tull Autodiscography." *Trouser Press* (October 1982). http://www.tullpress.com/tpoct82.htm.

Simon, John Alan. "The Codpiece Chronicles." *Down Beat* 43 (March 11, 1976). http://www.tullpress.com/db11mar76.htm.

"Songwriter Interviews: Ian Anderson of Jethro Tull." Songfacts. http://www.songfacts.com/blog/interviews/ian_anderson_of_jethro_tull.

Spicer, Mark S. "Large-Scale Strategy and Compositional Design in the Early Music of Genesis." In *Expression in Pop-Rock Music: A Collection of Critical and Analytical Essays*, edited by Walter Everett, 77–111. New York: Garland, 2000.

Stephenson, Ken. *What to Listen for in Rock: A Stylistic Analysis*. New Haven, CT: Yale University Press, 2002.

"The Story of the Hare Who Lost His Spectacles." YouTube. http://www.youtube.com/watch?v=0QCTe_50Sy8.

Stuessy, Joe. *Rock and Roll: Its History and Stylistic Development*. 2nd ed. Englewood Cliffs, NJ: Prentice Hall, 1994.

Stump, Paul. *The Music's All That Matters: A History of Progressive Rock*. London: Quartet Books, 1997.

Sweers, Britta. *Electric Folk: The Changing Face of English Traditional Music*. New York: Oxford University Press, 2005.

Tamm, Eric. *Robert Fripp: From King Crimson to Guitar Craft*. Boston: Faber and Faber, 1990.

Thomason, Neil. Ministry of Information. http://www.ministry-of-information.co.uk.

Tiven, Jon. "Jethro Tull." *Melody Maker* (November 25, 1972). http://www.tullpress.com/mm25nov72.htm.

TullTapes. "Part 1 of 4 Jethro Tull *A Passion Play* Concert Film 8mm Oakland CA, New York NY, 1973 Tulltapes." http://www.youtube.com/watch?v=44sHDZlQ_5p0.

———. "Part 2 Jethro Tull *Thick as a Brick* Making of 1972 8mm Film + Pics, Real Sound." http://www.youtube.com/watch?v=nnbeI2EZfPM&feature=related.

Valdez, Stephen. Interview by Tim Smolko. March 16, 2012.

Voltaire. *Candide, or Optimism*. New Haven, CT: Yale University Press, 2005.

Von der Horst, Dirk. "Precarious Pleasures: Situating 'Close to the Edge' in Conflicting Male Desires." In *Progressive Rock Reconsidered*, edited by Kevin Holm-Hudson, 167–182. New York: Routledge, 2002.

Voorbij, Jan. Cup of Wonder. http://www.cupofwonder.com/index2.html.

Warwick, Neil, Jon Kutner, and Tony Brown. *The Complete Book of the British Charts: Singles and Albums*, 3rd ed. London: Omnibus Press, 2004.

Webb, Martin, and David Rees. *Jethro Tull 25th Anniversary Programme*. England: Adrian Hopkins Promotions, Ltd., 1993.

Williams, Dick. "Hit Scene: Jethro Tull 1972." Interview with Ian Anderson in Australia. Broadcast on July 22, 1972. http://www.youtube.com/watch?v=EsMYOO_lZeo.

Young, Rob. *Electric Eden: Unearthing Britain's Visionary Music*. New York: Faber and Faber, 2010.

Discography

Anderson, Ian. *Divinities: Twelve Dances with God*. Angel 5 55262 2, 1995, CD.
———. *Rupi's Dance*. Fuel 2000 302 061 328 2, 2003, CD.
———. *The Secret Language of Birds*. Fuel 2000 FLDPRO 1118, 2000, CD.
———. *Thick as a Brick 2: Whatever Happened to Gerald Bostock?* Chrysalis Records 5099963872729, 2012, CD/DVD.
———. *Walk into Light*. Chrysalis Records CHR 41443, 1983, 33 1/3 rpm.
Jethro Tull. *A*. Chrysalis Records CHR 1301, 1980, 33 1/3 rpm; Chrysalis 72435 97103 0 3, 2004, Remastered CD with "Slipstream" DVD.
———. *Aqualung*. Chrysalis Records CHR 1044, 1971, 33 1/3 rpm; 40th Anniversary Special Edition, Chrysalis 5099908799920, 2011, 2 CDs.
———. *Aqualung Live*. Fuel 2000 302 061 509 2, 2005, CD.
———. *Benefit*. Reprise Records RS 6400, 1970, 33 1/3 rpm; Chrysalis 5 35457 2, 2001, Remastered CD.
———. *The Best of Acoustic Jethro Tull*. Capitol/EMI 388 8962, 2007, CD.
———. *The Broadsword and the Beast*. Chrysalis Records CHR 1380, 1982, 33 1/3 rpm; Chrysalis/EMI 72434 73411 2 0, 2005, Remastered CD.
———. *Catfish Rising*. Chrysalis Records 09463 21886 2 5, 1991, CD.
———. *A Classic Case: The London Symphony Orchestra Plays the Music of Jethro Tull: Featuring Ian Anderson*. Arranged, conducted and produced by David Palmer. RCA Red Seal XRL1 7067, 1985, 33 1/3 rpm.
———. *Crest of a Knave*. Chrysalis Records FV 41590, 1987, 33 1/3 rpm; Chrysalis/EMI 72434 73413 2 8, 2005, Remastered CD.
———. *Heavy Horses*. Chrysalis Records CHR 1175, 1978, 33 1/3 rpm; Chrysalis/EMI 72435 81571 2 3, 2003, Remastered CD.
———. *The Jethro Tull Christmas Album*. Fuel 2000 302 061 340 2, 2003, CD.
———. *J-Tull Dot Com*. Fuel 2000 FLD 1043, 1999, CD.
———. *A Little Light Music*. Chrysalis/EMI F2 21954, 1992, CD.
———. *Live: Bursting Out*. Chrysalis Records CH2 1201, 1978, 33 1/3 rpm, 2 LPs; Chrysalis/EMI F2 21201, 1992, CD.
———. *Living in the Past*. Chrysalis Records CHR 1035, 1972, 33 1/3 rpm, 2 LPs; Chrysalis Records F2 21035, 1999, CD.
———. *Minstrel in the Gallery*. Chrysalis Records CHR 1082, 1975, 33 1/3 rpm; Chrysalis/EMI 72435 41572 2 6, 2002, Remastered CD.
———. *M.U. The Best of Jethro Tull*. Chrysalis Records FV 41078, 1976, 33 1/3 rpm; Chrysalis/EMI F2 21078, 1992, CD.

———. *Nightcap: The Unreleased Masters 1973–1991.* Chrysalis Records/EMI CHR 8 28157 2, 1993, 2 CDs.
———. *A Passion Play.* Chrysalis Records CHR 1040, 1973, 33 1/3 rpm.
———. *A Passion Play.* Chrysalis Records F2 21040, DIDX 2936, 1992, CD.
———. *A Passion Play.* Original Master Recording. Mobile Fidelity Sound Lab UDCD 720, 1998, CD.
———. *A Passion Play..* Chrysalis Records 7243 5 81569 0 4, 2003, Remastered CD.
———. *Repeat. The Best of Jethro Tull Vol. 2.* Chrysalis Records PV 41135, 1977, 33 1/3 rpm; Chrysalis/EMI F2 21135, 1992, CD.
———. *Rock Island.* Chrysalis Records F1 21708, 1989, 33 1/3 rpm; Chrysalis/EMI 09463 70976 2 5, 2006, Remastered CD.
———. *Roots to Branches.* Chrysalis Records/EMI 8 35418 2, 1995, CD.
———. *Songs from the Wood.* Chrysalis Records CHR 1132, 1977, 33 1/3 rpm; Chrysalis/EMI 72435 81570 2 4, 2003, Remastered CD.
———. *Stand Up.* Reprise Records RS 6360, 1969, 33 1/3 rpm; Chrysalis CHRX 1042, 2010, 2 CD & DVD Edition.
———. *Stormwatch.* Chrysalis Records CHR 1238, 1979, 33 1/3 rpm; Chrysalis 72435 93399 2 4, 2004, Remastered CD.
———. *Thick as a Brick.* Reprise Records MS 2072, 1972, 33 1/3 rpm.
———. *Thick as a Brick.* Chrysalis Records F2 21003, DIDX 401, 1992, CD.
———. *Thick as a Brick.* Chrysalis Records 7243 4 95400 2 6, 1997, Remastered CD.
———. *Thick as a Brick.* Special Collector's Edition 40th Anniversary Set. Chrysalis Records 5099970461923, 2012, CD and audio DVD.
———. *Thick as a Brick/Thick as a Brick 2.* Special Vinyl Collection Box Set. Chrysalis Records 5099970462210, 2012, 33 1/3 rpm, 2 LPs.
———. *This Was.* Reprise Records RS 6336, 1968, 33 1/3 rpm; Chrysalis/EMI 8 52213 2, 2006, Remastered CD.
———. *Too Old to Rock 'n' Roll, Too Young to Die!* Chrysalis Records CHR 1111, 1976, 33 1/3 rpm; Chrysalis/EMI 72435 41573 2 5, 2002, Remastered CD.
———. *20 Years of Jethro Tull: The Definitive Collection.* Liner notes by David Rees and Martin Webb. Chrysalis Records V5X 41653, 1988, 5 LP box set.
———. *25th Anniversary Box Set.* Chrysalis Records/EMI 0946 3 26004 2 4, 1993, 4 CDs.
———. *Under Wraps.* Chrysalis Records FV 41461, 1984, 33 1/3 rpm; Chrysalis/EMI 72434 73415 0 2, 2005, Remastered CD.
———. *War Child.* Chrysalis Records CHR 1067, 1974, 33 1/3 rpm; Chrysalis/EMI 72435 41571 2 7, 2002, Remastered CD.

Videography

Anderson, Ian. *Ian Anderson Plays the Orchestral Jethro Tull.* ZYX Music 3082, 2005, DVD.

Jethro Tull. *Jack in the Green, Live in Germany.* Eagle Rock Entertainment EV 30250 9, 2008, DVD.

———. *Jethro Tull: Classic Artists: Their Fully Authorized Story.* Produced and directed by Jon Brewer. Image Entertainment, 2008, DVD.

———. *Live at AVO Session Basel.* MVD Visual MVD4955D, 2009, DVD.

———. *Live at Madison Square Garden 1978.* Chrysalis Records 509999 67920 25, 2009, DVD.

———. *Live at Montreux 2003.* Eagle Vision EE 39153 9, 2007, DVD.

———. *Living with the Past.* Produced by Ian Anderson and Classic Rock Productions. Fuel 2000 Records 302 061 201 9, 2002, DVD.

———. *A New Day Yesterday: The 25th Anniversary Collection.* EMI 724349071391, 2003, DVD.

———. *Nothing Is Easy: Live at the Isle of Wight 1970.* Eagle Vision EV 30103 9, 2005, DVD.

———. *The Rolling Stones Rock and Roll Circus.* Abkco 1003 9, 2004, DVD.

———. *Slipstream.* RCA Videodiscs, 12116, 1983, VHS.

———. *20 Years of Jethro Tull.* Virgin Music Video 3 50136, 1989, VHS.

Index

AABA form, 62–63, 74; in *APP*, 136–138, 148, 201–203; in *TAAB*, 58, 60, 65, 68, 75, 98, 109, 185, 188–189

Abbey Road, 5, 12, 17

Abrahams, Mick, 9, 28

absurdism, xiii, 37, 39–40, 44, 48, 119, 158–161, 166, 181. *See also* surrealism

acoustic guitar, 7, 10, 27–29, 69–71, 75–76, 78–79, 96, 98–105, 133, 141, 150, 152–153, 169, 181–182, 205–209

Adorno, Theodor, 60–61

album covers, xiii, 4, 26–27, 33–42, 92, 118–122

"All You Need Is," 11

"All You Need Is Love," 63

Allman Brothers Band, The, 166, 212n26

Alpert, Herb, 34

American Beauty, 33

Anderson, Ian, xi, 9–10; acoustic guitar (*see separate entry*); on the counterculture, 4–5; flute (*see separate entry*); humor, 26, 158–161; influences, 10–11; live performance, 25–26, 55, 59–60, 61, 166–175; lyrics, 24–25, 43–54, 112–116, 122–128; songwriting, 10–11, 14–15, 30–32, 48, 52, 61–71, 74–77, 88–93, 117–118, 136–141; vocal style, 26, 102; youth, 7–9, 43–44, 46

Andrews, Mike, 179

"Animelée," 113

"Another Brick in the Wall, Part 2," 46

Another Side of Bob Dylan, 35

Anthems in Eden, 23

Aoxomoxoa, 34

Aqualung (album), xv, 9, 11, 13, 26, 27, 29, 43, 44, 46, 117, 169, 174, 182; influence on *TAAB*, 14, 24, 64, 91, 92, 102, 165; place in Jethro Tull's *oeuvre*, 6, 102, 124, 165; tour, 36, 59, 88

"Aqualung" (song), 14, 64, 102, 104, 181, 182

Arlen, Harold, 62

As You Like It, 113–114

"At Last, Forever," 15

Atom Heart Mother, 2, 212n26

Bach, Johann Sebastian, 24, 134, 160

"Back-Door Angels," 25

Baez, Joan, 23

balalaika, 28–29

ballads, 22–24, 102

Bangs, Lester, 42, 122, 161

Barlow, Barrie, 7–10, 29, 41, 55, 69–70, 78–79, 80, 83, 85, 93, 94, 97, 99, 100–101, 106, 117, 134, 152–153, 154, 161, 182, 205–209, 218n8

Baroque era music, 29, 30, 31, 72, 73, 105, 118, 130, 133–134

Barre, Martin, 4–5, 9, 10, 28, 103, 181; on *APP*, 131, 141, 152–153, 208–209; on *TAAB*, 7, 29, 40, 55, 69, 70, 82, 85, 88, 94, 97, 99, 100–101, 104–105, 107, 170, 171, 172, 205–207; on *The Château d'Isaster Tapes*, 113, 117

Barrett, Syd, 55

"Battle of Evermore, The," 20

bass guitar, 3, 7–9, 55, 69, 76, 78, 80–86, 93, 94, 97, 99, 100–101, 104–106, 131, 133, 152–153, 171, 172, 181, 205–208
Beatles, The, xiv, 1–2, 3, 4, 5, 8, 10, 11, 12, 17, 33, 34–35, 41, 55, 62, 63, 75, 91, 107, 159, 176
"Beautiful Day," 64
Beethoven, Ludwig van, 14, 73, 109, 181
Beggar's Banquet, 5
Benefit, 5, 9, 24, 169, 174, 213n10
"Bennie the Bouncer," 160
Beowulf, 20
Berlioz, Hector, 135
Beyond the Fringe, 158
Bible, The, 124, 126, 127
Billboard record chart, xiv, 1, 2, 17, 60, 110, 122, 165, 179
binary dance form, 72–73
Black Moses, 33
Black Sabbath (album), 135
Black Sabbath (band), 32, 135
"Black Sabbath" (song), 135
Blackpool (city), xviii, 7–10, 212n21
"Blackpool" (song), 10
Blades, The, 7–9, 106
Blonde on Blonde, 41, 122
"Blowin' in the Wind," 62–63
Blues, The, 3, 10, 27–29, 31, 102, 213n10
"Bohemian Rhapsody," 63
Bostock, Gerald, xiii, 39, 44, 48, 64, 179, 181, 183
"Bourrée," 24, 160
bouzouki, 28–29
Bowie, David, 55, 168
Brahms, Johannes, 73
Brain Salad Surgery, 160
Britten, Benjamin, 22
Broadsword and the Beast, 27, 46
Brubeck, Dave, 37
Bruford, Bill, 93, 106
"Budapest," 15
Buddhism, 124
"Bungle in the Jungle," 15, 63, 112–113
Bunker, Clive, 9
Bursting Out, 170
"By Kind Permission Of," 14, 63
Byrds, The, 3, 213n4

Camelot, 21
Campbell, Joseph, 216
Candide, 45–46
Canned Heat, 20
Cantos, The, 123
Captain Beefheart, 20, 34
Carroll, Lewis, 127
Carson, Rachel, 20
"Cat Food," 160
Catch a Fire, 33
CD, 34, 41–42, 128–129, 181, 216n13, 220n7
"Celebration of the Lizard, The," 35, 214n5
celesta, 180
chamber orchestra, 99, 149, 152–154. *See also* string section
Château d'Hérouville, 111, 116
Château d'Isaster Tapes, The, 111–118, 123, 134, 165–166
"Cheap Day Return," 63
Child, James Francis, 22–24
Christianity, 124
Christie, Agatha, 5
"Christmas Song," 27
"Circle," 11
Classic Artists: Jethro Tull (DVD), 37
Classical era music, 72–73, 96
classical music, xiv, 3, 11, 18, 57–61, 68, 72–74, 77, 93, 96, 110, 215n3
Cleese, John, 158, 161
climax, musical, 63, 68–71, 86, 87, 93, 102, 140–141, 170
Coleridge, Samuel Taylor, 89
Collins, Dolly, 20, 23
Collins, Phil, 93
Collins, Shirley, 20, 22–23
"Come All Ye," 23, 24, 102
Come Out Fighting Genghis Smith, 10–11
compact disc. *See* CD
compound form, 62, 63–64
concept album, 11–12, 15–17, 37, 39, 43–44, 51, 71, 111, 112, 113, 134, 159, 160, 172, 178, 180
concerto, 74, 99
Cooper, Alice, 33, 168
Cornick, Glenn, 9
counterculture, 1960s, 3–6, 19–21
Country Joe and the Fish, 3

court jesters. *See* jesters
courtly love, 30
Covach, John, xiv, xv, 12–13, 40, 42, 47, 63, 177
"Crazy Man Michael," 23
Cream, 3, 6, 13
Creem, 31, 122
Crest of a Knave, 15, 27
"Crimson and Clover," 103
"Critique Oblique," 114–117, 129
"Cup of Wonder" (song), 214n24
Cup of Wonder (website), xviii, 214n24
"Cycling Tour, The," 161

Dance of Death, 130, 135, 136
Danse Macabre. *See* Dance of Death
Dante Alighieri, 124, 127
Dark Side of the Moon, 2, 94, 128
"Dark Star," 167
Dasein, 114, 125
Dave Brubeck at Storyville: 1954, 37
Davis, Miles, 2, 176
"Dazed and Confused," 167
Dean, Roger, 4, 34, 92
Debussy, Claude, 14
Deep Purple, 11, 105
Denny, Sandy, 20
Dickens, Charles, 167, 213n2
Divinities: Twelve Dances with God, 124
"Dog-Ear Years, The," 160, 178
Doors, The, 2, 35, 63, 176, 214n5
"Down at the End of Your Road," 160
Dream Theater, 6
drugs, 4
drums, 3, 7–10, 29, 69–70, 78–79, 80, 83, 85, 93, 94, 97, 99, 100–101, 106, 117, 134, 152–153, 154, 161, 182, 205–209
"Dun Ringill," 32
Dylan, Bob, 23, 35, 41, 62–63, 122
dynamics, 13, 70, 81, 91, 93, 95, 97, 143

Early Music Consort of London, 23
eccentricity, 54–56
ecology movement, 20–21
education system, British, 45–47, 45, 47, 102
Eldridge, Royston, 36–37, 40, 179

electric folk, 14, 20, 23, 24, 26, 99, 213n4
electric guitar, 7, 9, 19, 29, 69, 76, 78, 80, 82–86, 93, 96–101, 103–105, 107, 131, 133, 141, 144–146, 152–153, 170, 173, 180, 205–209
Electric Ladyland, 2
electronic music, 14, 20, 70, 173
Eliot, T. S., 123
Ellis, Terry, 37, 165
Elvis Sails!, 37
Emerson, Keith, 105
Emerson, Lake & Palmer, 1, 2, 6, 11, 149, 160, 177
English and Scottish Popular Ballads, The, 22
English Folk Dance and Song Society (EFDSS), 22
EP, 7, 9, 106, 212n14
"Eternal Recurrence," 128
extended-play record. *See* EP
Evans, John, 7–10, 14, 36, 55, 218n8; on APP, 131, 134, 147, 151, 152–153, 154, 155, 208–209; on TAAB, 7, 9, 36, 69, 79, 82, 83, 88, 94, 97, 99, 100–101, 104, 105, 106, 107, 182, 205–207; on *The Château d'Isaster Tapes*, 117, 127
Everett, Walter, xiv, 63

fables, 16, 24, 113, 115, 122, 127, 140, 151
Fagin, 213n2
Fairport Convention, 20, 23, 24
fairy tales, 24, 127, 159, 164
fantasy literature, 3, 20, 21
"Farm on the Freeway," 21
"Fat Man," 160
fiddle. *See* violin
flute, 5, 7, 9, 13, 27–29, 32, 70, 76, 82–86, 94–104, 131–133, 140–141, 150–154, 160, 167, 170–173, 176, 178, 180, 181, 205–209, 213n2
folk music, 3, 10, 19–24, 26–28, 31–32, 48, 58–60, 62, 74, 77, 81, 92–95, 99, 102, 105, 107, 109, 150, 172, 176, 183, 213n4. *See also* electric folk
form, musical. *See* AABA form; compound form; large-scale form; small-scale form; strophic form; through-

composed form; verse-chorus form; verse-chorus-bridge form
fortspinnung, 80–81, 94, 95, 106, 207
45. *See* single
Four Seasons, The, 37
Foxtrot, 95
Freak Out!, 91
"Free Bird," 68
French Suite in E-flat major, BWV 815, 134
Fripp, Robert, 55
"From a Pebble Thrown," 180
Frost Report, The, 158
Fulham Road, 126, 128, 144–145, 195, 196, 198, 203

G N' R Lies, 37
Gabriel, Peter, 35, 55, 92, 126, 160, 168
Gazette Vol. 2, 37
Genesis, xiv, 1, 6, 20, 35, 55, 58, 92, 93, 95, 107, 126, 149, 160, 168, 177
Gentle Giant, 20, 180
Genuine Imitation Life Gazette, The, 37
Gethsemane, 9
Geworfenheit, 114, 125
Giddings, Andrew, 172
gigue, 131, 133–135, 142–143, 208
Gilliam, Terry, 158, 161–164
"Girlie," 11
Glascock, John, 221n19
glockenspiel, 83, 99–101, 103, 106, 152–154, 180
Going for the One, 2
"Going Up the Country," 20
Goodier, David, 181
Goon Show, The, 158
Grateful Dead, The, 3, 33, 34, 166–167
Guillaume de Machaut, 30, 32
guitar. *See* acoustic guitar; electric guitar
Guns N' Roses, 37
Guthrie, Woody, 62

Hammond, Jeffrey, 7–10, 36, 40–41, 45, 55, 76, 78, 80–86, 88, 94, 99, 100–101, 104–106, 115, 127, 131, 133, 151–155, 205–208, 218n8
Hammond, Scott, 181

"Happiest Days of Our Lives, The," 46
"Happy Family," 160
Harburg, E. Y., 62
harmony: 66–67, 103, 107–110, 132, 139, 154–156
Harper, Roy, 10–11, 28
harpsichord, 99, 100–101, 103, 105, 117, 134, 180, 207
Haydn, Joseph, 73
Hayes, Isaac, 33
Head, Gilbert, 168, 174
Head Hands & Feet, 169
heartbeat, 124, 126, 128, 130–133, 141–144, 148, 156, 163, 174, 175, 208, 209
Heavy Horses, 15, 24, 25, 31
Heidegger, Martin, 114, 125
Hendrix, Jimi, 2, 3, 13
Henry VII, King, 25
Henry VIII, King, 21, 24
Hergest Ridge, 2
"Hey Jude," 62
Highway 61 Revisited, 122
Holm-Hudson, Kevin, xiv, xviii, 6, 126, 177
Holst, Gustav, 22
homophony. *See* texture
Hooker, John Lee, 10
"How to Recognize Different Types of Trees from Quite a Long Way Away," 163–164
humor, 17, 26, 39–40, 44, 158–164, 166, 176
"Hymn 43," 62

"I am the Walrus," 159
"(I Can't Get No) Satisfaction," 72
"I Don't Want to Be Me," 178
"I Want to Hold Your Hand," 63
Idle, Eric, 158, 164
"I-Feel-Like-I'm-Fixin'-To-Die Rag," 3
In the Wake of Poseidon, 160
"In-A-Gadda-Da-Vida," 12, 106
Incredible String Band, The, 20
individualism, 45–47, 55–56
Inferno, 124, 127
instrumental passages, 12, 51–52, 64, 68, 95–98, 110, 149–150, 162, 205–209
instrumentation, 3, 27–29, 76–77, 98–107, 150–153

Iommi, Tony, 135
Iron Butterfly, 12, 106

Jack in the Green: Live in Germany 1970–1993 (DVD), 171
Jackson, Andrew, xv, xviii, 168
James, William, 126
Jansch, Bert, 10, 20, 28
Jarrett, Keith, 92
Jefferson Airplane, 3, 20, 33, 37
jesters, 21, 24–26, 55
Jethro Tull, 176; history, 1–10; influences, 3, 10–11; live performance, 25–26, 55–56, 166–175; place in rock history, 1–6, 176–178. *See also names of individual members, albums, and songs*
Jethro Tull (agriculturist), 21
Jethro Tull Christmas Album, The, 24, 27
Jethro Tull Press (website), xviii, 168
"John Barleycorn," 24
John, Elton, 111
John Evan Band, The, 7–8, 56, 106
John Evan Smash, The, 7, 106
Johnny Breeze and the Atlantics, 8
Jones, Terry, 158, 161
Journey to the Centre of the Earth, 2
J-Tull Dot Com, 178
Jung, Carl, 126
"Just Trying to Be," 180

Kansas, 6
King, B. B., 28
King Crimson, xiv, 1, 3, 20, 55, 93, 95, 160, 176, 177
"King Henry's Madrigal," 24
Kinks, The, 159
Kinks are the Village Green Preservation Society, The, 159
Kirk, Rashaan Roland, 10

lai, 23, 29–32, 58, 177, 214n24
Lamb Lies Down on Broadway, The, 35, 126
large-scale form, xiv, 1, 11–16, 30–32, 57–60, 63, 66–73, 91–93, 138–141, 177, 215n3
"Larks' Tongue in Aspic Part 1," 95
"Last Time, The," 72
"Law of the Bungle," 112–113, 115, 117, 134, 166

"Law of the Bungle Part II," 113, 115
Led Zeppelin, 5, 6, 20, 33, 63, 68, 166–167
Led Zeppelin, 6
Led Zeppelin II, 6
Led Zeppelin III, 33
Led Zeppelin IV, 20
"Left Right," 114, 116
Leibniz, Gottfried, 45–46
leitmotif. *See* motive (musical)
Lennon, John, 11, 37, 55, 159
Let it Bleed, 5
Liege and Lief, 23
Life is a Long Song (EP), 7, 9, 10–11, 106
Lifemask, 11
Linwell, 41, 179
Lion in Winter, The, 21
Liszt, Franz, 73–74, 135
Little Cruddock, 179
Live at AVO Session Basel (DVD), 172
Live at Madison Square Garden 1978 (DVD), 117, 170, 172, 175
Live/Dead, 167
Living in the Past (album), 7, 10–11, 14, 24, 26, 118, 165, 180
"Living in the Past" (single), 5, 181
Living with the Past (DVD), 172
Lizard, 160
"Locomotive Breath," 62, 181–182
Lomax, Alan, 22
London, 3, 8, 9, 20, 22, 36, 39, 117, 126, 172
Long John Silver, 33
"Look at the Animals," 112–113, 166
"Look into the Sun," 103
Lord, John, 105
Lord of the Rings, The, 20
"Lord's Prayer, The," 11
"Love Story," 27
LP (long-playing record), xiv, 33–35, 41–42, 182
Lucifer, 127–129, 143
lute, 24, 25, 160
Lynyrd Skynyrd, 68

M. U.–The Best of Jethro Tull, xiii, 76
Macan, Edward, xiv, xviii, 3, 4, 5, 13, 28, 102, 107, 108, 177
Mackie, Rob, 138

Magical Mystery Tour, 159
Magus Perdé, 122, 123, 128, 129, 202
Mahler, Gustav, 143
Man for All Seasons, A, 21
mandolin, 27, 28–29, 32
Marie de France, 30
Marillion, 6
marimba, 152–154, 208
Marley, Bob, and the Wailers, 33
Marquee Club, 167
"Matty Groves," 23
maypole dance, 25, 201
Meatloaf, 63
Medieval era music, 19–32, 107–108, 124, 133–136
Meet the Beatles!, 2
mellotron, 9
Melody Maker, 5, 36, 57, 117
Mercury, Freddie, 55
meter, 66–67, 78–86, 93–97, 139, 154–155, 205–209
Middle Earth (concert venue), 20
Middleton, Richard, 60, 73–74
Mill, John Stuart, 56
Milne, A. A., 127
Milton, John, 128
Ministry of Information (website), xviii, 123
Minstrel in the Gallery, 7, 15, 26
"Minstrel in the Gallery," 25
minstrels, 21, 25–27, 107
Mitchell, Joni, 20, 35
Monty Python and the Holy Grail, 161
Monty Python's Flying Circus, 40, 44, 124, 158, 161–164, 168
Moody Blues, The, 3, 11
Moore, Allan, xiv, xv, 93, 107, 177
Morgan Studios, 36, 117, 126
Morris, Desmond, 112–113
Morrison, Jim, 35, 214n5
"Mother Goose," 24, 29, 113
motive (musical), 77–90, 96, 109, 130–136, 142–149, 162–164, 205–209
moto perpetuo, 80, 82, 87
"Move on Alone," 107
Mozart, Wolfgang Amadeus, 73
MP3, 34, 41–42, 181
"Mr. Neutron," 161

Munrow, David, 23
music hall, British, 158–159, 160, 161, 168
"Musical Box, The," 168
Mussorgsky, Modest, 12
"My God," 11, 13–14, 29, 59, 64
"My Sunday Feeling," 28, 62

Naked Ape, The, 112
nakers, 29
"Neapolitan Tarantella," 136
"New Day Yesterday, A," 5, 103
New Day Yesterday: The 25th Anniversary Collection, A (DVD), 174
Nice, The, 13
Nietzsche, Friedrich, 128
Nightcap, 116, 134
Nollen, Scott Allen, xviii, 151, 166, 168
Nothing Is Easy: Live at the Isle of Wight 1970 (DVD), 4
Nursery Cryme, 160
nursery rhymes, 24, 29
"Nursie," 11

O'Donnell, Ryan, 181
Ogdens' Nut Gone Flake, 159, 160
O'Hara, John, 174, 180, 181
"Old School Song," 180
Oldfield, Mike, 2
Oliver!, 213n2
Oliver Twist, 213n2
Once and Future King, The, 21
"Only Solitaire," 25, 114, 218n7 (chap6). *See also* "Solitaire"
Opahle, Florian, 180, 181
organ, 9, 23, 29, 94–101, 105, 107, 117, 151–154, 170, 173, 180, 182, 205–209
organic form, 16, 52, 73–74, 89–91
ornamentation, 29, 133
"Over the Rainbow," 62
Overture, 117, 126, 130–136, 140–143, 155–156, 208

Palin, Michael, 158, 162
Palmer, Dee (formerly David), 7, 10, 29, 88, 99, 100–101, 107, 151, 152–153, 219n17
Panglos, Prof., 45, 45

Pangloss, 45–46
"Paradise by the Dashboard Light," 63
Paradise Lost, 128
parody. *See* spoof
Passion Play, A: album cover, 118–122, *119–121*; form, 136–141; harmony, 139, 155–156; instrumental passages, 149–150, 208–209; instrumentation, 150–153; lyrics, 122–129, 195–203; meter, 139, 154–155; overture, 130–136; thematic development, 142–149
passion play (sacred drama), 124
"Pastime with Good Company." *See* "King Henry's Madrigal"
Peacock, Steve, 115
Peart, Neil, 93
Pegg, Dave, 171, 172
"Penny Lane," 63
Pentangle, 20
percussion. *See* drums
Perry, Doane, 74, 171, 172
Peter and the Wolf, 151
"Philosophers' Football Match, The," 40
piano, 8, 9, 14, 28, 92, 99, 100–101, 103, 105, 151–154, 181, 206, 209
Pilgrim, Ronnie, 17, 118, 120, 122–128, 133–134, 142–143, 149, 151
Pink Floyd, xiv, 2, 3, 6, 20, 46, 55, 94, 107, 128, 149, 176
plainchant, 29
"Play in Time," 5, 213n10
polyphony. *See* texture
popular music, 1–2, 11, 16, 17, 19–21, 52, 58–64, 72–73, 165, 177
popular music forms, 58–68, 72–77, 136–138, 148, 185–203. *See also* AABA form; compound form; small-scale form; strophic form; through-composed form; verse-chorus form; verse-chorus-bridge form
portative organ, 23, 29, 107
"Post Last," 115, 117
Pound, Ezra, 123
Presley, Elvis, 37
Procol Harum, 11
Prof. Panglos. *See* Panglos, Prof.
program music, 73

progressive rock, xiv–xv, 1–7, 11–15, 18, 19–21, 23, 28–29, 41, 58–61, 63, 73, 88–95, 107, 149, 159–160, 166, 172, 177
Prokofiev, Serge, 151
psychedelic rock, 3

Queen, 63, 107

R & B. *See* Rhythm and Blues
Rachmaninoff, Sergei, 14
Radiohead, 6, 43
"Reasons for Waiting," 11
reception, 6, 151, 165–166, 174
recorder, 27, 29
Rees, David, xviii, 36, 116, 165, 168, 176
Renaissance (band), 20
Renaissance era music, 19–32, 105, 107–108, 133–136
Renbourn, John, 10, 20, 22, 28
Repeat – The Best of Jethro Tull – Vol II, 76, 173
repetition, exact, 72–73, 137–138
repetition, local, 75–76, 138, 148
repetition, musical, 12, 51, 63, 72–77, 80–81, 89–90, 98, 133, 136–138, 141, 162–163, 177, 206–209
repetition, textual, 51–54, 136–137, 148
reprise, 12, 65, 67, 70, 75–77, 102, 126–127, 137–138, 141, 145, 166, 169, 171, 172, 173
"Return of the Giant Hogweed, The," 160
Rhythm and blues, 3, 7, 8
Ring des Nibelungen, Der, 88
Rock and Roll Hall of Fame, 6
Rockin' Vickers, The, 8
Rolling Stones, The, 5, 8, 25, 33, 36, 72
Rolling Stones Rock and Roll Circus, The, 25
Romantic era music, 73–75, 89, 130, 135–136, 142, 177
Romeo and Juliet, 21
Roots to Branches, 15
"Roundabout," 57
Rush, 6, 93
Russo, Greg, xv, xviii, 10, 14, 165, 168

Saint-Saëns, Camille, 135
satire, 37, 42, 44–46, 48, 113, 158–163. *See also* spoof

"satire boom," 158–163
Saturday Night Live, 161
saxophone, 9, 29, 85, 96, 100–101, 103–104, 131–134, 140–141, 144, 150–156, 205–209
"Scenario/Audition/No Rehearsal," 114, 116
Schlegel, August Wilhelm, 89
School's Out, 33
"Sea Lion," 113
sectional form. *See* compound form
Seeger, Pete, 26, 37
sex, 5, 34
Sgt. Pepper's Lonely Hearts Club Band, 2, 4, 11, 35, 75
Shakespeare, William, 21, 89, 113
Sharp, Cecil, 22
Shelton, Pete, xviii, 8
Shulman, Derek, 180
"Silly Olympics," 40
silver cord, 124, 126, 129, 195, 219n24
Simon and Garfunkel, 23, 62
Sinfield, Peter, 160
single, xiii, 2, 5, 6, 9, 15, 16, 23, 27, 60, 75–76, 138, 155, 163, 172, 177, 181, 211n1 (preface)
"Skating Away on the Thin Ice of the New Day," 114–115, 125, 218n8 (chap6)
skiffle, 8, 22
Slipstream (DVD), 32, 160
Small Faces, The, 159, 160
small-scale form, 58–68, 71, 110, 136–138, 185–203
social commentary, 4, 21, 24–26, 44–47, 45, 47, 53
Soft Machine, 20
"Soft Parade, The," 63
"Solitaire," 114, 115. *See also* "Only Solitaire"
Some Time in New York City, 37
sonata form, 72–73, 96
Song Remains the Same, The, 167
Song to a Seagull, 35
Songs from the Wood, 15, 24, 25, 29, 31, 43
"Song-Story, A," 23
Sophisticated Beggar, 10–11
soprano saxophone. *See* saxophone
"Sossity; You're a Woman," 24
"Sound of Silence, The," 62
Sounds, 36, 115, 138

Spinal Tap, 32, 214n17
spoken-word, 16, 39, 45, 97, 100–101, 113, 115, 124, 152–153, 180, 181, 190, 198–200, 206
spoof, xiv, 17, 32, 37, 44, 50–51, 71, 91, 140, 159–160. *See also* satire
"Stagnation," 92
"Stairway to Heaven," 63, 68
Stand Up, 2, 5, 7, 11, 23, 24, 27, 28–29, 92, 103, 169
St. Cleve, xii, 41, 179
St. Cleve Chronicle & Linwell Advertiser, The, 33, 35–42, 38, 45–51, 45, 47, 50–51, 57, 60, 64, 98, 118, 119, 138, 179, 183
Steeleye Span, 20, 24
Sticky Fingers, 33
Stonehenge, 32
"Stonehenge" (Black Sabbath song), 32
"Stonehenge" (Spinal Tap song), 32
Stone-Mason, Adrian, xi–xii, 214n15
Stone-Mason, Julian, 40, 57, 103
Stormwatch, 15, 31, 32, 43
"Story of the Hare Who Lost His Spectacle, The," 16–17, 113, 115, 118, 122–124, 127, 129–130, 140, 142, 151–154, 156, 160, 164, 166, 173–174, 198–200
Strawbs, The, 20
string section, 11, 58, 81, 83–84, 87, 88, 93, 97, 99, 100–101, 107, 149, 152–154, 170, 207
strolling minstrels. *See* minstrels
strophic form, 14, 58, 60, 62–65, 68, 75, 109, 136–138, 148, 188, 190–191, 195–198, 200
Styx, 6
Suite for Lute in E minor, BWV 996, 24, 160
Sun Bear Concerts, The, 92
surrealism, 3–4, 26, 158–162, 168. *See also* absurdism
"Swing it Far," 180
symphonic poem, 58, 73–74, 110, 177
Symphonie Fantastique, 135
synthesizer, 99, 100–101, 105, 117, 131–134, 141, 143, 145, 147, 151, 153–155, 173, 208–209

TAAB2. *See Thick as a Brick 2: Whatever Happened to Gerald Bostock?*

tabor, 29
Tales from Topographic Oceans, 2
"Tam Lin," 23
tarantella, 136
Tarkus, 2
"Teacher," 9, 15
tempo, 16, 68, 70, 91, 94–95, 117, 133, 143, 146, 207–209
texture, 1, 69, 91–92, 94, 102–103, 133, 153, 182
That Was the Week That Was, 158
thematic development, 16–17, 72–90, 142–149, 162–164, 217n17
theme and variations, 58
Thick as a Brick: album cover, xiii, 33–42, 38, 45, 47, 50–51, 92; form, 57–71; harmony, 66–67, 107–110; instrumental passages, 95–98, 205–207; instrumentation, 98–107; lyrics, 43–54, 185–193; meter, 66–67, 78–86, 93–97; stylistic diversity, 91–93; thematic development, 72–90
Thick as a Brick 2: Whatever Happened to Gerald Bostock?, xiv, xvi, 11, 15, 169, 177–183
"thick as a brick" (expression), 46
"Thick as a Brick" (single), xiii, 16, 75–76, 163, 172
This is Spinal Tap, 32, 214n17
This Was, 7, 27, 28, 55, 107, 178
Thomason, Neil, xv, xviii, 123, 125–126
through-composed form, 62, 63, 65–68, 95, 109–110, 137–138, 186–188, 190–191, 196–200
Tibetan Book of the Dead, 124, 126, 128
"Tiger Toon," 113, 117, 134
timpani, 93, 99, 100–101, 103, 106, 152–153, 207
Tiven, Jon, 117
"To Cry You a Song," 104
To Cry You a Song: A Collection of Tull Tales, 10
Tolkien, J. R. R., 20
Tommy, 6, 11, 49
Tommy James and the Shondells, 103
"Too Many Too," 46
"Too Old to Rock 'n' Roll: Too Young to Die," 160, 176

Too Old to Rock 'n' Roll: Too Young to Die!, 15, 43, 178
Totentanz, 135
Trespass, 92
troubadours, 27–28, 30, 107
Trout Mask Replica, 34
trouvères, 27–28, 30, 32, 107
trumpet, 29, 98, 100–101, 103–104, 154
tubular bells, 83, 99–101, 103, 106, 206
Tubular Bells, 2
Tull, Jethro (agriculturist), 21
20 Years of Jethro Tull, 116, 176
25th Anniversary Box Set, 171–172

U2, 64
UK Albums Chart, 1, 2, 5, 23
Ummagumma, 6
Unwin, Stanley, 159
"Up the 'Pool," 10, 212n15
"Upper Class Twit of the Year," 40

Valdez, Steve, xvii, 168, 213n16
Van Vliet, Don. *See* Captain Beefheart
Vaughan Williams, Ralph, 22
"Velvet Green," 21, 29
Velvet Underground, The, 2
verse-chorus form, 14, 52, 54, 58–65, 68, 72, 75, 109, 136–138, 148, 186–187, 191–192, 201–202
verse-chorus-bridge form, 63
Vettese, Peter-John, 171
Vietnam War, 19, 24
vinyl. *See* LP (long-playing record)
violin, 29, 83–84, 98, 100–101, 103–104
Voltaire, 45
Volunteers, 37
Voorbij, Jan, xv, xviii, 123, 125

Wagner, Richard, 73, 88
Waiting for the Sun, 35, 214n5
Wakeman, Rick, 2, 105
Walker, T-Bone, 10
Wall, The (album), 2, 46, 128
Wall, The (film), 46
War Child, 7, 14–15, 25, 104, 112–114, 150, 161
"Waste Land, The," 123
"Watcher of the Skies," 95

Waters, Muddy, 10, 28, 62
Watt, 25
Whipped Cream & Other Delights, 34
White, T. H., 21
White Album (The Beatles), 33, 41, 91
Who, The, 6, 11, 20, 159
Who Sell Out, The, 159
Williams, Tony, 221n19
Wilson, Steven, 182
"Wind Up," 11, 59, 102
"Winter Snowscape, A," 21
Wish You Were Here, 2
"Witch's Promise, The," 9, 19, 24
"With You There to Help Me," 5

"Wond'ring Again," 21, 24, 180
"Woodstock," 20
Woodstock Festival, 5
wordplay, 124, 127, 129
world music, 14

Yardbirds, 3
Yes, xiv, 1–6, 34, 57, 58, 92, 93, 106, 107, 149, 177
"Yesterday," 62
"You Can't Always Get What You Want," 5

Zappa, Frank, xiv, 2, 16, 63, 91, 176
Zeffirelli, Franco, 21

TIM SMOLKO holds master's degrees in Musicology and in Library Science and is monographs original cataloger at the University of Georgia.

www.ingramcontent.com/pod-product-compliance
Lightning Source LLC
Chambersburg PA
CBHW050105170426
43198CB00014B/2467